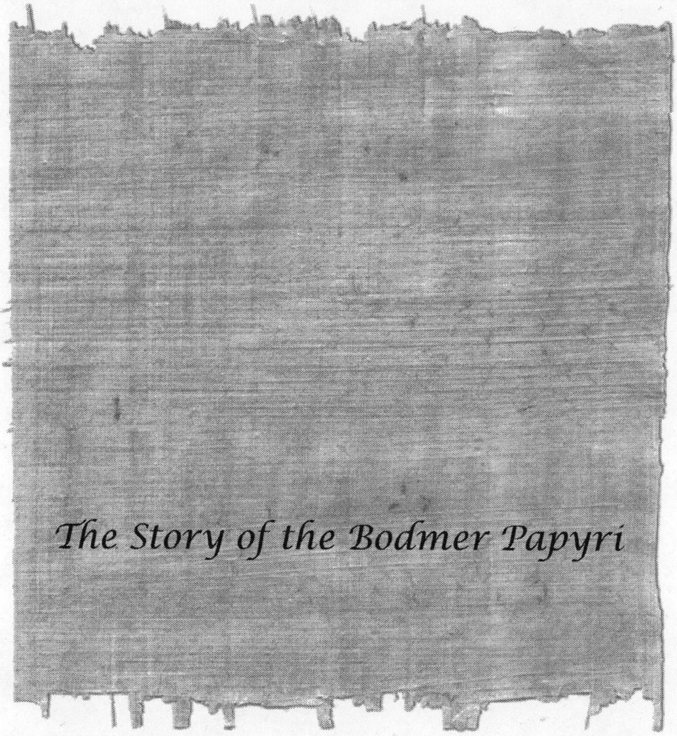

The Story of the Bodmer Papyri

The Story of the Bodmer Papyri

From the First Monastery's Library in Upper Egypt to Geneva and Dublin

James M. Robinson

CASCADE *Books* • Eugene, Oregon

THE STORY OF THE BODMER PAPYRI
From the First Monastery's Library in Upper Egypt to Geneva and Dublin

Cascade Books
An Imprint of Wipf and Stock Publishers
199 W. 8th Ave., Suite 3
Eugene, OR 97401

ISBN 13: 978-1-59752-882-5

Cataloging-in-Publication data:

Robinson, James M. (James McConkey), 1924–.

The story of the Bodmer papryi : from the first monastery's library in Upper Egypt to Geneva and Dublin / James M. Robinson.

ISBN 13: 978-1-59752-882-5

viii + 216 p. ; 23 cm. —Includes bibliographic references and index.

1. Bible. N. T.—Criticism, Textual. 2. Bible. N. T.—Manuscripts. 3. Manuscripts, Greek (Papyri). 4. Bibliotheca Bodmeriana. 5. Bodmer, Martin, 1899–1971. 6. Beatty, Alfred Chester, Sir, 1875–1968. I. Title.

BS1904.5 R65 2011

Manufactured in the U.S.A.

Contents

Preface

This book has to do with a manuscript discovery whose contents were scattered over a series of depositories, but which are primarily known as the Bodmer Papyri. Hence the book begins with those manuscripts that are at the Bibliothèque Bodmer near Geneva. But a large number of manuscripts are at the Chester Beatty Library in Dublin, which is the focus of the second chapter. Indeed, a few manuscripts were widely dispersed, in Mississippi, Cologne, and Barcelona, to which the third chapter is devoted. In Egypt, the manuscripts are known as the Dishnā papers, since that is the large town where they were sold, which the fourth chapter investigates. Finally, a last chapter shows that the manuscripts derive from the library of the Pachomian monastic order.

I also include as an Appendix my last publication in the field, an essay titled "The Pachomian Monastic Library at the Chester Beatty Library and the Bibliothèque Bodmer," which in more abbreviated form traces the manuscripts more in chronological sequence, from the Pachomian Monastery Library to the Dishnā Papers, then to the libraries of Sir Chester Beatty in Dublin and Martin Bodmer near Geneva. It then presents an Inventory of the texts found in the discovery.

I am deeply indebted to K. C. Hanson, editor in chief at Cascade Books, for editing and publishing *The Story of the Bodmer Papyri*, which I composed two decades ago but did not prepare for publication at the time. To facilitate following the course of the narrative, he has added the four sections at the end, where the bibliography also makes it possible to reduce the length of the footnotes throughout.

Part One

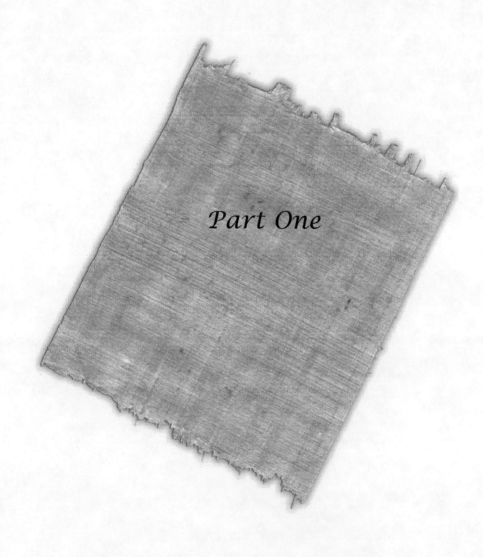

Introduction

THE BIBLIOTHÈQUE BODMER

During the 1950s and 60s there came to scholarly attention manuscripts of an importance for determining the original wording of the New Testament equaled only by the Chester Beatty Biblical Papyri of the 1930s. For Bodmer Papyrus II (abbreviated P^{66}, the Gospel of John) and Bodmer Papyrus XIV–XV (P^{75}, the Gospels of Luke and John) have now emerged alongside of the Chester Beatty Biblical Papyri P^{45} (the Gospels and Acts), P^{46} (the Pauline Epistles), and P^{47} (the book of Revelation) as priceless witnesses to the third-century Greek text, much as Codex Sinaiticus (א) and Codex Vaticanus (B) had provided nineteenth-century scholarship equally unexpected access back to the fourth-century text. These most recently emerging manuscripts are part of the fabulous Bibliothèque Bodmer created by the Swiss bibliophile Martin Bodmer at Cologny near Geneva.

Martin Bodmer (1899–1971) came from a distinguished Zurich family that had, at the dawn of the German Enlightenment, as its most distinguished ancestor Johann Jakob Bodmer, one of the rediscoverers of the Middle Ages. Before he was twenty-five Martin Bodmer himself had endowed a foundation to fund an annual literary prize named after the Zurich author Gottfried Keller. Bodmer came to focus his own energies toward creating a library of "world literature," "what has shown itself to be decisive for the growth and refinement of the human spirit and thereby conquered the world." "Ultimately world literature means what is valid across national and temporal limits in the writing of the various peoples."[1] The Bodmer collection came to have five foci: Homer and antiquity; the Bible; Dante and the Middle Ages; Shakespeare; and Goethe.

At the opening of the Second World War, Bodmer offered his services to the International Committee of the Red Cross, for which purpose he moved in 1940 to its headquarters in Geneva. He helped that organization distribute a million and a half books to internees and prisoners of war. After the war he traveled for the Red Cross to troubled areas around the world. About a month before his death, he created a private foundation for the maintenance of his library and the publication of its more important manuscripts, controlled by a self-perpetuating board currently made up of: a member of the Bodmer family, a representative of the Department of Education of the Canton of Geneva, two professors from the University of Geneva, and a lawyer. The library is located near the center of the village of Cologny, a suburb of Geneva. It consists of two older buildings connected by a newer underground vault and exhibit hall.[2] It is open to the public on Thursdays and for scholars by appointment.

Already in 1947, Bodmer published a book titled *A Library of World Literature*[3] in which he presented a rationale for the acquisition policy and the arrangement of his library. Although his own focus was more on German literature than on papyrology, and though at the time his library contained "only" 70,000 volumes,[4] the list of manuscripts[5] already included seventeen papyri from 1000 BCE to the eighth century CE. And yet none of these are what have come to be known as the "Bodmer Papyri." Rather, this term refers somewhat imprecisely to a series of publications—beginning in 1954, continuing in rapid succession until 1969, and resumed in 1984—titled *Bodmer Papyrus I*, et cetera. Although no details had been given prior to 1984 about the provenience or acquisition of these Bodmer papyri in the narrower sense, most were assumed to have come from a shared provenience. Hence the term by extension has come to refer to a manuscript discovery made presumably not too much earlier than the commencement of their publication in

1. Bodmer, *Eine Bibliothek der Weltliteratur*, 8–9.

2. Described by Albert Bettex in a brochure published in April 1971 by the Swiss fraternity Pro Helvetia.

3. Bodmer, *Bibliothek der Weltliteratur*.

4. Ibid., 33.

5. Ibid., 139–41

1954. In this way the term "Bodmer Papyri" comes to have a modified delimitation, excluding the earlier acquisitions of papyri and even one item in the series *Papyrus Bodmer* but not to be attributed to that discovery, and including in addition whatever papyri, though not published in that series, may be attributed to the same provenience. In this way the term "Bodmer Papyri" as used here has come to have both a narrower and a broader meaning.

To get some impression of what the Bodmer Papyri must have meant to Bodmer at the time when he was busy acquiring and publishing them, one may cite his second major book published at just that time:

> But by far the most dangerous enemy of ancient literary works was the fragility and flimsiness of the material! The fact that the papyrus roll maintained itself relatively well in Egypt, its land of origin, is the exception to the rule and an incredible stroke of luck, since otherwise we would possess for all practical purposes nothing! But the texts that mattered were the most endangered. So we must accept it as our fate that the primary sources of humanity, that which make life worth living and humans humane, survive only in tatters. These are doubly remarkable in view of the fact that it is upon them that the best of our being builds.[6]

Specifically with regard to the Gospels: "Everywhere the same text comes to meet us, and yet nowhere more upsetting than in the sparse papyrus rags that reach back near to the days 'when still, unknown and very small, our Lord walked on earth.' The same text, and yet again and again basically different!"[7] These are the words of a bibliophile who only the year before had acquired, and then the same year published, the oldest extant copy of the Gospel of John (P. Bodmer II = P^{66} of the early third century). Indeed, earlier the very same year, on the return trip from a Red Cross mission in Indonesia, he had stopped off in Cairo long enough to acquire a previously lost play by Menander (P. Bodmer IV, *The Misanthrope*) as well as the oldest extant copy of the Gospel of Luke, along with another copy of the Gospel of John (P. Bodmer XIV–XV = P^{75}, from the middle of the third century). For *this* is the priceless treasure that echoes in the minds of biblical scholarship at the very idea of "Bodmer Papyri"! Indeed this and much more.

6. Bodmer, *Variationen*, 67.

7. Ibid., 65.

It is not necessarily the case that once a book has entered the Bibliothèque Bodmer one can assume it is still there. When Pope Paul VI visited Geneva in 1969, Bodmer gave him a copy of the two letters of his most famous predecessor, P. Bodmer VIII (the [pseudonymous] First and Second Epistles of Peter from the New Testament). They are now in the Vatican Library. Indeed much more recently, on January 22, 2007, the Vatican Library was given P. Bodmer XIV-XV = P^{75}. Bodmer was also generous in providing fragments from codices from the same discovery that had been acquired by other libraries to those libraries, such as an exchange of such fragments with Barcelona and the gift of fragments belonging to the Savery Codex (then the Crosby Codex of the University of Mississippi). But the major loss to the holdings of the Bibliothèque Bodmer took place in order to produce the capital needed to endow the foundation that now administers the Bibliothèque Bodmer. For the German rare book dealer of New York, H. P. Kraus, who had been buying from and selling to Bodmer for years, was invited to come and choose several million dollars' worth of books:

> I sold great books to Bodmer and bought equally great ones from him. My association with him began inauspiciously. As a young dealer in Vienna in 1935 I received a postal card from Bodmer ordering several books from one of my catalogues . . . One of the more exotic sales I made to Bodmer was a papyrus Book of the Dead of late dynastic Egypt (715–525 B.C.) . . . In 1960 I bought this fine example from Dr. Otto Fischer of Detroit, who passed away shortly thereafter . . . Later I came into possession of a large, valuable collection of Greek and Coptic papyri assembled by a well-known collector. Along with it came a remarkable object, a silver dedicatory plate or plaque from the foundation of the Serapeum . . . Though he chose not to install the plaque in the cornerstone of his new library building, Bodmer recognized that such an item belonged in his collection . . . I saw him usually once a year . . . The greatness of books sold to Bodmer over the years can be equalled only by the greatness of books bought from him. The volumes I succeeded in purchasing from Bodmer were, to put it mildly, of fabulous beauty and importance . . . An offer of sixty million dollars was made in a letter from me to Bodmer [for the whole Bibliothèque Bodmer], received in time for his 70th birthday celebration. At the party that evening in Rome he took out the letter with a flourish and read it aloud to the members of his family. Flattered and impressed, he nevertheless answered no

> . . . He had decided to leave his library as a public foundation. A man of grand design, he had doubtless had this in mind for years. Two to three million dollars would have to be raised, he explained, to establish an endowment. I had been repeatedly trying to buy from Bodmer over the years and he had repeatedly declined, except in the few instances mentioned earlier. So, selling a number of his books to me was, he felt, not only an act of business but of friendship, giving me the long-denied chance to make a selection from his shelves . . . On June 20 [1970] I returned to Geneva and began going through the library . . . My purchases from Bodmer are certainly among the most notable transactions ever to take place in the book trade. They far outclassed the famous Holford purchase, both in the sums of money involved ($500,000 for the Holford books, several millions for the Bodmer deal), and in the intrinsic importance of the materials. The Bodmer purchases covered a great range in time—from the Adler papyri of the 2nd century B.C., to the Moliere *Oeuvres* of 1682 . . . The vast range of the collection is a reflection of Dr. Bodmer's all-encompassing interests; the books he sold me came from every corner of his library . . . But the crowning glory of the Bodmer purchase was the group of manuscripts.[8]

This report by Kraus suggests that the transaction took place just before Bodmer's death (on March 22, 1971). But Dr. Braun, currently the director of the Bibliothèque Bodmer, reports that it was just after Bodmer's death that the family had Kraus come. This is also suggested in the published catalogue of Latin manuscripts, which lists twenty that were "sold after the death of Martin Bodmer," though an introductory statement reports that they "have been sold, before the existence of the Foundation, by the good offices of the book dealer H. P. Kraus of New York."[9] This suggests the transaction was actually consummated between the death of Bodmer and the assumption of authority by the Foundation, at a time when presumably the heirs of Bodmer were in control. In the preface to Kraus's book, he reported that "during a period of several years in the early 1970s I bought many great treasures from the library of the late Dr. Martin Bodmer of Geneva."[10]

8. Kraus, *Rare Book Saga*, 273, 275–76, 278, 281–83, 286.

9. Pellegrin, *Manuscrits Latins*, 457–62, where one finds the list titled "Latin manuscripts from the collection sold after the death of Martin Bodmer."

10. Ibid., xv.

It is unknown if any "Bodmer Papyri" were involved in this massive transaction, since there is no published catalogue of papyri comparable to that of the Latin manuscripts. Nor are there any allusions identifiable as "Bodmer Papyri" in Kraus's report. But his informed comments about the actuality of Bodmer's dealings in the rare book market may serve to correct any naive assumption one might have, to the effect that he bought whatever manuscript discoveries came his way and, once acquired, retained all he had purchased.

If the manuscripts here listed that are not in the Bibliothèque Bodmer are to be associated with those that are, in that they may be of the same provenience, conversely some of the Bodmer Papyri may not be of this same provenience, and hence should perhaps be excluded from consideration here, where the focus is on a single manuscript discovery. Although the present volume seeks to provide whatever clarity can be achieved in each instance, by the very nature of the case absolute certainty is hardly attainable and degrees of probability are all that can be reasonably achieved.

—1—

The Bodmer Papyri

THEIR QUANTITY

> It is quite certain that this find of some thirty codices (in the region of Nag Hamadi, like the Gnostic papyri) cannot remain the act of a single individual.
>
> —Louis Doutreleau in a letter to Victor Martin on July 26, 1956

> Riyāḍ counted out to the priest of Dishnā, "al-Qummuṣ" Manqaryūs, one by one thirty-three books . . .
>
> —From an interview with Riyāḍ Jirjis Fām in Heliopolis on January 15, 1980

When one tries to correlate the concept of the Bodmer Papyri with a concrete, physical reality, one realizes how abstract our thinking often is. This is true is several regards.

A number of the Bodmer Papyri are in fact not in the Bibliothèque Bodmer in Cologny near Geneva, but scattered rather widely around the world. The present investigation seeks to include all that were involved in the discovery, irrespective of their present repository.

The designation of them as "papyri" is quite misleading. Among papyrologists it has become common, if confusing, usage to refer to ancient manuscripts studied by "papyrologists," whatever the writing surface may be, as "papyri." Thus they no doubt came to be called "papyri" quite casually without further reflection. But it would be inaccurate to assume that the Bodmer Papyri are all written on papyrus. Many are, but many are written on parchment. They could hardly be referred to as codices, as in the case of the Nag Hammadi Codices, in view of the fact that P. Bodmer I, XXVIII, XXXIX, XLVIII, and XLIX consist of what is left of rolls; and the Pachomian archives include rolls. Furthermore, the Bibliothèque Bodmer uses the term *codex* for the numeration system in its catalogue of Latin manuscripts, where the concept of codicology is at home.[1]

The numeration of the monograph series *Papyrus Bodmer* I, et cetera, is misleading to the extent that one might be tempted to take the highest number in the series as a relevant quantity of something (XLVI among those published, L among those assigned a number). For the numeration is neither the number of ancient books, nor of texts written in such books, nor of modern books publishing the ancient material. The numeration of the series thus has unintentionally served to obscure the fact that there is no clear picture as to the size of the collection.

The first objective in what follows is hence to make a survey of the available information: to seek to establish just how many ancient books are involved, where they are, the material they are written on, the language, and the nature of their contents. This will be relevant as an indication of the size, contents, and variety of a collection buried in late antiquity, which is valuable information in its own right. It will also be relevant in seeking to correlate the Bodmer Papyri with reports emanating from Egypt as to the quantity and kinds of books involved in the discovery referred to there as the Dishnā Papers.

The number of ancient books that emanated from the same discovery is very difficult even to approximate on the basis of what has been published thus far. Appendix 2, a bibliography of Bodmer Papyri, will indicate what Bodmer Papyri have been published as well as what is not yet published but known to exist. The bibliography will make it possible to limit footnote references to these editions to the title and page references.

One may conjecture that the numeration of the monograph series *Papyrus Bodmer*[2] was originally intended to reflect both the number

1. Thus the Bodmer "Codices" are cataloged by Pellegrin in her *Manuscrits Latins*.

2. Initially the *Papyrus Bodmer* series was presented as a subseries within a larger series of publications of the Bibliothèque Bodmer listed at the end of each of the first

of ancient books and the number of volumes published in the modern *editiones principes*. This policy did apply when a codex contained only a single text: P. Bodmer II (though two supplementary volumes were required before this codex was more or less adequately published), VI, XVI, XVIII, XXI (the part at the Bibliothèque Bodmer), XXIII, and XXIV. But it was not carried through consistently in other instances.

Already in the first publication, a certain vacillation can be noted. For here a roll containing documentary texts on the front had been secondarily cut into two rolls containing on the back the *Iliad*, books 5 and 6. The two books of the *Iliad* were published with a comment in the introduction to the effect that, since they are distinct entities, "from a bibliological point of view," they would be designated P. Bodmer I and P. Bodmer II.[3] But yet they were actually published in a single volume that was designated *Papyrus Bodmer* I. Perhaps this outcome resulted from the recognition that all that was left of the roll that had contained book 6 of the Iliad was a relatively few fragments, which did not call for a separate volume for their publication. The decision to publish both rolls in a single volume may thus have led to the decision to give them a single number, perhaps with the rationalization that the documentary texts on the front had been a single roll or that the *Iliad* is a single work. The documentary texts will, however, only be published in a concluding volume of miscellanea as *Papyrus Bodmer* L. Then, somewhat more simply, a codex containing only the Gospel of John was published as *Papyrus Bodmer* II.

A Coptic codex was ready next, as *Papyrus Bodmer* III. But, no doubt in view of the esoteric language, it was published in the Coptic subseries of the CSCO of Louvain, a series with the policy of publishing the transcription and the translation in separate volumes. The Bibliothèque Bodmer then adapted this policy to its own format: for its own distribution, it brought the two volumes together into a single

volumes (except at the end of the more recently published *Supplement* to *Papyrus Bodmer* II: *Evangile de Jean chap. 14–21*). For *Papyrus Bodmer* I and *Papyrus Bodmer* II were listed on a half-title page as *Bibliotheca Bodmeriana* III and IV respectively. But beginning with *Papyrus Bodmer* III, this broader series title, *Bibliotheca Bodmeriana*, was omitted, presumably because this codex, like *Papyrus Bodmer* VI, was published in the CSCO series of Louvain. Then beginning with *Papyrus Bodmer* IV, the listing of the broader Bodmer series at the end of the volumes was resumed but without numeration. This eliminated the double numeration, while still integrating the *Papyrus Bodmer* series into the whole listing of publications of the Bibliothèque Bodmer.

3. *Papyrus Bodmer* I, 9.

folder that was comparable in appearance to the covers of the volumes that had been published by the Bibliothèque Bodmer itself.

The next codex contained three plays by Menander. But the play that stood in first place in the codex (*The Girl from Samos*, P. Bodmer XXV) and the play that stood in third place (*The Shield*, P. Bodmer XXVI) were very fragmentary. Since rumors indicated that missing parts of them might ultimately be acquired,[4] the second, relatively complete, play was published first, in a volume to itself, as *Papyrus Bodmer* IV. Thereupon the policy seems to have been adopted, at least for Greek texts, of publishing each and every text from a codex in a volume to itself, or if too small, at least with a distinct number. For this is the policy followed in the cases of the two other Greek codices containing more than one text: One codex was published in five volumes as *Papyrus Bodmer* V, *Papyrus Bodmer* VII–IX, *Papyrus Bodmer* X–XII, *Papyrus Bodmer* XIII, and *Papyrus Bodmer* XX (or, to follow the order in which the texts occur in the codex, as P. Bodmer V, X, XI, VII, XIII, XII, XX, IX and VIII); the other was published as *Papyrus Bodmer* XIV and XV (in two volumes).[5] After the publication of P. Bodmer VI in 1960, Coptic codices were no longer included in the CSCO series of Louvain.[6] The practice became to publish a whole Coptic codex, even though containing more than one text, in a single volume under a single number: P. Bodmer XVII, XIX, and XXII. As a result, the monograph series *Papyrus Bodmer* I–XXVI, which is the amount published prior to the hiatus marked by Bodmer's death in 1971, presents the *editiones principes* of sixteen ancient books containing thirty-nine ancient texts (or, if one remove from the calculation P. Bodmer XVII that is clearly from another provenience, fifteen ancient books containing thirty-one ancient texts). Thus, the numeration of the series itself is misleading on both accounts: It is considerably

4. *Papyrus Bodmer* XXV, 5 (and almost identically *Papyrus Bodmer* XXVI, 5): "These regrettable lacunae, and the hope that existed of seeing them filled, had motivated Mr. Martin Bodmer to delay for a long time the publication of the fragments that had come to his Library."

5. There is a vacillation in the case of P. Bodmer XIV (Luke)—P. Bodner XV (John), the two texts of P[75]. Luke is published in one volume as *Papyrus Bodmer* XIV and John in a separate volume as *Papyrus Bodmer* XV, according to the title pages. Yet the cover of each volume is inscribed *Papyrus Bodmer* XIV–XV: *Evangile de Luc et Jean*, the one being distinguished from the other as *Tome I, XIV: Luc chap. 3–24*, and *Tome II, XV: Jean chap. 1–15*.

6. The suspension of that publication arrangement was reported in a letter of January 31, 1961, from R. Draguet, the editor of CSCO, to Jean Doresse.

higher than the number of ancient books published therein, but somewhat lower than the number of texts they contain.[7]

Bodmer Papyri of brief extent have also been published in articles. This has taken place only after the death of Martin Bodmer, and hence reflected a new policy of the Library when administered as a Foundation. Indeed, there was a lapse of six years between the last publication in book form (P. Bodmer XXVI in 1969) and the first in journal format (P. Bodmer XXVII in 1975), when the publication of three papyrus sheets from a Greek codex[8] was begun in a Swiss journal *Museum Helveticum*. The article of 1975 contains Thucydides 6.1,1–2,6 (P. Bodmer XXVII).

7. The numeration of the series also does not conform to the number of modern volumes in the series. As in the case of P. Bodmer III, the Coptic P. Bodmer VI was published in two volumes in the CSCO series. In two cases, a single volume of the series *Papyrus Bodmer* contains more than one brief text but not a whole codex, though now each text is given a separate number (VII–IX; X–XII). This breaks down in the converse way from that of P. Bodmer III and VI the correlation between the numeration of the series and the number of modern volumes, in that one modern volume carries more than one number in the series. The correlation between the numeration and the number of modern volumes is also not retained in the case of P. Bodmer II, where an initial publication was followed by a *Supplément* and then a *Nouvelle Édition augmentée et corrigée* of the *Supplément*, with the result that three publications relate to one number.

8. Turner, *Typology*, 81, provided fuller information:

> Parts of two or possibly three gatherings survive. Gathering 1 and the beginning of gathering 2 contain *Susanna* in Greek. It is followed by some other apocryphal work and then the beginning of Daniel, perhaps extending into gathering 3. After a blank page, Thucydides VI, 1–3 was copied, breaking off where the gathering ends. It is impossible to say whether the whole of Thucydides VI would have been copied in a series of subsequent gatherings.

Already in 1963, Willis, "Papyrus Fragment of Cicero," 325, referred to a codex "containing a part of Thucydides." In the *editio princeps* of this text in 1975, the contents of the four leaves are listed: Antonio Carlini, "Il papiro di Tucidide della Bibliotheca Bodmeriana (P. Bodmer XXVII)," 33:

> In the Bibliotheca Bodmeriana of Cologny-Geneva there is conserved a fascicle [quire] composed of three bifolios [sheets] of papyrus without numeration, coming from an imprecise locality of Upper Egypt . . . The first two pages (pp. 1a, 1b) contain the biblical text "Susanna" (1:53 ΤΟΥΣ ΑΙΤΙΟΥΣ–end) in the version of Theodotion; pp. 2a, 2b, 3a, 3b contain, still in the version of Theodotion, "Daniel" 1:1–20 ΚΑΙ ΤΟΥΣ. These two biblical texts were copied at a careful scriptorium attributable according to G. Cavallo and M. Manfredi to the Third Century A.D., according to E. G. Turner to the Fourth Century A.D. On p. 4a is found, in a heavy and irregular script difficult to date, moral exhortations. P. 4b is blank. The final four pages, pp. 5a, 5b, 6a, 6b, contain in a chancellery hand the beginning of book 6 of the History of Thucydides (6.1,1–2,6 ΟΙ ΕΛΛΗΝΕΣ).

Then in 1981 Susanna 1:53–64 (in the translation of Theodotion) and Daniel 1:1–20 (also Theodotion) were published together as P. Bodmer XLV and XLVI. An "apocryphal work" (E. G. Turner), "moral exhortations" (Antonio Carlini) from these three sheets, is to be published as P. Bodmer XLVII. Also, six fragments from a papyrus roll of a satyr-play were published as P. Bodmer XXVIII in the same journal. Though not in the monograph series, these joined publications do continue the numeration of the monograph series. Thus the original numeration system came to apply no longer to the monograph series but rather to refer only to the publication of papyri that (mostly) belonged (at the time of publication) to the Bibliothèque Bodmer.

"With Papyrus Bodmer XXIX," published in 1984, the first text of the so-called Codex Visionum, "the publication of Bodmer Papyri in book form resumes."[9] The rest of the Codex Visionum, P. Bodmer XXX–XXXVIII, is to be published.[10]

The presumably minor residue of still further materials at the Bibliothèque Bodmer from the same discovery, about which more precise information apparently must await their publication, includes the following:

- P. Bodmer XXXIX, a small parchment roll containing Pachomius's Letter 11b in the Sahidic dialect of Coptic;[11]
- P. Bodmer XL, leaves from a parchment codex containing the Song of Songs in the Sahidic dialect of Coptic, assigned to Roldophe Kasser for publication;[12]

9. *Papyrus Bodmer* XXIX 5.

10. See already Reverdin, "Les Genevois et Menandre," as presented on the French-language Swiss radio on March 15, 1975, 1: "Vision of Dorothea, an unknown poem in epic verse by Quintus of Smyrna, for which three professors of the University of Geneva are currently preparing the edition." E. G. Turner, in a letter of October 13, 1980, has clarified:

> Smyrna is a guess, and in my view a bad one. The author simply calls himself Quintos. And he is obviously a member of the imperial bodyguard, and also a Christian. I have seen the original. My impression of date is c. iv or v; size I don't have, but I don't think it is the same size as any of the other Bodmer codices—that is, it is an independent book.

The volume that appeared in 1984 is titled *Papyrus Bodmer* XXIX: *Vision de Dorotheos*.

11. Veilleux, *Pachomian Koinonia*, 3:77–78. The Coptic text is to appear in a volume by Tito Orlandi, et al., *Pachomiana Coptica*.

12. Listed already by Till, "Coptic Biblical Texts," 240. According to information

- P. Bodmer XLI, seven partially published papyrus leaves in the Sub-Achmimic dialect of Coptic containing the Ephesus episode from the *Acts of Paul*, assigned to Rodolphe Kasser for publication;[13]
- P. Bodmer XLII, Second Corinthians in Coptic, whose dialect and writing material has not been divulged, assigned to Rodolphe Kasser for publication;
- P. Bodmer XLIII, an unidentified apocryphon in Coptic, whose dialect and writing material has not been divulged, assigned to Rodolphe Kasser for publication;
- P. Bodmer XLIV, papyrus fragments of Daniel in the Bohairic dialect of Coptic;
- P. Bodmer XLVII, Greek "moral exhortations" an "apocryphal work" from the three papyrus sheets mentioned above; and
- P. Bodmer XLVIII, fragments of the *Iliad* and P. Bodmer XLIX, the *Odyssey* from papyrus rolls not belonging to P. Bodmer I.
- P. Bodmer L will contain the documentary texts from the recto of P. Bodmer I and miscellaneous addenda to the previous volumes, such as unpublished facsimiles.

THEIR PROVENIENCE

> One knows what little credence one can give to the reports of antiquities dealers when they cannot be confirmed by any archeological investigation.
> —Rodolphe Kasser[14]

Shortly before his death, however, the antiquities dealer who had sold them lifted the secret. He revealed that these papyri came

obtained by Hans Quecke in the Bibliothèque Bodmer and transmitted by Tito Orlandi in a letter of June 9, 1976, the leaf containing 6:9b—7:9 was not included by Till since it was acquired later than the rest. The date on which Rodolphe Kasser prepared the inventory that he provided to Till for this purpose is not known. In various regards this inventory is less complete than that found in Kasser, *Compléments au Dictionnaire Copte de Crum*, xv. But the additional material may be due to further study rather than to further acquisitions.

13. Kasser, "Acta Pauli 1959," 45–57. See also Kasser, "Anfang des Aufenhaltes," 268–70. Note also the English translation, "Beginning of the Stay in Ephesus," 387–90.

14. Kasser, *Papyrus Bodmer VI*, viii, n. 1.

> from a village near Nag Hammadi . . . It is to Mr. Rodolphe Kasser . . . that he made his confession.
> —Olivier Reverdin[15]

> . . . a little to the east of Nag Hammadi . . .
> —Rodolphe Kasser[16]

The *provenience* of a book is its "place of origin." However, this may be taken to refer either to the place where it was produced, or, in the case of discovered manuscripts, to the place where it was discovered. Internal evidence, such as the scribal hand or codicological details, would tend to point to the place where a book was produced, and only by inference to the place where it was discovered. External evidence, such as reports accompanying the material to the antiquities market, would tend to point to the place where a book was discovered and only by inference to the place where it was produced. Since books could be readily carried up and down the Nile, the two senses of provenience need not coincide. But the assumption has been, when there are no indications to the contrary, that they would be the same. As long as the two senses of provenience may reasonably be assumed to coincide, the discussion may be carried on in this inclusive sense. Yet, one should be aware of the theoretical possibility of a divergence in terms of provenience in order that evidence not be used in an inappropriate way. And when the dates, languages, writing material, cultural matrix, and other qualities of individual books diverge as much as is the case with the Bodmer Papyri, it is wisest to limit the term to refer to the place of discovery.

In the case of most manuscripts reaching scholarly hands through the antiquities market, the provenience is not known. Thus manuscripts discovered in the process of legitimate archaeological excavation not only have the advantage of being free from the shadows of impropriety in their acquisition and avoid the dangers of mishandling and loss at the hands of discoverers and middlemen, but also have the added value that inheres in an artifact found *in situ*. An instance would be the Oxyrhynchus Papyri, where knowledge of their provenience has made possible the reconstruction of the history of that location.[17] Even when the manuscripts result from a clandestine discovery, an identification of

15. Reverdin, "Les Genevois et Ménandre," 1.

16. Kasser, *Papyrus Bodmer* XXIX, 100, n. 2.

17. Turner, "Roman Oxyrhynchus," 78–93.

the provenience would make them amenable to such a use. Father Louis Doutreleau urged Victor Martin (unsuccessfully) to prepare an inventory of the Bodmer Papyri, since he thought this would "make it possible to discover the *raison d'être* of Nag Hammadi" (see below). Indeed the thesis of this book as to the provenience of the Bodmer Papyri from the Pachomian Monastic Order provides the most important new information about the Pachomian Order to have emerged in recent times.

The knowledge of the provenience of a manuscript also augments what can be inferred about the manuscript itself. The lack of information concerning the provenience of the Bodmer Papyri early led to whimsical regret over this limitation of their usefulness: "The editor concludes that the [Bohairic] text was translated from an archaic Sahidic model by someone whose knowledge of Bohairic was not perfect. It is regrettable in this connection that there is no satisfactory information as to the provenience of BO [P. Bodmer III]."[18]

Rodolphe Kasser has similarly expressed the importance for the localization of Coptic dialects that would be attached to establishing the provenience of the Bodmer Papyri:

> The *place* of discovery of a papyrus is an extremely important indication for the study of the text that it contains (and that all the more when it has to do with an ancient Coptic copy). But often, too often, this place cannot be known with certitude. Such is unfortunately the case with the Bodmer Papyri that have occupied us until now. And even if one would expect a bit that a copy like P. Bodmer XXI would come from Upper Egypt, it is impossible to prove what is only an assumption. Let us hope that one day we will be better informed on this point, capital for the study of Coptic linguistics, in particular with regard to what concerns the localization of the different dialects in Egypt, their geographic origin, their field of expansion, there zones of superimposition and reciprocal influences.[19]

Martin Krause has drawn attention to the greater usefulness of the Nag Hammadi codices over the Bodmer Papyri due to knowledge as to the provenience of the Nag Hammadi Codices and the lack of specificity concerning the provenience of the Bodmer Papyri, with the result that

18. Kuhn, "Review of *Papyrus Bodmer* III," 364.
19. *Papyrus Bodmer* XXI, 7.

the two collections can hardly be fruitfully brought into interaction with each other:

> Especially it is so important that both the place of discovery as well as the time of inscribing the texts be assured, because both form the presupposition for well-grounded work in the area of Coptic dialect research. But this presupposition is given in only the rarest cases with regard to early Coptic manuscripts. It is largely missing for the already mentioned manuscript discovery that R. Kasser has edited for the largest part: As place of discovery only quite generally Upper Egypt is known. The dating of the Coptic manuscripts is very crude: P. Bodmer XVIII and XXI, for example, are said to be "probably from the Fourth Century." P. Bodmer XIX and XXII come from the "Fourth to Fifth Century." Before these texts can be evaluated for the history of the Coptic language and dialects and compared with the linguistic situation of the library of Nag Hammadi, these manuscripts must first be more precisely dated and one must attempt to determine the place of their origin.[20]

To be sure, such reasoning seems to assume that the location of the discovery is the same as that of the scribe or translator, whereas, in fact, the contrary seems to be the case, once the ensemble of the Bodmer Papyri is considered as a whole. For example, the plurality of dialects represented makes it difficult to assume the provenience of the discovery would help identify the nomes in which that dialect was spoken. But the striking divergence among the Bodmer Papyri with regard to the plurality of Coptic dialects and indeed of non-Coptic languages has been hard to appreciate, due to the lack of an overview of the whole of the Bodmer Papyri discovery.

Published information has been sparse and even then ambivalent concerning just what material in the Bibliothèque Bodmer is of a shared provenience. The Introduction of *Papyrus Bodmer* III of 1958 reported that P. Bodmer II and III were part of a batch of documents offered in a block, whose provenience, though unknown, is referred to in the singular.[21] This would tend to suggest that a discovery of manuscripts had been kept together and sold together to the Bibliothèque Bodmer. Similarly the Introduction to *Papyrus Bodmer* XVI of 1961 spoke of a

20. Krause, "Zur Bedeutung des gnostisch-hermetischen Handschriftenfundes," 73.
21. *Papyrus Bodmer* III, 3.

single provenience for the "ensemble" of the Coptic material;[22] and the Introduction to *Papyrus Bodmer* XXIII of 1965 attributed to a single discovery the Greek and Coptic documents on papyrus and parchment that arrived together.[23]

Yet the publication in 1956 of P. Bodmer II had been accompanied by a small green chit of paper reporting that a new batch of papyri containing fragments of P. Bodmer II had been acquired while the volume was in the press.[24] This tends to suggest that the material from the one discovery had been divided and was acquired by the Bibliothèque Bodmer in more than one transaction. The introduction to *Papyrus Bodmer* XXII of 1964 suggested that this manuscript, after passing by the Bibliothèque Bodmer only to be examined, was absent for over a year before it finally came back in altered condition, and, one might be led to infer, only then acquired.[25] However, the codex, after its first passage at the Bibliothèque Bodmer, seems less to have returned to the antiquities market than, in view of its balled-up condition, to have undergone a not fully successful effort to flatten and conserve it.[26] The inaccurate numeration written in

22. *Papyrus Bodmer* XVI, 7.

23. *Papyrus Bodmer* XXIII, 7: "the discovery of Greek or Coptic documents on papyrus or parchment that arrived together at the Bibliothèque Bodmer."

24. The chit of paper was as follows:

> Important Notice: The present volume was already in the press when the Bibliothèque Bodmer was able to acquire a new batch of papyri. On examining it, it became clear that it contained a good number of fragments, though of very small size, belonging to the last chapters of our manuscript of the Fourth Gospel. Since the identification and assembly of these scraps will require considerable time, it has seemed fitting not to delay the publication that was in progress, and to reserve the remainder for an appendix that will be prepared as quickly as possible.

25. *Papyrus Bodmer* XXII, 7: "In effect, the manuscript that must have been entrusted to the Bibliothèque only for examination, disappeared from it again for more than a year. When it returned, most of the folios had been separated the one from the other; furthermore they had been carefully unglued, flattened and polished, which had not taken place without altering the clarity of the script."

26. William H. Willis has reported in a letter of June 8, 1980:

> On a visit to the Bodmeriana in the course of Kasser's and my collaboration (1962), I saw the Bodmer leaves and learned the story to which Kasser obliquely alludes . . .When the ball-shaped first half came to Geneva (along with all the rest from Tano), at the time when Testuz was the house scholar and before Kasser, still at Combas, had been recommended to Testuz by Draguet, Bodmer sent it to Zürich (where he had business interests) to have it

pencil on the pages during their absence has been explained as an error due to the fact that some of the material was in a different lot only later acquired by the Bibliothèque Bodmer,[27] which again suggests more than one stage in the acquisition process. (The parts of this same P. Bodmer XXII that were to become Mississippi Coptic Codex II, which were also originally in a balled-up state,[28] did not pass through the Bibliothèque Bodmer, but represent a completely independent transaction.) The preface to *Papyrus Bodmer* XXV of 1969 also suggested in a still different way a process rather than a single acquisition, in that its publication was deferred in 1958 in hopes that rumors of more to come would prove to be true, a hope that by 1969 had for all practical purposes been abandoned.[29] One may conclude that the acquisition extended over a period of years, which seems to have been largely limited to the 1950s rather than extending significantly over into the 1960s. One should,

> relaxed and photographed; somehow Bodmer's son was involved. The relaxing and "consolidation" was very crudely done, with a hot iron in fact, with resulting splits in the parchment leaves; folds in some leaves were pressed into overlaps with resulting loss of letters; and the photos were made by a newspaper photographer, rather poorly. This is the "year of disappearance" to which Kasser later alluded, I believe. His allusion was purposefully obscure because he didn't want to offend Bodmer (or his watchdog Mlle. Bongard), whom he thought to have acted incompetently.

27. *Papyrus Bodmer* XXII, 7, n. 2: "If they [the penciled page numbers] do not correspond exactly to the actual position of the leaves, it is because other folios (e.g., pp. 1/2) were acquired later by the Bibliothèque Bodmer."

28. Willis, "New Collection of Papyri," 382–83: "While the papyrus codex [Mississippi Coptic Codex I = the Crosby Codex] was found flat and undistorted, the parchment one was on arrival so curled as to appear almost ball-shaped, suggesting it may have been preserved in the bottom of a small pot."

29. *Papyrus Bodmer* XXV, 5 (and almost identically, *Papyrus Bodmer* XXVI, 5):

> Ten years have run past since V. Martin published the *Dyscolos* of Menander (*Papyrus Bodmer* IV), a comedy almost entirely unpublished until then, and conserved practically intact in this new document. The manuscript of the Third Century that has restored the *Dyscolos* to us contains also other pieces by Menander. However none of them is complete (several folios of the codex are still completely lacking). These regrettable lacunae, and the hope that there was of seeing them filled, had led Mr. Martin Bodmer to delay for a long time the publication of the fragments that had come to his library. But now, after so many years of largely fruitless patience, the decision has been made not to deny to papyrologists and Hellenists any longer the knowledge of texts that they have been awaiting with great impatience.

A footnote explained the hope: "The rumor was circulating that the pages still absent could be recuperated soon."

however, note the feeble and unfulfilled hope still expressed at the conclusion to the supplements to *Papyrus Bodmer* IV, published in 1969 with *Papyrus Bodmer* XXVI.[30]

The very fact that parts of the same discovery emerged in so many other collections (see chapters 2–3 below) would suggest that the discovery was not sold as an ensemble but rather in a series of transactions, in which process the Bibliothèque Bodmer might be expected to have been involved more than once. It is this situation that is reflected in a parenthetical comment of 1969 to the effect that almost all of an ancient library finally reached the Bibliothèque Bodmer.[31] Since the Bibliothèque Bodmer did not itself have an overview of the total contents of the discovery, this comment probably means no more than that Bodmer bought most of what was offered to him.

If thus the material reached the Bibliothèque Bodmer in a series of transactions, a shared provenience for all the material is not certain. Only when materials from different transactions belong to the same manuscript are the two batches in question thereby obviously related. Yet the statements cited above implying a shared provenience may be assumed to be intended to apply to all of the collection except where specific exceptions are made. An exception to the shared provenience is most probable in the case of P. Bodmer XVII, stated to be of unknown provenience, but with no relation to the other documents published in the series, and "different from them in every regard."[32]

In the introduction to *Papyrus Bodmer* XXIV of 1967, this codex was added to P. Bodmer (I and) XVII as having a separate provenience from the bulk of the Bodmer Papyri.[33] This separation of P. Bodmer

30. *Papyrus Bodmer* XXVI, 49: "Let us hope that other fragments of this codex will still appear and permit us to have a still more complete and precise picture of the work of Menander."

31. *Papyrus Bodmer* XXXVI, 17: "Manuscripts that, almost all, have finally come to the Bodmeriana."

32. *Papyrus Bodmer* XVII, 7: "P. Bodmer XVII (P^{74}) is a rather large papyrus codex whose exact provenience is unknown to us. In any case one cannot establish any relation between this document and the other ancient codices (Greek or Coptic, on papyrus or parchment) belonging to the Bibliothèque Bodmer and published in this same series. Besides, P^{74} is different from them in every regard."

33. *Papyrus Bodmer* XXIV, 7: "Only one thing is sure: It [P. Bodmer XXIV] is not part of the batch including the Greek or Coptic P. Bodmer II to XVI and XVIII to XXIII, and, furthermore, it is not of the same *origin* as P. Bodmer I or P. Bodmer XVII."

XXIV from the main collection was apparently not based on specific information concerning a distinct provenience, since that is said to be unknown.[34] It may be because P. Bodmer XXIV was known to come from a different dealer (see chapter 4 below). In any case, in 1969, in the introduction to *Papyrus Bodmer* XXV, P. Bodmer XXIV was dropped from the list of exceptions to the shared provenience.[35] Similarly, in 1972 Rodolphe Kasser listed only P. Bodmer (I and) XVII as exceptions to the collection's having been copied (he must have meant discovered!) at the same place.[36] Thus, one may infer that the initial exclusion of P. Bodmer XXIV from the shared provenience was soon suspended.

In 1963, George D. Kilpatrick reported that "it has been questioned whether the Homer [P. Bodmer I] is part of the same find as the Biblical and Christian texts."[37] William H. Willis has also reported having been told early in the 1960s that only P. Bodmer I and XVII were of a distinct provenience.[38] The distinguishing of the provenience of P. Bodmer I from that of the bulk of the collection does not seem to have been published prior to the introduction to *Papyrus Bodmer* XXIV in 1967. The *editio princeps* of P. Bodmer I in 1954 did not affirm or deny a shared provenience, since what other papyri may have been at the Bibliothèque Bodmer at that time were unpublished; in any case no reference was made to them.

34. *Papyrus Bodmer* XXIV, 7: "We do not know from what part of Egypt P. Bodmer XXIV comes."

35. *Papyrus Bodmer* XXV, 7, the matter of provenience is relegated to: "Cf. *P. Bodmer XXIII*, p. 7; P. Bodmer I and XVII are of a different origin." The reference back to the equivalent passage in the Introduction to *Papyrus Bodmer* XXIII, rather than to that of *Papyrus Bodmer* XXIV, would also seem to suggest a tacit disavowal of the exclusion of P. Bodmer XXIV from the shared provenience maintained in the introduction to *Papyrus Bodmer* XXIV.

36. Kasser, "Fragments du livre biblique," 80, n. 23.

37. Kilpatrick, "Bodmer and Mississippi Collection," 34.

38. In a letter of May 27, 1980, from Willis:

> In Geneva nearly twenty years ago I was told positively by both Mlle Bongard and Professor Kasser that P. Bodmer I and XVII had no connection with the other Bodmer codices . . . P. Bodmer I comprises two rolls (probably from Panopolis) which M. Bodmer purchased because he was interested in Homer, well before he had the opportunity to buy the subsequent find of codices; and well after he had bought the other codices, his agents turned up P. Bodmer XVII, a much later (seventh-century) papyrus codex of entirely different format, style and script from the Dishnā group. All the other codices, so far as I could learn, belonged to the big find.

On December 25, 1958, Victor Martin had written to Willis concerning the provenience of the Bodmer Papyri: "That they were found in Achmim, though probable, is by no means certain.[39] Willis took this to refer in general to the Bodmer Papyri and hence inferred that it also applied to Mississippi Coptic Codices I and II. Yet the association with Achmim was at the time derived from P. Bodmer I.[40] Martin had recognized that once the land registry of Panopolis (Achmim), dated to 208–209 CE and inscribed on the recto of both rolls of P. Bodmer I, was no longer of value, it could have been moved elsewhere prior to the use of the verso to inscribe books 5 and 6 of the *Iliad*.[41] Yet, in the absence of any reason to suggest a different provenience, Achmim seemed a logical conjecture.[42] Thus the association of the Bodmer Papyri with Achmim presupposes the inclusion of P. Bodmer I in the same discovery as the bulk of the Bodmer Papyri. Hence as late as 1961, the introduction to *Papyrus Bodmer* XVI apparently still presupposed the inclusion of P. Bodmer I in the main collection, in suggesting that the scriptorium of the Coptic material was somewhere "between Achmim and Thebes," though apparently for linguistic reasons tending to prefer Thebes.[43]

39. Willis, "New Collections of Papyri," 383, n. 1.

40. *Papyrus Bodmer* I, 21: "With regard to their provenience, the recto also furnishes indications. The administrative register that it contains concerns the nome of Panopolis in Upper Egypt. Hence one has every reason to think that it is at Panopolis (today Achmim) that the Homeric roll was created, and doubtless also discovered." P. Beatty Panop., which has for similar reasons also been attributed to Panopolis, had not yet been published, much less associated with the Bodmer Papyri.

41. Turner, "Roman Oxyrhynchus," 89–90, cited by Martin, *Papyrus Bodmer* I, 21, had drawn attention to such material found at Oxyrhynchus but originating from other nomes of Egypt. See also Turner, "Recto and Verso," 102–6.

42. *Papyrus Bodmer* I, 21–22:

> In any case nothing obliges us to disassociate the text of Homer here published from the land registry on the recto with regard to the place of their transcription. Panopolis was a provincial metropolis of a certain importance, where one knows that classical culture was in high repute. If this region became in the Fourth Century a center of monastic life, we also know that it remained until much later a center of resistance on the part of intellectual paganism to the new religion . . . We can hence, without mental reservations, see in our Homeric papyrus both a product of the local "bookstore" and a witness to the interest of the Panopolitans of the imperial epoch for classical Greek literature.

43. *Papyrus Bodmer* XVI, 7: "For the moment, in the absence of more precise indications, we can admit, as a possibility if not probability, that these texts were copied between Achmim and Thebes, and, by preference, in the neighborhood of the latter site."

Achmim has hence been widely accepted as the provenience of the bulk of the Bodmer Papyri. In 1958, E. G. Turner advocated Achmim and, indeed, a single discovery as the provenience of all the Bodmer Papyri, as well as of other manuscripts that have emerged since 1930.[44] In 1970, Richard Seider listed as the site of the discovery of P. Bodmer IV "Panopolis(?)."[45] In 1976, Joseph van Haelst listed Panopolis as the probable provenience of all the Christian codices among the Bodmer Papyri that had been published up to that time.[46] In 1979, Colin H. Roberts

44. Turner, *Greek Papyri* 52–53:

> Classical scholars will think, however, of Panopolis as the possible source of another codex of Menander, P. Bodmer IV . . . Within the thirty-year period 1930 to 1960 a considerable number of intact or nearly intact papyrus books were acquired by collectors, some by M. Bodmer, some by Sir Chester Beatty, others by institutions which include the University of Mississippi and the papyrological Institutes of Cologne and Barcelona. The earliest of these texts are to be dated about A. D. 200, the latest are of the sixth and seventh centuries . . . It is an economical hypothesis that all these papyri, whether works of Greek literature, documents, or Christian texts, are from one source and constitute a unitary find . . . The proved connection of P. Bodmer I and P. Beatty Panop. with Panopolis (leaving P. Gen. Inv. 108 and P. Leit. 10 out of account) is not evidence that would be sufficient in a court of law to establish Panopolitan origin for either the Menander codex or the rest of the manuscripts enumerated. There may have been more than one find (it is said, for instance, that P. Bodmer XVII did not belong to the original find). With this find it may be wrong to associate P. Bodmer I *and* the Chester Beatty codex *and* the documents mentioned in (5) [P. Gen. Inv. 108 and P. Leit. 10]. Yet these points are worth bearing in mind, especially as Panopolis was noted for its monasteries.

In the Supplementary Notes of the paperback edition of 1980, page 201, Turner withdraws P. Gen. Inv. 108 and P. Leit. 10 from such a shared provenience, since they were acquired by Geneva in 1900 and 1922 respectively. However, he indicates explicitly that the Chester Beatty Biblical Papyri may also be from Panopolis, and casts doubt on the report of Rodolphe Kasser to the effect that the dealer said the Bodmer Papyri came from a village near Nag Hammadi. "I am skeptical whether the dealer got his details right." However, in a letter of October 13, 1980, in response to an earlier draft of the present chapter, Turner has retracted this position: "You could help by slipping in a footnote to say that what I wrote in *Greek Papyri* 1968, 2nd ed. paperback, I am convinced is wrong, after reading your account."

45. Seider, *Paläographie*, vol. 2, *Literarische Papyri*, 136.

46. Van Haelst, *Catalogue des papyrus littéraires juifs et chrétiens* 156, item 426 (P. Bodmer II); 212, item 599 (P. Bodmer V); 196, item 557 (P. Bodmer VII); 193, item 548 (P. Bodmer VIII); 69, item 138 (P. Bodmer IX); 217, item 611 (P. Bodmer X); 199-200, item 569 (P. Bodmer XI); 244, item 681 (P. Bodmer XII); 243, item 678 (P. Bodmer XIII); 148, item 406 (P. Bodmer XIV-XV); 258, item 710 (P. Bodmer XX); and 62, item 118 (P. Bodmer XXIV). This includes all the Christian Bodmer Papyri

supported Turner's pan-Panopolitan argument on the basis of similarities in the use of *nomina sacra*, including the attribution of the Chester Beatty Biblical Papyri to the same discovery as the Bodmer Papyri,[47] although he did recall Carl Schmidt's report of having been told that the Chester Beatty Biblical Papyri were found "in the ruins of a church or monastery near Atfih (Aphroditopolis)."[48]

Thus the inclusion of P. Bodmer I in the same discovery as the rest of the Bodmer Papyri seems, at least indirectly, to have gained widespread acceptance, to judge by the trend to derive the bulk of the material from Panopolis. But this could also cut the other way: The ultimate provenience in Panopolis of material secondarily used for two books

---

that had at that time been published except P. Bodmer XVII, which he attributed to an "unknown provenience," p. 171, item 470. Haelst made the same statement for each of the other codices: "Uncertain provenience (purchase); probably Upper Egypt (the region of Panopolis)."

47. Roberts, *Manuscript, Society and Belief*, 28, n. 1.

48. Ibid., 7, referring to Schmidt, "Die neuesten Bibelfunde," 292–93:

> The determining of the location of a discovery is of course always very difficult, since the discoverer as well as the middleman has the greatest interest in erasing all traces, so as not to be called in to give account before the authorities or the administration of the museum. Nonetheless I have continued the investigation of the mysterious location of the discovery on my last visit, and could obtain from my old trusted contact man, who himself had possessed a number of leaves, first of all the admission that the Fayyum, of which one thinks first, did not come in question. A location of the discovery in Upper Egypt is excluded because of the group of middlemen into whose possession the leaves had come. In any case the location of the discovery could not lie far from the Fayyum. So I believe I possess an important pointer in the explanation of my contact man, when he described how to reach the site of the discovery, to the effect that I must go to the shore of the Nile east from Bush, a train station between El-Wasta and Beni Suef (115 km from Cairo), and cross over the Nile to the village Alalme. Alalme is the village from which a street leads to the monasteries of Anthony and Paul on the Red Sea, and from which toward the north the old Monastery of Anthony lies, and still further to the north, also on the east shore, the hamlet Atfih, old Aphroditopolis, from which Anthony, the founder of Egyptian monasticism, came. Here churches and monasteries must have existed that in old times possessed Christian sacred writings on papyrus and that copied them onto parchment after they were worn out.

Roberts also refers to Schmidt, "Evangelienhandschrift," 225: "Still this spring I interrogated the Fayyum dealer again and received the same information, to the effect that a locality Alame on the east bank of the Nile in the region of Atfih, old Aphroditopolis, is to be considered the location of the discovery."

of the *Iliad* (P. Bodmer I) need not mitigate against a shared secondary provenience near Dishnā, once one reflects upon the absorption of a monastic cluster near Panopolis led by Petronius into the Pachomian order, and the inclusion of Dishnā in the Panopolitan nome.

A somewhat similar situation obtains with regard to a Chester Beatty codex, where the quire was made of two rolls pasted together so that the writing surfaces faced each other, and the uninscribed back sides of the rolls became the exposed sides that were the pages in the codex. For the text on the two rolls are administrative documents from Panopolis of 298 and 300 CE (whereas the pages of the codex, largely uninscribed, do present a few tax receipts between 340 and 345 CE). Hence the codex has been designated P. Beatty Panop.[49] These tax receipts have to do in large part with a Panopolitan fairly prominent in documentary papyri at the Institut für Altertumskunde of the University of Cologne (see chapter 3 below). Thus one has to do with the three main repositories of the bulk of the Bodmer Papyri: Either these repositories share materials both from the main discovery near Dishnā and from a second provenience near Panopolis, or Panopolitan documentary papyri were in late antiquity incorporated among the Bodmer Papyri and were thus included in the shared burial near Dishnā (see chapters 2 and 3 below).

The assumption that P. Bodmer I (published two years before P. Bodmer II) was acquired separately and prior to the bulk of the collection does not necessarily indicate a different provenience. It was not a very early acquisition since it was not included by Bodmer among the papyri listed in *Eine Bibliothek der Weltliteratur* (1947). Bodmer had contacted the Cairo dealer from whom the bulk of the Bodmer Papyri were acquired as early as 1950, so that acquisitions made prior to the bulk purchases beginning in 1955 could have been from the same dealer and provenience. Bodmer had assembled the material conceded to be from the shared provenience in a series of transactions over a period of time, and the acquisition of P. Bodmer I could have been the beginning of this process.

Since nothing is reported from the antiquities market about a divergent provenience for P. Bodmer I, one may suspect that this view is a mere inference from perhaps misinterpreted circumstantial evidence. Doubt as to whether P. Bodmer I was of the shared provenience may have been increased by the observation that it was a roll, whereas the

49. Skeat, "Papyri from Panopolis," 194–99.

other books were codices. For when fragments of another roll, also with a classical text, were subsequently identified and published as *Papyrus Bodmer* XXVIII, this new fact was brought into conformity with the concept of a library exclusively of codices by the hypothesis of W. E. H. Cockle that the fragments may be from the cartonnage from the cover of a codex. Yet this view was put in question by Rodolphe Kasser's insistence that the removal of the fragments from a cover would have to have been done prior to the arrival of the material at the Bibliothèque Bodmer.[50] And now further fragments of rolls of the *Iliad* (P. Bodmer XLVIII) and the *Odyssey* (P. Bodmer XLIX) have been identified, in the residue of fragments that were among the various batches. If, therefore, fragments of rolls, and indeed rolls of Homer, accompanied the bulk of the Bodmer Papyri, the case for excluding P. Bodmer I from the shared provenience is correspondingly weakened.

It may have been that the publication of a New Testament text (P^{66}: John) next after Homer may have led to the assumption of a different provenience, especially since the editor of P. Bodmer II conjectured a monastery as its provenience. Thus Turner's pan-Panopolitan theory had to emphasize both the pagan and the monastic environment of Panopolis. But the investigations by Bodmer's secretary, Odile Bongard, had also produced what was in effect and probably in fact Tano's information that the material came from a monastery near Dishnā. This would have served to separate off the material thought to be from Panopolis: P. Bodmer I. But then Menander and other non-Christian material from the shared provenience may have led gradually to the abandonment both of the monastery hypothesis and of a divergent provenience for the non-Christian material, to whatever extent this played a role in the case of P. Bodmer I.

The absence or inaccessibility of information at the Bibliothèque Bodmer or from within the Bodmer family, together with the unwillingness of Mlle Bongard to divulge, prior to her testament, what she

50. Turner, "Papyrus Bodmer XXVIIII: Satyr-Play," 2. Evidence that this might have been cartonnage had been seen in the condition of the fragments:

> Clearly observable folds run obliquely down the height of the two large fragments A and D. In A the area on the upper right of this fold, in D that on the lower right is dirtyish, and covered by a whitish powder which could be remaining traces of paste; the areas on the other side of the fold are clean and bright golden in colour. A and D have in fact been put together to reconstitute the roll as here published. It might well have been torn up and the torn pieces folded to pack behind a leather outer cover.

knows, eliminates the more obvious sources of information concerning the relatedness of the Bodmer Papyri. The willingness on the part of the Chester Beatty Library to make Beatty's correspondence, the registry of accessions, and the other archival material accessible to scholarship produces in some cases a higher degree of certainty that some items in the Chester Beatty Library are Bodmer Papyri in the sense of a shared provenience (see chapter 2 below) than can be said of some items in the Bibliothèque Bodmer, for which such an assumption is quite reasonable but actually lacking any specific confirmation. And the same is true of the Institut für Altertumskunde of the University of Cologne, where willingness to make available the in-house reports on accessions and records about each accession has made possible a sifting between what is probable and what is merely possible in terms of a shared provenience (see chapter 3 below).

In addition to the association of P. Bodmer I with Achmim, the *editiones principes* of other Bodmer Papyri have assumed various positions with regard to provenience. Victor Martin's introduction to P. Bodmer II in 1956 proposed "a scriptorium attached to some monastery."[51] But Kurt Aland pointed out that there were no Christian monasteries at the time.[52] He suggested, as possibilities, a scriptorium at the catechetical school of Alexandria or one resulting from Bishop Demetrius's organization of the Egyptian church, but he pointed out that nothing is known of such scriptoria. The hand of P. Bodmer II makes it clear that it is the work of a professional scribe at the scriptorium of a publishing house.[53] Yet it is doubtful that such publishers at the time produced Christian texts for the public market, though it could have been commissioned by the church.

51. *Papyrus Bodmer* II, 10: "One can think of a scriptorium attached to some monastery that, without pretending to produce luxury copies, strove nonetheless for a certain quality."

52. Aland, "Papyrus Bodmer II: Ein erster Bericht," 180:

"That is in any case very unlikely. For Christian monasteries in the genuine sense did not exist around 200 either in Egypt or elsewhere." This judgment is not altered even if one were to date P. Bodmer II as late as 200–250 AD, as does Eric G. Turner, *Greek Manuscripts of the Ancient World* (Oxford: Clarendon, 1971), 108, item 63. E. A. Wallace Budge, *Coptic Biblical Texts in the Dialect of Upper Egypt* (London: British Museum, 1912) 1.xxviii, pointed out that when Anthony was a young man (around 270 AD) "there were no monasteries in existence."

53. Ibid., 180–81: "That it comes from the hand of a professional scribe and hence from a workshop seems in any case to be certain based on the character of the script."

Aland also doubts that it was produced by a professional Christian scribe for his own use, in that the quantity of omissions and scribal errors would suggest that the scribe was not a Christian.[54] The idea of a monastery as provenience was dropped in the *editiones principes*.[55] In the introduction of 1958 to *Papyrus Bodmer* IV, a play by Menander for which a monastic provenience would not suggest itself, Victor Martin simply stated that the provenience was unknown.[56] Indeed the suggestion of a monastic provenience did not reemerge until information from the antiquities market began to be reported (see below).[57]

Here one can already observe that the location of the scribe of one book would not necessarily be that of another, much less that of the whole collection. If the hand of P. Bodmer II (Greek!) reflects a professional scribe at a scriptorium, the hands of P. Bodmer III and VI (Coptic!) have been characterized as reflecting the reverse.[58]

54. Ibid., 181.

55. The introduction to *Papyrus Bodmer* XIX, 8, n. 2, in order to explain the rapid deterioration of the papyrus, postulated frequent use "by a Christian community, no doubt." Even several communities are postulated, on p. 9: "One could ask oneself also if this decayed codex, venerable souvenir of a past epoch, was not divided, like a precious relic, between several Christian communities." But it is not clear that such Christian groups were envisaged by the editor as monasteries rather than as local churches. Michel Testuz, *Papyrus Bodmer* VII–IX, 9, used the term *community* to refer to a congregation rather than a monastery, as is evident from the fact that he had in view a wealthy member of such a community: "The content of this anthology shows that the book was produced by Christians of Egypt, probably on the order of a well-to-do member of their community, who intended it for his own library." But Turner, *Greek Papyri* (1968), 53, used the association of Achmim with monasteries and the fact of manuscript discoveries in the White Monastery there as a final argument in favor of this provenience: "Yet these pointers are worth bearing in mind, especially as Panopolis was noted for its monasteries. Just across the river from Panopolis lies the White Monastery presided over by Schenute in the late fourth century. The stones of this monastery have already furnished the British Museum with a unitary find of a Coptic Psalter and homilies, and a number of other Coptic texts." The concept of a monastic library would, however, reemerge in connection with the reports of antiquities dealers and middlemen (see below).

56. *Papyrus Bodmer* IV, 7: "The place and the conditions of the discovery of the papyrus of the *Dyscolos* are unfortunately unknown, as is almost always the case for pieces of this kind acquired on the antiquities market."

57. Reverdin, "Les Genevois et Ménandre," 1: It has to do, in all probability, with what survives of the library of a monastery.

58. *Papyrus Bodmer* III, CSCO, 178.i: "We have shown how, in our view, this private copy was made: Very probably it was the work of a rather awkward scribe . . ." Kuhn, Review of *Papyrus Bodmer* III, 364: "The erratic orthography and the many errors and corrections indicate that BO [P. Bodmer III] was copied privately and that it is not the

Rodolphe Kasser's introduction to *Papyrus Bodmer* III in 1958 also expressed ignorance as to the provenience, suggesting only that the papyri had all been found together in Upper Egypt and emanated from a private library,[59] a view also presented in his introductions to *Papyrus Bodmer* VI and *Papyrus Bodmer* XVI in 1960–1961, as well as in Jean Guitton's preface to the deluxe edition of P. Bodmer VIII in 1968.[60] Michel Testuz's introduction to *Papyrus Bodmer* VII–IX in 1959[61] had provided the explanation for the conjecture of a private library: The small format of a codex has traditionally been so explained, in distinction from the large format used in the church.[62] However, this is hardly a reliable indication. For other factors have come to be recognized as influencing the size, such as changing style and the material used.[63]

Even if some specific use were in mind in choosing a format, that would apply to the original setting of the copying of the book rather than to the provenience of the discovery. If the collection covers more than

product of a scriptorium. *Papyrus Bodmer* VI, CSCO, 194.xxix: A scribe who had none of the professionalism of a scriptorium . . ."

59. *Papyrus Bodmer* III, CSCO, 177.iii: "This papyrus [P. Bodmer II] and ours were part of a group of Coptic and Greek documents that, offered in a block to the Bodmeriana, were acquired by the latter without their exact provenience having been revealed thus far. One said that all the pieces had been found together in Upper Egypt, and that it had to do with a private library. We do not know anything more."

60. *Papyrus Bodmer* VI, CSCO, 194.viii. *Papyrus Bodmer XVI* 7. Jean Guitton, "Preface," in Carolus M. Martini, *Beati Petri Apostoli Epistulae*, viii: "A rich and spiritual person of Egypt in the Third Century A. D., rather like the excellent Theophilus to whom Luke dedicated his work, commissioned his scribe to copy for him certain canonical texts of the New Testament." This is very similar to Father Louis Doutreleau's assumption that the Bodmer Papyri were the library of "an educated Christian." In a letter of August 29, 1980, L. Doutreleau stated: "In my view, NH II [the Bodmer Papyri] was a different library [from the Nag Hammadi codices], that of an educated Christian."

61. *Papyrus Bodmer* VII–IX, 9–10: "The content of this anthology shows that the book was produced by the Christians of Egypt, probably on the commission of a well-to-do member of their community, who intended it for his own library. The small format of the codex (about 15.5 x 14.2 cm) indicates that it had been made for private use rather than for reading in church."

62. Budge, *Coptic Biblical Texts*, 1.xxxiii–1.xxxiv: "It is tolerably certain that the Codex was not used as a service-book in a church, for it is not large enough, and the extraordinary selection of books of the Bible in it suggests that it was written for or by a private individual, most probably a monk who was a trained scribe, for private use."

63. Turner, *Typology*, 13–34. See also Drescher, "Review of *Papyrus Bodmer* XXII," 228: "The manuscript is a parchment one and, like other early parchment manuscripts, is of small format."

three centuries of scribal activity, the final situation at the time of burial would hardly be the same as that prevalent when at least the older books were produced. If size were a factor in determining the provenience, in terms of the place of manufacture, plurality of provenience would be evident from the wide divergences especially in height within the collection XXV–IV–XXVI: 12 cm broad by 27.5 or 28 cm high (though as a collection of Menander's plays, hardly a book for use in the church!); P. Bodmer VI: 12 cm broad by 14.5 cm high. It has also been noted that the earlier codices tend to be in Greek, the later ones in Coptic, indicative of the changing situation as Coptic wins out over Greek.[64] This tendency is also reflected in Coptic words written in the margin of a Greek text (P. Bodmer VIII) to facilitate comprehension.[65]

The fact that the late material is only in Coptic, with its implications that Greek had died out in the community whose library is involved, may explain some oddities regarding the Greek material: The non-Christian materials may no longer be recognizable as such, since they are no longer read; the fact that they were known as part of the older holdings of the library would have given them a status as relics that would account for their burial with the Christian material. In fact the repairs made on some of the older Greek codices are such as to render them largely unusable, an observation which has led to the conjecture that, at least in their case, their final use was that of a relic.[66] P. Bodmer XIV–XV, though a canonical

64. Kilpatrtick, "Bodmer and Mississippi Collection," 35:

> Let us try to imagine the circumstances in which such a library might come into being. First, the oldest texts in the collection are, as we shall see, Greek, both Christian and Classical. Next, the later their date, the more Coptic predominates. I know of no Greek texts in the collection which can be dated to the fifth century though this seems a likely enough date for some of the Coptic items. This observation suggests that we have a monument of the gradual triumph of Coptic power in the Christianity of upper Egypt during the Byzantine period.

65. *Papyrus Bodmer* VII–IX, 66 (to P. Bodmer VIII). See p. 33: "A Copt has hence written this word to explain his Greek text, and this Copt seems to be the scribe who made the copy." See also *Papyrus Bodmer* XIV, 24; *Papyrus Bodmer* XV, 76–77.

66. *Papyrus Bodmer* XXV, 15–17, especially p. 17:

> All of that is not without interest, and permits one to imagine a bit in what spirit in those times the books destined for this ancient library were assembled (manuscripts that, almost all, finally arrived at the Bodmeriana); this library was not only a place where one assembled works in good condition, usable for intellectual work. One also conserved there, preciously, old books very abused by time, use, and perhaps also the persecutions of the Third

text, was rebound before burial in such a way that part of the text became inaccessible, perhaps because as Greek it was unintelligible. Fragments of the text were pasted together into cardboard as the cartonnage lining the cover. And the binding thongs of the rebinding did not go through the center of the spine, as is usually the case, but through the front and back covers near the inner margin, making it impossible to open the book out wide enough to read the text at the inner margin. To treat Luke and John this way must mean their Greek texts were no longer read.

Michel Testuz also advocated in 1959 a provenience in the region of Thebes (= Luxor) on the basis of the confusion of /g/ and /k/ by Coptic scribes,[67] a trait to which already W. H. Worrell had drawn attention[68] and which Rodolphe Kasser had then noted in Papyrus Bodmer VI.[69]

> Century, books with which one could not do much, to be sure, but to which the memory of a prestigious past was attached.

The two codices classified as relics, P. Bodmer XXV–IV–XXVI and P. Bodmer XIV–XV, do not share a date prior to the Diocletianic persecution, but what they do have in common is that they are in Greek. At a time when Greek was becoming a dead language in Upper Egypt, in favor of Coptic, such codices would in any case tend to serve only as relics.

67. Testuz, *Papyrus Bodmer* VII–IX, 32:

> In a personal communication that he was kind enough to send me, and for which I wish to thank him, Pastor R. Kasser, the specialist who has to do with Coptic manuscripts at the Bibliothèque Bodmer, has given me the following information: It is a Coptic characteristic to confuse the sounds of /g/ and /k/, and also the /r/ and the /l/. But this phenomenon is very localized and is found only among the scribes of the region of Thebes. P. Bodmer VI, which contains the book of Proverbs in a quite distinctive Coptic dialect, makes this confusion regularly, to the point that he has completely omitted the use of /g/ in Coptic words, but not in terms of Greek origin. Our papyrus seems to us to present a beginning of the contamination of Greek words themselves with this habit of Coptic scribes of Thebes to replace the *g*'s with the *k*'s. Our copyist writes naturally a *k*, and he has to make an effort and correct himself, in order to reestablish the Gamma of correct orthography. We think then that this gives us a clear indication to determine the place where our codex was made: This would be at Thebes, by a Coptic scribe.

68. Worrell, *Coptic Sounds*, 106. "All three letters—Gamma, Kabba, and Schima—have the same value, /g/, in the Theban dialect." See also Kahle, *Bala'izah*, 1:147: "Some early examples [of interchanging *Kabba* and *Schima*], it may be noted that all these examples are from Achmimic, semi-Achmimic or Theban manuscripts; nearly all the non-literary examples are likewise from Thebes . . . Several examples could be cited from the unpublished part of the Berlin Gnostic text."

See also Nagel, "Der frühkoptische Dialekt von Theben," 38–40, and Kasser, "Les dialectes coptes," 81.

69. *Papyrus Bodmer* XXIII, 7, n. 1.

As recently as 1965, Kasser has stated: "Various indications, internal or external, would tend to orient our research a bit to the north of Thebes."[70] Yet the collection includes Coptic texts in a plurality of dialects, including Paleo-Theban, Sahidic, Sub-Achmimic (Lycopolitan) and Bohairic (influenced by Sahidic). Hence traits of dialect can hardly be used to establish the provenience of the collection as a whole but at best might indicate the provenience of the translator or scribe of an individual text.

It is not surprising that the suggestions made thus far as to provenience based on internal evidence—Panopolis, a monastery, a private library, Thebes—have largely been dropped for lack of adequate grounding. For the time being, the conclusion to be drawn from internal evidence is that the sight of the burial is unknown.

In terms of external evidence, one might think that by this time the track would have gotten cold. In 1964, it was stated that no new element had emerged to overcome the profound obscurity in which the circumstances of the discovery lay.[71] But then in 1972, Rodolphe Kasser announced that the Bodmer Papyri had been found at a place near Nag Hammadi.[72] A year later he was even more specific: a little to the east (northeast) of Nag Hammadi.[73] The source of this new information was

70. *Papyrus Bodmer* XXI, 7, n. 1: "Of course an admission of uncertainty is worth more than the affirmation of a certainty based on false information."

71. Kasser, "Fragments du livre biblique," 80: "I have serious reasons to believe that they were found, like the Gnostic codices mentioned above, in a place near Nag Hammadi."

72. Kasser, "Les dialectes coptes," 81, with regard to the dialect of P. Bodmer VI: "The manuscript that let us know this seems to have been found a bit to the east (northeast) of Nag Hammadi."

73. Reverdin, "Les Genevois et Ménandre," 1:

> Around 1956, Martin Bodmer acquired in Cairo for his library of Cologny a very important group of Greek and Coptic papyri. For a long time one had only quite vague indications about their provenience. Shortly before his death, however, the antiquities dealer who had sold them lifted the secret. He revealed that these papyri came from a village near Nag Hammadi, in Upper Egypt, a locality made famous by the discovery around the same time of Coptic Gnostic texts; that he had acquired the whole group, with the exception of some fragments that were detached at the time of the discovery; and that he had sold it, without diverting anything, to Mr. Bodmer. It has to do, in all probability, with what remains of the library of a monastery.

A footnote documents the reference to the divulging of the secret by a dealer: "It is to Mr. Rodolphe Kasser, Professor of Coptic Language and Literature at the Faculty of Letters of Geneva, and editor of a large part of these papyri in the series *Papyrus Bodmer*, that he made his confession."

divulged by Olivier Reverdin in his preface to a popularized translation of P. Bodmer XXV, Menander's play *The Girl from Samos*, as presented on Swiss radio in 1975: Shortly before his death, the antiquities dealer through whose hands the papyri had passed revealed to Rodolphe Kasser that they came from a village near Nag Hammadi.[74] It was in this context that the concept of a monastic provenience re-emerged. The dealer in question was the Cypriote Phokion J. Tano of Cairo, who died on February 9, 1972. Kasser had interviewed him in Cairo several times in the period between 1969 and 1971, and most recently in December 1971. Thus the question of the provenience was answered by relying on the word of a dealer, an approach that had been discounted a decade and a half earlier.[75] If this answer could not to be verified by supporting evidence, it too might ultimately be ignored as a moot question, much as was the identification by Carl Schmidt of the provenience of the Chester Beatty Biblical Papyri, in that it too was based only on the word of a middleman he trusted.[76]

Upon the resumption in 1984 of the publication of the monograph series with *Papyrus Bodmer* XXIX, Rodolphe Kasser and Guglielmo Cavallo for the first time report the provenience with some confidence in the *Papyrus Bodmer* series.[77]

74. *Papyrus Bodmer* VI, viii, n. 1: "One knows the little credence one can give to the reports of antiquities dealers when they cannot be confirmed by any archeological investigation."

75. Roberts, *Greek Papyri: An Introduction* (paperback edition 1980), 201, is skeptical whether the dealer got his details right, but in a letter of October 13, 1980, accepts the provenience near Nag Hammadi, i.e., near Dishnā, on the basis of a draft of the present text.

76. *Papyrus Bodmer XXIX*, Kasser and Cavallo, "Appendice," 100, nn. 2–3. Note 2 also refers to the publication in the *Bulletin* of the Institute for Antiquity and Christianity, 7.1 (March 1980) 6–7, "rather imprudently," of this information, criticized as consisting of "information gathered at the location itself some thirty years after their discovery." On June 23, 1980, I had mailed to Kasser the manuscript of the present chapter, which he acknowledged with gratitude, as he had the receipt of the *Bulletin*. Of course Kasser's own information was gathered at much the same time as was mine (actually some twenty rather than thirty years after the discovery), with the main difference being that his source was a Cairo dealer, a procedure he had previously explicitly repudiated, whereas mine was a series of villagers and middlemen through whom the manuscripts and the identification of the provenience reached Tano, as well as confirmatory documentation provided by the Chester Beatty Library and the Institut für Papyrusforschung of the University of Cologne, as well as Father Doutreleau. See also the discussion of the relative value of information limited to a Cairo dealer in Robinson, *Facsimile*, 3–4, n. 1.

77. Kasser and Cavallo, "Appendice."

Various converging indications (among them the dialects of the Coptic texts) make very plausible the localization of this discovery in Upper Egypt, a bit to the east of Nag Hammadi.

The dealer is identified as the same as in the case of the Nag Hammadi materials, whereby Tano is clearly intended. Thus Kasser's interview with Tano (confirmed by my investigation) has provided the Bibliothèque Bodmer solid enough information to publish the provenience and the identity of the main dealer.

THEIR ACQUISITION

Father Louis Doutreleau, SJ, one of the editors of the patristics series *Sources chrétiennes* (SC), worked in Cairo in the 1950s, during which time he served as a link between Tano and the Bibliothèque Bodmer. He has explained the cryptic nature of the prefaces to the Bodmer Papyri as due to a concern to keep from the Egyptian authorities information concerning the departure of the material from Egypt. Tano had close contacts with middlemen, antiquities dealers, and peasants of Upper Egypt, and thus was able to find those who had papyrus. He bought locally through his agents and sold far and wide, or at times profited from his international contacts to serve simply as an intermediary for other sellers.[78] By paying relatively low prices in Egypt and selling outside Egypt at inflated prices he could make high profits.[79] And yet his pricings may well have been more reliable than the average.

On a visit to Egypt in about 1950, Martin Bodmer secured the services of Tano and Doutreleau in his search for manuscripts,[80] and

78. Doutreleau explained this procedure in a letter of July 28, 1976:

> The Prefaces of the Bodmer Papyri are intentionally imprecise, for it was a matter of not revealing to the Egyptian police when and how all that had escaped from Egypt . . . Tano was in relation with many informers (hagglers, colleagues, amateurs, peasants . . .) from Upper Egypt. Hence in this way he knew the owners of papyrus. He bought at the local level by means of his agents and sold to distant places; or he was merely an intermediary (as in the case of *The Girl from Samos*) and assumed responsibility for finding a purchaser.

79. Doutreleau, July 28, 1976: "Another time Tano explained to me that he proceeded in this way for important pieces that he 'exported': He paid relatively little in Egypt, but overseas he resold them for very high prices."

80. Doutreleau, July 28, 1976: "Mr. Bodmer, beginning with the trip that had taken him by Egypt around 1950, entrusted himself to Tano to procure for him good papyrus, and he counted a bit on me for good advice to Tano."

is reported to have met with him again in Cairo in February 1956. In March or April 1956, Bodmer's secretary, Odile Bongard, visited Cairo to reactivate Tano, at which time she received assurance from Doutreleau that he would continue in his role of giving an assessment of what Tano had to offer Bodmer for sale.[81]

Tano also made use of the diplomatic pouch. Indeed, this is responsible for the regrettable report that Menander's *The Girl of Samos* was long delayed in arriving, and on arrival lacked leaves that had been intact at the time of Doutreleau's inventory in Tano's shop. This mishap is reported to have been due to the closing of the Tunisian embassy in Cairo by the Egyptian authorities as a result of the rupture of diplomatic relations between the two states just at the moment when the papyrus had been deposited there for export by diplomatic courier.[82]

Doutreleau has explained the references, in the prefaces to the Bodmer Papyri, to one or more batches of material, as referring to the three or four (actually more!) stages in which the material was purchased for and arrived at the Bibliothèque Bodmer, but not as alluding to distinct discoveries. For Doutreleau was convinced by his talks with Tano

81. See Doutreleau's letter of July 28, 1976 (see note 3 above) and his letter of July 28, 1980: "She had come to Cairo about 1954 to relaunch Tano. She received groups of papyrus at the Bodmeriana and she watched over them in the vault of the Library. She knew the prices and she saw to it that one did not profit excessively from the wealth of Mr. Bodmer." On August 29, 1980 Doutreleau added:

> Rectification: From another letter from me to V. Martin, 6 v 56, it becomes clear that Mlle B. passed by Cairo in March or April 1956 (a more precise date not found). I recall having seen her and assured her that I would continue to expertize in a disinterested way whatever Tano could put before me for Mr. Bodmer. Apart from what I have already said to you, I knew nothing of the precise purpose of her stopover, which lasted, it seems to me, more than a week.

82. Doutreleau, July 28, 1980:

> Of course Tano used the diplomatic pouches to which he was able to gain access. It is thus—I can tell it now that almost a quarter of a century has passed—that the group that contained *The Girl from Samos* was deposited at the embassy of Tunisia to make use of the service of the pouch. Alas! Just at that moment the relations between Egypt and Tunisia were broken and the embassy closed. Nothing more exited by this means until, several years later, the litigation that divided the two countries was resolved. When Mr. Bodmer finally received the package, missing were the leaves of *The Girl from Samos* whose stupid disappearance I still deplore, leaves that I had seen at Tano's and that it would be so desirable to find again.

that most of the material was from a single discovery, even though there may have been a plurality of middlemen behind Tano.[83]

It was not Tano's practice to divulge information concerning the provenience to the purchaser, and hence Doutreleau assumes that neither Bodmer nor Martin obtained such information, whereas Doutreleau himself had indeed gradually obtained such information from Tano over the period of time he was in Egypt.[84] On February 18, 1956, Victor Martin had written Doutreleau expressing curiosity as to the place and date of the discovery, a curiosity he doubted would ever be satisfied. But Mlle Bongard may have obtained information from Tano on her visit to Cairo a month or so later. For whereas Bodmer told William H. Willis that he knew the provenience but could not divulge it, Mlle Bongard told Willis that Bodmer was misinformed, but that she had reason to think the material came from the ruins of a fourth-century church at Dishnā.[85] This is the same way Tano described the site of the discovery to Beatty (see chapter 3 below). Although there are no such ruins at Dishnā, the well-known ruins of the (fifth-century) Basilica of St. Pachomius at the headquarters monastery of the Pachomian Order at Phbow (= Fāw Qiblī) founded in the fourth century are quite visible on the surface, only 6.5 km from Dishnā. Doutreleau provided Martin with information concerning the discovery, to the effect that the some thirty (!) codices came from the Nag Hammadi region.[86] Thereupon Martin

83. Doutreleau, July 28, 1976:

> At the Bibliothèque Bodmer the papyri—which were sold, for the most part, by Tano—arrived at three or four times. This is what explains to you the term "batch" used in the Prefaces of the Bodmer Papyri: batches in terms of purchase, batches in terms of shipment, but never batch in terms of discovery. I believe—this is a conviction at which I arrived following my conversations with Tano—that most of the Bodmer Papyri have the same origin, although the intermediaries who procured them could have been different.

84. Doutreleau, August 31, 1976: "This correspondence with Mr. Bodmer shows you that the Bodmer Papyri came almost all from Tano's, and that Mr. Martin, like Mr. Bodmer, was ignorant of their origin. Tano, who knew much more on this topic, said nothing about it to the purchasers. It is in chatting with him that I learned what I have already said to you in my first letter."

85. Willis, February 25, 1980: "Bodmer told me knowingly that he 'knew' where it had come from, but 'couldn't tell'; Mlle Bongard, who had her own connections, told me (in confidence!) that Bodmer was misinformed, because she 'had reason to believe' that the codices were found in the ruins of a iv-cent church at Dishnā."

86. Doutreleau wrote Martin on July 26, 1956: "It is quite certain that this find of some thirty codices (in the region of Nag Hamadi, like the Gnostic papyri) cannot

reported both Bodmer's interest in this information and his hopes of receiving more information when Doutreleau visited Geneva in October 1956.[87] On February 24, 1957, Martin wrote Doutreleau conceding the validity of Doutreleau's frequent suggestion that Martin should prepare a comprehensive inventory of the manuscripts, in that their origin seemed identical. But Martin questioned what he mistakenly took to be Doutreleau's view that the Bodmer Papyri were part of the same discovery as the Nag Hammadi Codices.[88] Yet he did not argue on the basis of divergent information at his disposal. Rather, he pointed to the (ungnostic) Menander codex, which he saw no reason to separate from the rest of the material, and expressed his (inaccurate) view that it was not necessary to date any of the Bodmer Papyri later than the Diocletianic persecution, at which time the material could have been hidden for safekeeping.[89] Martin seems ultimately to have given preference to the internal evidence from the front of P. Bodmer I in favor of Panopolis, in suggesting Achmim to Willis on December 25, 1958.

Jean Doresse, who had been consulted by Doutreleau, has also reported having heard talk of a provenience near Dishnā, but had discounted it on the assumption it had been invented to increase interest in the Bodmer Papyri.[90] Though the report may well have been circulated for this purpose, it was nevertheless a valid report.

---

remain the act of a single individual. To suppose that the discoverer were a single individual, reasons of security and profit would persuade him to address himself to a number of middlemen."

87. In a letter from Martin to Doutreleau of September 1, 1956.

88. Doutreleau, August 29, 1980:

> On the topic of the letter of V. Martin of 24 ii 57 . . . I can tell you that it is he who mixed up the two NH, to connect everything to the Gnostic papyri. The idea never came to me to do so, for very early I had had information from [Jean] Doresse and [Abbot Étienne] Drioton [Director of the Department of Antiquities of Egypt] on the Gnostic papyri, and I knew the distinctiveness of NH I. I probably had not distinguished, in talking or writing to Martin, NH I and NH II. In my mind NH II was another library, that of an educated Christian, put in safe-keeping and miraculously preserved in a grotte, of which the bulk, when one had made an inventory of it, should (in my mind) make it possible to discover the *raison d'être* of Nag Hammadi.

89. Colin Roberts, "The Codex," presented this thesis concerning a Philo codex.

90. In a letter of November 28, 1980, Doresse reported:

> I had already heard it said that the Bodmer Papyri had been found near Dishnā. But I had had the impression that the sellers, then Bodmer, were in this way trying to make one suppose that they were of the same origin

Doutreleau has also recorded Tano's version of the story of the find, to the effect that there were two Nag Hammadi discoveries, the Bodmer Papyri in a grotto near the site of the discovery of the gnostic manuscripts, though taking place five or six years later (actually the two discoveries were in 1945 and 1952) as a result of increased clandestine digging resulting from rumors of the profits from the first. Hence, Doutreleau himself refers to the two discoveries as Nag Hammadi I (the Nag Hammadi Codices) and Nag Hammadi II (the Bodmer Papyri), and this justifies the nomenclature for the Bodmer Papyri with the observation that it "gives adequate account of the origin and is general enough not to provoke unwelcome investigations on the part of the Egyptian authorities."[91]

> as the Gnostic ones, which would have been of interest, no doubt, but on the condition that the origin had really been one and the same. In fact, the Bodmer Papyri did not contain, in their group, a single fragment that could come from the jar at Chenoboskion.

91. Doutreleau, July 28, 1976:

> I had been on friendly terms with Tano, who had told and shown me a good number of things and had given me photographs of several pieces of papyrus. To put it succinctly—this is of some interest—, Tano spoke of two discoveries at Nag Hammadi, one in a buried jar, this the Gnostic manuscripts, the other in a grotto quite close to there, what has become the bulk of the Bodmer collection. The second discovery would have taken place following upon the first, but a number of months later, the first having provoked among the *fallahin* a resurgence of excavations . . . These discoveries . . . I have always chosen to call, for my part, Nag Hammadi I and Nag Hammadi II.

In his letter of July 28, 1980, Doutreleau rectified a lapse of memory concerning the date of the discovery and included a photocopy of a letter he had written on March 31, 1960, to Georg Maldfield documenting his recollections as of 1960:

> Here is what I know on the papyri that I have designated P. Nag Hamadi I and P. Nag Hamadi II in talking with you and with several colleagues. P. Nag Hamadi I = the Gnostic manuscripts in Coptic . . . They were found in a jar buried in a cemetery at the ancient location called Chenoboskion . . . Not far from the cemetery (between 50 and 200 meters) and *no doubt* (these are *suspect* reports of Egyptian antiquities dealers who informed me—this is why I insist on the *doubtful* character of this information) in a grotto at the cliff, which at this location is very near to the Nile (100 meters approximately), one found, five or six years after the Gnostic papyri, a group of diverse papyri of which Mr. Bodmer received the largest part and the University of Mississippi a few. It seems that the peasants that found these papyri had been very prudent: They spoke of them very little; they dribbled out their discovery bit by bit, and at present there are still a few papyri of this group that one is trying to sell in Egypt. The nomenclature, that I propose as *Nag Hamadi* II, gives adequate account of the origin and is general enough not to provoke unwelcome investigations on the part of the Egyptian authorities.—That is all that I know.

When one seeks to organize chronologically or at least sequentially various scattered allusions to transactions, something like the following six transactions or batches can be distinguished.

1. The reference by Willis to the effect that "the Bodmer papyri were purchased from a dealer in 1954" may apply to Papyrus Bodmer I, since it was published already by 1954, but apparently also applies to one or more codices. For it was in that year that Bodmer addressed himself to Rolf Ibscher for advice in conserving papyrus codices.[92] However it did not apply to material still seen in Egypt early in 1955,[93] as well as to other material whose purchase can be documented as later.

2. Tano's plans for the summer of 1955 were to be on Cyprus (from which his family came) toward the beginning of July 1955 and in Switzerland in September 1955.[94] Doutreleau has reported that the

---

The nearness of the site of the two discoveries is here highly exaggerated. Since the caves at the Jabal al-Tarif are spread over a distance of almost two kilometers, a site fifty to two hundred meters away from the cemetery would actually be part of the cemetery. The nearness is in terms of a much larger area (see below). This also applies to the proximity to the Nile. Doutreleau had not himself visited the sites, though Tano had. Doutreleau, August 29, 1980: "I did not go to the site of N.H. I only passed by in a car, and all that I have said either to Maldfeld or to you comes from Tano and the imprecise memory of his words."

92. Ibscher, "Wiederherstellung des Berliner Proverbiencodex," 362:

> When I was asked in 1954 by Dr. Bodmer, the enviable owner of the wonderfully preserved papyrus manuscripts of the Bodmeriana in Geneva, to provide an expertise as to how one could save from further deterioration one of these papyrus codices which, in spite of its exemplary preservation, was crumbling in the quires that are on the outside, I proposed, after a brief examination of the "patient," to make this manuscript secure by imbedding it between panes of glass in the usual procedure, no matter how uncomfortable this thought was for me of "destroying" such a beautiful example in its original form as book.

93. Gilles Quispel, in a letter of July 23, 1980, reported on his visit to Egypt early in April 1955: "Tano showed and offered me 'John' [P^{66}] in Greek in 1955. He was then furious about the confiscation of the Nag Hammadi papyri and said: 'If they [the authorities] burn me, I'll burn them [the Bodmer Papyri].' He intended to smuggle them to Cyprus. Could it be that *all* the Bodmer Papyri were brought there then, and that the different installments came from Cyprus!" The fact that Doutreleau saw considerable material still in Cairo in 1956 indicates that not all was "exported" in 1955 (see below).

94. Tano wrote Quispel on June 4, 1955: "I hope, God-willing, to be in Switzerland around next September and on Cyprus toward the beginning of July. If there is something to write to me please do it in July so I can arrange my schedule."

Bibliothèque Bodmer "possessed a first batch" prior to 1956,[95] which may be a reference to a transaction consummated at this time. A shipment had indeed been received from Tano late in 1955, containing P. Bodmer II and Coptic books,[96] one of which was P. Bodmer III.[97]

Ludwig Keimer, an Egyptologist and ethnologist of Austrian origin who had lived in Egypt so long that he had taken out Egyptian citizenship, was in the confidence of Tano to the extent that he was privy to the prices of the items, information that even Doutreleau did not have. Early in December 1955, Keimer had an appointment with the major middleman supplying Tano, known to Doutreleau only under the nickname of "Bey of Papyrus." Keimer sensed that the middleman had lost interest in a sale and inferred that, through intermediaries, the Bey of Papyrus must have been in contact with Martin. In any case, his policy was to sell to the first one who brought him money.[98] Since the Mississippi Coptic Codices were purchased "late in 1955" "from a different dealer" than were the Bodmer Papyri, one may assume that the Bey of Papyrus was indeed selling at this juncture to a plurality of persons. For Willis has clarified his published statement with the information that the Cairo antiquities dealer Maguid Sameda had delivered the Mississippi Coptic Codices, which he had apparently not had on hand a year earlier, in the autumn of 1955 (see chapter 3 below).[99]

95. Doutreleau, July 28, 1976.

96. On February18, 1956, Martin had written Doutreleau that, several months prior to the date of writing, Tano had sent a shipment of Coptic books including P. Bodmer II.

97. *Papyrus Bodmer* III, CSCO, 177.iii, quoted above, note 59.

98. Keimer wrote Doutreleau on December 17, 1955:

> I have seen (or rather I had made an appointment, last week, with the Bey) the Bey of Papyrus. He was very polite, but I understood right away that he was no longer interested in the sale of his papyri. Something had changed . . . I have the impression (that is really all!) that one of these persons has left for Paris and perhaps gone to Switzerland to see the professor who is a confidant of M.B. (??). In any case, the Bey told me (but his words are not worth much) that whoever would bring money first would have both papyri and jewels.

99. Willis in a letter of February 25, 1980:

> The additional information I can give you about the provenience of the Mississippi papyri is not very much. They all came to us from Maguid Sameda, Sultan's father. He had sold the "third group" of Robinson Papyri to David M. Robinson in 1954, a miscellany of Greek and Coptic texts (including the IX-cent. Coptic bifolium) which so far as I know had nothing to do with the two Coptic codices and miscellaneous papyri which he sent us the

3. Doutreleau waited impatiently for an opportunity for himself to visit the Bey of Papyrus.[100] Keimer took Doutreleau to him in a Cairo suburb in January or February 1956[101] so that Doutreleau might provide Bodmer with an expert opinion on what was to become P. Bodmer IV and XIV–XV, as well as fragments of P. Bodmer XXV–XXVI and various other items in Greek and Coptic,[102] including burnt parchment. Doutreleau wrote Martin promptly about what he had been shown, and on February 18, 1956, Martin could reply that they had arrived at the Bibliothèque Bodmer. On September 1, 1956, Martin reported to Doutreleau that the first batch of Menander had included parts of all three plays that were to become P. Bodmer IV, XXV, and XXVI. On November 11, 1956, Doutreleau wrote Keimer that he had seen in the Bibliothèque Bodmer the papyri they had seen on the visit with the Bey of Papyrus.[103]

> following year and which I eventually was able to buy for the University of Mississippi. In fact, I am reasonably sure that Sameda hadn't yet acquired the codices and later texts in the summer of 1954, when Robinson visited him; Robinson believed he had bought all the stock Sameda had at that time.

100. Doutreleau, August 29, 1980: "Since December 1955 I had held myself from one moment to the next ready to go to the Bey of Papyrus, and this moment, I recall, was delayed a long time."

101. Doutreleau, August 29, 1980: "It was hence in February 1956 that I went with Keimer, who at the request of Tano had prepared the Bey for this visit, to expertize the papyri." In a letter of September 2, 1980, Doutreleau clarified:

> Even what I wrote you in my last letter of 30 [29?] viii, namely that I wrote to Keimer 11 x 56: ". . . what I had already seen with you in February," that too must be passed through the filter of criticism. For it is true that I had written to Keimer, but one must recognize that it was nine months after the event that I placed it in February. It comes back to me now, like a distant impression, that I had hesitated then about the date of the event and that the end of January seemed to me to fit just as well; in doubt, I had leaned toward February.

102. Doutreleau, July 28, 1976: "One day in 1954 (or 1955?) I inventoried the papyri in the suburb of Cairo, at the home of a middleman (who was not Tano, but of whom Tano was not ignorant), a peasant, rather rich and without culture, from Upper Egypt, whose name I never had known." Doutreleau, on consulting his records, on August 31, 1976, corrected the date: "It was following that [a letter from Ludwig Keimer of December 17, 1955], that one day in the first months of 1956 I went to expertize for Mr. Bodmer the papyri of the group where there was the *Dyscolos* [P. Bodmer IV], Luke [P. Bodmer XIV], John [P. Bodmer XV], etc."

103. On November 11, 1956, Doutreleau wrote Keimer: "I saw again [at the Bibliothèqueque Bodmer] what I had already seen with you in February."

At Bodmer's request, Martin had written to Doutreleau on January 2, 1956, reporting that Bodmer was to be in Cairo for five or six days beginning January 24, after which he would go to Upper Egypt. Doutreleau was asked to meet Bodmer in Cairo and update him on the papyrus market. Bodmer did not actually contact Doutreleau in Cairo. But on October 8, 1956, Gilles Quispel, in Cairo attending the meeting of the International Committee for the Study and Publication of the Coptic Gnostic Papyri, was told by Keimer that Bodmer had bought from Tano material involving a Gospel and "Aristophanes" (the latter was later corrected in Quispel's diary to read "Menander") at the beginning of February 1956.[104] On May 21, 1956, Chester Beatty wrote his librarian J. V. S. Wilkinson: "Bodmer, apparently, found one or two very important things from our friend. He indicated to me that he had an important deal on with Bodmer. I imagine it is in connection with that Gospels."

4. By July 1956, Tano had sent to Cyprus for the Bibliothèque Bodmer another batch of Christian texts, including P. Bodmer X, XIII, and XIX, as well as the *Vision of Dorotheos* and a few more leaves of P. Bodmer IV.[105] By September 1, 1956, the shipment had arrived at the Bibliothèque Bodmer.[106] It may be that Tano took them himself, for in September 1956 Reinhold Merkelbach characterized Tano as he experienced him in Cairo as follows:

> He is 60 years old, one of the most serious antiquities dealers in Egypt. Yet his business really blossomed only after the death of Nahman. Tanos had been invited by Bodmer and Chester Beatty

104. The entry in the diary of Gilles Quispel of October 8, 1956, was translated by him from Dutch into English on February 25, 1981: "Keimer: . . . Bodmer (a Swiss) bought from Tano a Gospel and 15 pages of Aristophanes [emended above the line: Menander] in the beginning of February: 12 February departed."

105. Doutreleau wrote Martin on August 26, 1956:

> Shortly before my departure from Cairo in July I had seen Tano. He was going to leave on vacation in Greece and had already had a certain number of pieces cross the sea, pieces he wanted to present to you, a thing that he has perhaps already done. There were among them more Christian papyri, with which you are saturated but which one must collect nonetheless, biblical texts (St. Paul) and apocrypha, supplements, if I have understood correctly, of those that you already have, Christian commentaries (Dorothea, Melito . . .), some leaves, unfortunately too rare, of Menander, on which I have read the names of the personages . . . [readily identified by Martin from the cast of the *Dyscolos*], which will let you know with which play you have to do.

106. Reported on September 1, 1956, by Martin to Doutreleau.

> to Europe (Geneva and Nice [where Beatty often stayed]), and had flown for the first time in his life. Having just arrived back, he was still so overwhelmed by the impression that he narrated the whole course of his trip to me—which according to the orient's rule of secrecy he would no longer have done a week later. First in this moment did I realize what path the great papyrus discoveries take today: Tanos is the permanent agent of Bodmer and Chester Beatty. He is advised by . . . Dr. Wild in the Institut Français. Everyone knows that he is constantly buying and sending to Europe interesting papyri for these two clients. Also Nisim Cohen [a Jewish rug dealer who had also sold manuscripts to Bodmer] has already made deliveries to Tanos. Tanos sends the texts to his clients even on approval to Europe.

5. Fragments that had been promised by Tano for several weeks prior to September 1, 1956, had not arrived by that date.[107] This is apparently a reference to the small fragments of P. Bodmer II that arrived in a lot while P. Bodmer II was in the press, according to the green chit of paper placed inside the publication of P. Bodmer II late in 1956. For that volume was in the press on September 1, 1956, and was due to appear late in October or in November 1956.[108] The fragments had not yet arrived when Doutreleau visited Geneva on or soon after October 5, but did arrive before October 19.[109] (Chester Beatty acquired one fragment of P. Bodmer II early in 1956, see chapter 2 below.) This batch also included more supplements to the previous lots, such as P. Bodmer VII–X and XIII, and three more leaves of Menander. Doutreleau was impressed by the quality and quantity of this batch.[110]

6. The last batch had apparently left Egypt just before the Suez Crisis of October 1956. Doutreleau thought this crisis would prevent further shipments in the near future but hoped Tano would hold in reserve what he could not transport.[111] But Tano may well have had no more.

107. Reported on September 1, 1956 by Martin to Doutreleau.

108. Reported on September 1, 1956, by Martin to Doutreleau.

109. Reported on October 19, 1956, by Martin to Doutreleau.

110. Doutreleau wrote Martin on November 22, 1956: "In any case, there you have a batch that is extremely important, as much for the nature of its content as for its quantity."

111. Doutreleau wrote Martin on November 22, 1956: "The letter by means of which you announce to me the arrival of the shipment of Tano is already a good time away! And what events since, besides, which without doubt will hinder new arrivals for a long time! Provided that Tano puts in reserve what he cannot transmit!"

On January 6, 1957, Martin wrote Doutreleau in Lyon that Mlle Bongard was doing all that could be done to secure the rest of the Menander codex with the help of Tano, who had been assured of the necessary means and had consequently held out the hope that some day good news might arrive. But on February 24, 1957, Martin wrote Doutreleau that the last news from Tano had arrived two months earlier, giving encouragement in symbolic language, encouragement that had not materialized. When Doutreleau notified Martin on September 18, 1957, of his return to Cairo, Martin wrote on September 23 that he had heard that Tano had been able to continue in business and that he would be grateful if Doutreleau would inquire about the papyrus market, especially the rest of the Menander codex.

In 1958, Tano showed Doutreleau about nine leaves of Menander he had on consignment, which were to become P. Bodmer XXV. This lot was deposited at the Tunisian embassy in Cairo complete, but only arrived at the Bibliothèque Bodmer several years later, and incomplete.[112] It must be that the reference in the preface to *Papyrus Bodmer* XXV in 1969 is to the ultimately disappointed hope that these would finally emerge.

A parchment leaf containing Song of Songs 6:9—7:9 was omitted from Till's list published in 1959, since it apparently had not yet arrived when Kasser made the inventory published by Till. But the precise date of

112. Doutreleau, July 28, 1976:

> Later, in 1958 I believe, Tano showed me a folio of *The Girl from Samos*. I wanted to see the others. Since they did not belong to him, I had to return on another occasion to be shown the eight others (eight, I believe, but I am not sure about the number). This *Girl from Samos* was complete. It resembled outwardly the *Dyscolos* and seemed to come from the same collection of pieces by Menander as did the *Dyscolos*. It had been sent complete to the Bibliothèque Bodmer, but only arrived a few years later, incomplete! About this extraordinary and clandestine trip, I cannot for the moment tell you more, but that explains to you why Mr. Bodmer had wanted to hold up publication until the missing folios could arrive.

See the further details from Doutreleau's letter of July 28, 1980, quoted above, and the following caution from his letter of September 2, 1980:

> Another point where my memory may be mistaken: The number of leaves of *The Girl from Samos* that I had seen at Tano's. I have always said, it seems to me, nine. But, in effect, should this happen to be ten or only eight, one should not be astonished. I saw them two times. Now did those I saw the second time contain the two of the first time? I get lost in the details of my recollections . . .

that inventory is not known. Hence whether it was part of the batch transmitted through the Tunisian embassy or of a different batch is not clear.

Doutreleau, who had left Cairo in the summer of 1958, heard from Martin on August 2, 1959, and again in September 1959 to the effect that there was no news from Tano. On a visit to the Bibliothèque Bodmer on December 2, 1959, Doutreleau learned that Bodmer was no longer in the market for papyri. Yet as late as March 31, 1960, Doutreleau conjectured that there was still material from this discovery for sale in Cairo, and has pointed to the fact that Ramon Roca-Puig and Jose O'Callaghan were acquiring Christian papyri.[113]

Thus the material reached the Bibliothèque Bodmer in at least six installments. If one may add the acquisitions at Dublin (in more than two transactions), Cologne, two repositories in Barcelona, and Mississippi, one may infer that the material was involved in at least twelve transactions.

In a few instances one can determine in which batch or batches a given book arrived, but, since complete inventories of the individual batches are not available, any detailed itemization remains fragmentary. No specific information associating P. Bodmer V, VI, XI, XII, XVI, XVIII, or XX–XXIV with any given installment(s) is available. Thus about half the material at the Bibliothèque Bodmer cannot be dated in terms of its arrival there.

Such a tabulation is rendered even more imprecise by the fact that a single book was often divided into parts and arrived in more than one installment. The Bibliothèque Bodmer received parts of the Menander codex in lots 3–6, parts of P^{66} in lots 2 and 5, and supplements to one or more earlier shipments of the composite biblical and apocryphal Greek codex V–X–XI–VII–XIII–XII–XX–IX–VIII in lots 4 and 5. Furthermore, of the twenty codices represented at least in part in the Bibliothèque Bodmer, parts of seven were acquired elsewhere:

- most of Mississippi Coptic Codex I (the Crosby Codex = the Savery Codex) by the University of Mississippi, with only fragments by the Bibliothèque Bodmer;
- almost half the leaves and the cover of P. Bodmer XXI by the Chester Beatty Library;

113. Doutreleau, August 29, 1980. See also the letter of Doutreleau to Georg Maldfeld of March 31, 1960, quoted above.

- almost half the leaves of P. Bodmer XXII by the University of Mississippi;
- isolated fragments of P. Bodmer II and XX by the Chester Beatty Library;
- P. Bodmer XXV by Barcelona;
- P. Bodmer XXVI by Cologne.

And Homer fragments at Cologne and others to be published as P. Bodmer XLVIII (the *Iliad*) and XLIX (the *Odyssey*) by the Bibliothèque Bodmer may be part of the same set of Homer rolls as those published as P. Bodmer I. Thus, the only materials at the Bibliothèque Bodmer of which there is no evidence of division into separate batches are the ten codices of P. Bodmer III, VI, XIV–XV, XVI, XVIII, XIX, XXIII, XXIV, XXVII, and XXIX–XXXVIII, and the presumably smaller and largely unpublished texts of the Bibliothèque Bodmer: P. Bodmer XXIX–XXXVIII, XLI, XLII, XLIII, and XLIV, a total of hardly more than half the material at the Bibliothèque Bodmer. But since large parts of some of these rolls and codices are missing, they too may well have been divided and the missing parts either destroyed or left unidentified in some public or private collections.

Supplementary documentation of what went through Tano's hands is found in the series of photographs Tano gave to Doutreleau in 1958 of material from this discovery. They included sample pages from P. Bodmer IV, V, VII, VIII, X, XIII, XV, XXIX, XXXVIII, and XLV.[114]

CONTENTS

It is of course possible that some of the Bodmer Papyri may not be of the same provenience, in which case they should be excluded from consideration here, where the focus is on a single manuscript discovery.

114. Doutreleau, September 2, 1980:

> Tano, in 1958, had given me a certain number of photos of the papyri of NH II: P. Bodmer IV, *Dyscolos*, 28, lines 405–52; P. Bodmer V, beginning and end of the *Genesis Marias*; P. Bodmer VII, beginning of *Epist. Judae*; P. Bodmer VIII, beginning and end of Ia Petri, beginning and end of IIa Petri; P. Bodmer X, *Acta Pauli*, Pag. Pap. N and NA; P. Bodmer XIII, Melito, end; P. Bodmer XV, John 3:34—4:14 . . . Suzanna 23–32; *Dorothea*, several leaves in thickness; *Dorothea*, a detached leaf . . . *Shepherd of Hermas*, Vis. 3.4–5.

And now further fragments of rolls of the *Iliad* (P. Bodmer XLVIII) and the *Odyssey* (P. Bodmer XLIX) have been identified. In any case, the numerical tabulations made above are to be reduced by the excluded P. Bodmer XVII, the present study of Bodmer Papyri emanating from a shared provenience. But there is insufficient reason to exclude P. Bodmer I. Thus the concluding summary of the preceding section could be reformulated, in terms of material that may at least tentatively be associated with a shared provenience, as follows:

> When one adds to the three rolls (one roll) or parts thereof and at least eighteen codices or parts thereof at the Bibliothèque Bodmer the two codices at the Chester Beatty Library, the two Barcelona codices, the Crosby Codex, the Minor Prophets codex, and the three New Testament codices in the Middle Egyptian (Oxyrhynchite) dialect, one reaches, for material at least in part extant, a total of three (one) rolls and twenty-six codices, a grand total of twenty-nine (twenty-seven) books.

The following is a preliminary inventory of the ancient books that are to be investigated in terms of a shared provenience (omitting P. Bodmer XVII, since it is clearly of a different provenience). There are represented, though in a few cases quite fragmentarily, thirty-two ancient books: Three papyrus Greek rolls and twenty-nine codices, twenty-two made of papyrus, and five of parchment. (Two unpublished texts at the Bibliothèque Bodmer have not been identified in terms of the writing material.) Twelve papyrus codices are in Greek, six in Coptic, two in Latin (both of which are partially in Greek). All five parchment codices are in Coptic. In Greek are only the twelve papyrus codices (two of which are partially in Latin). In Coptic are the five parchment codices and ten papyrus codices, plus the two whose writing surface is unknown, a total of seventeen Coptic codices. In Latin are two papyrus codices (both of which are partially in Greek). Non-Christian are, in addition to the three papyrus rolls, one Greek codex as well as a part of two more (one Greek and one Latin and Greek); there is also one in Greek with documentary contents. Codices that are (at least predominantly) Christian are ten Greek codices (two of which are largely in Latin) and all seventeen Coptic codices, a total of twenty-seven codices. The Old Testament is represented in five Greek and ten Coptic codices, a total of fifteen codices. The New Testament is represented in three Greek and five Coptic codices, a total of nine codices. Three of these codices contain material from both Testaments, so that the Bible is represented in a total of only twenty-one codices. Thus there are six non-canonical Christian codices.

Such raw statistics may have no apparent significance beyond a numerical impression of what is involved in the discovery. Some trends, however, may be apparent. Rolls are all non-Christian, but non-Christian material is rare among the codices. The papyrus codices are predominantly Greek but with a visible minority in Coptic. The parchment codices are all in Coptic. (Latin is rare, confined to papyrus codices that also have some Greek.) Rolls are all papyrus. They and the papyrus codices tend to be early, parchment codices to be late. Greek tends to be early (from the second to the fourth centuries), Coptic late (perhaps the third, century but predominantly the fourth to fifth centuries). These trends are not surprising, but either reflect what is typical or are based on too limited a quantity to be very relevant. For an itemization of the inventory one may be referred to the essay "The Pachomian Monastic Library at the Chester Beatty Library and the Biblioteque Bodmer" appended below.

To be sure, the coordination of such statistics can only be approximate, in that the numbers given by peasants in Egypt do not have precision. But even more, one need not assume that an ancient book of which only fragments survive would have been counted by them as a book. Thus from the total number of works known to have survived in whole or part, one would need to subtract some items as too small to have been included in their count. Conversely when books were divided and sold in two separate transactions (P. Bodmer XXI and XXII), they might have been counted each as two books. There is as well also the unfortunate possibility that books may have been counted but then burnt, discarded, or fragmented. Of course there may be Bodmer Papyri in museums, libraries, and private collections that have not been identified as such and therefore are not included in such a statistical survey. And the survey may in fact be too inclusive, in that it may suggest that some books that are not from the same discovery may be from the shared provenience. The cut-off point in such a survey will, by the nature of the case, be fluid. Yet in spite of all of these factors of imprecision, it is important to assess as accurately as possible the size and nature of the discovery known as the Bodmer Papyri.

THE BODMER PAPYRI IN THE BROADER SENSE

Some of the material published in the *Papyrus Bodmer* is not actually at the Bibliothèque Bodmer: A fragment from P. Bodmer II 139/40 (John 19:25–28, 30–32) is at the Chester Beatty Library,[115] as is a fragment or fragments of P. Bodmer XX, 135/136 (*Apology of Phileas*).[116] The eighteen leaves of P. Bodmer VIII (1 and 2 Peter) were presented, first in the form of a facsimile (one of which was in the possession of Frank W. Beare), then the original itself, by Martin Bodmer to Pope Paul VI on the occasion of the Pope's visit to Geneva in 1969 and are now in the Vatican Library.[117] Thirty-five leaves of P. Bodmer XII were at the Library of the University of Mississippi as Mississippi Coptic Codex II.[118] They were then sold in 1981 to the rare book dealer of New York H. P. Kraus, who offered them to the Bibliothèque Bodmer for SFr300,000 (some $150,000). A fragment of P. Bodmer XXV, prepublished as P. Barc. 45 by the Fundacio Sant Lluc Evangelista of Barcelona, was at the suggestion of Rodolphe Kasser and E. G. Turner given to the Bibliothèque Bodmer in exchange for fragments of Cicero's *In Catilinam* from the remains of a Barcelona codex, P. Barcin. Inventory Numbers 149–57.[119] A fragment

115. Treu, "Christliche Papyri 1940–1961," 182, lists the passage as John 19:25–28, 31–32. Aland, *Repertorium*, 296, lists the fragment under the folio 135/136, which is the numeration of the plates but not that of the (restored) pagination in Papyrus Bodmer II, *Supplément, Nouvelle edition*. Similarly, van Haelst, *Catalogue*, 156, entry 426, lists it as "fragment" of a leaf paginated [*sic*!] 135–136." It is due to the fact that pages 35–38 are missing that the numeration of the plates became four digits lower than the missing pagination.

116. Turner, *Greek Papyri*, 52, states that "a few scraps were found among Sir Chester Beatty's texts," and Haelst, *Catalogue*, 258, item 710, reports "miniscule fragments at Dublin"; *Papyrus Bodmer* XX lists only one such fragment with acknowledgment to T. C. Skeat for identifying it, pages 34, 36. This fragment at the Chester Beatty Library can be distinguished by the darker coloration of its photograph on plates 7 (135, 13–16) and 8 (136, 14–17). A cut-out of the fragment from a photograph is glassed with the rest of the leaf at the Bibliothèque Bodmer.

117. Aland, *Repertorium*, 1.303; Haelst, *Catalogue*, 193, item 148; Turner, *Typology*, 80.

118. Willis, "New Collections of Papyri," 383 n. 1, quoted in a letter of January 21, 1959, from Rodolphe Kasser, identifying Mississippi Coptic Codex II as part of the *Papyrus Bodmer* XXII.

119. According to a letter of October 13, 1980, from E. G. Turner.

of P. Bodmer XXVI is at the University of Cologne, where it was prepublished as P. Colon. 904.[120]

Thus it is clear from the *Papyrus Bodmer* series itself that parts of Bodmer Papyri found repositories initially at the Chester Beatty Library in Dublin, the Institut für Altertumskunde of the University of Cologne, the University of Mississippi, and the Fundacio Sant Lluc Evangelista of Barcelona, and secondarily at the Vatican Library and the rare book dealer of New York, H. P. Kraus. But still more are from the same provenience, such as the large segment of P. Bodmer XXI at the Chester Beatty Library, Accession Number 1389, published in 1963. Among the acquisitions of the Bibliothèque Bodmer are fragments from Cicero's *In Catilinam*, part of the remains of the codex in Barcelona, P. Barcin. Inventory Numbers 149–57 (with Cicero on 149a), which the Bibliothèque Bodmer exchanged for Barcelona's fragment of P. Bodmer XXV. Thus P. Barcin. 149–57 is what is left of another manuscript that must come from the shared provenience. And a further fragment of Cicero *In Catilinam* was found tucked into Mississippi Coptic Codex I (the Crosby Codex), which would indicate that this codex too was from the shared provenience, as one might hypothetically infer already from the fact that Mississippi Coptic Codex II, acquired in the same batch, is part of P. Bodmer XXII. Fragments of Mississippi Codex I were also identified at the Bibliothèque Bodmer, which has turned them over to William Willis, who now has them at Duke University, thus providing further confirmation that Mississippi Coptic Codex I is from the shared provenience. Thus the scattering of parts of the same codex at different repositories makes it possible to add two codices, or what survives of them, to the list of Bodmer Papyri, though themselves not published in the series of the Bibliothèque Bodmer: P. Barcin. Inventory Numbers 1249–57 and Mississippi Coptic Codex I (the Crosby Codex).

The four repositories in addition to the Bibliothèque Bodmer that have been identified thus far as having acquired parts of Bodmer Papyri may also have acquired still other materials from the same discovery, though there happen to be no parts of them identified with what are known to be Bodmer Papyri. Of course such further holdings may be from other acquisitions or even from the same acquisition but a separate provenience. Thus their attribution to the shared provenience is

120. *Papyrus Bodmer* XXVI, 6.

hypothetical and must be weighed in each case in terms of whatever indications they may be. To attribute such manuscripts to the shared provenience will remain to some degree speculative. However to attribute to each a separate provenience is also speculative, in that otherwise unattested manuscript discoveries must thereby be conjectured.

There are also secondary repositories, in that some materials have moved from their original repositories to other locations. P. Bodmer VIII and XIV/XV are now at the Vatican Library in Rome; Mississippi Coptic Codex I (the Crosby Codex) was sold to H. P. Kraus, who sold it to a consortium with headquarters in Vaduz, Liechtenstein; Mississippi Coptic Codex III was sold to H. P. Kraus, who had it in New York; and the Bibliothèque Bodmer's fragments of Mississippi Coptic Codex I were with Willis in Durham, North Carolina. If one may then remove the University of Mississippi from the roster of repositories, there remain seven locations at which materials from the same provenience were deposited in addition to the Bibliothèque Bodmer:

- the Chester Beatty Library at Dublin
- the University of Cologne
- the Vatican Library
- the rare book dealer H. P. Kraus in New York
- a consortium in Vaduz, Liechtenstein
- Durham, North Carolina
- the Fundacio Sant Lluc Evangelista of Barcelona.

The term *Bodmer Papyri* is to be broadened beyond the holdings of the Bibliothèque Bodmer or texts published in the monograph series *Papyrus Bodmer* to include all that come from the same discovery, just as, conversely, it is to be narrowed to exclude papyri of various other proveniences housed in the Bibliothèque Bodmer.

The question as to how many of these manuscripts actually derive from the same discovery is at least on first glance most acutely posed by those that were not acquired by the Bibliothèque Bodmer. For they are not in a narrower, literal sense Bodmer Papyri. But in several instances, parts of manuscripts that are at the Bibliothèque Bodmer have emerged elsewhere. It is very unlikely that a book was dismembered in late antiquity and then the parts buried separately and both burials discovered in modern times. Thus when the parts of the same codex emerge at different repositories, the natural assumption is that both places acquired material from the same discovery. Then it becomes relevant to investigate whatever other materials may come in question at each of the repositories where parts of such dismembered manuscripts are known to have been acquired. In this way, one may include in the list not only parts of the Bodmer manuscripts in other repositories but any other materials in these repositories for which there are reasons that would tend to indicate that they too came from the shared provenience.

As has already been determined, parts of the Bodmer Papyri were acquired by the Chester Beatty Library, the University of Cologne, the University of Mississippi, and the Fundacio Sant Lluc Evangelista of Barcelona (not to mention secondary repositories that received materials from these places). These four repositories may hence have still other materials from the same discovery, though there happen to be no parts of these other papyri that have been identified at the Bibliothèque Bodmer. Of course such further holdings acquired by these four supplemental repositories may be from other acquisitions or even from the same acquisition but a separate provenience. Thus their attribution to the shared provenience is hypothetical and must be weighed in each case in terms of whatever indications there may be. To attribute such a manuscript to the shared provenience will, by the nature of the case, remain to some degree speculative. However, to attribute each to a separate provenience is also speculative, in that to do so would involve conjecturing a series of otherwise unattested manuscript discoveries. In some instances, a simple *non liquet* is advisable, but in others the inclusion of given materials in the analysis of the Bodmer Papyri may seem quite appropriate. It is in fact a very normal occurrence for the books in a discovery to be separated early from each other as they are marketed. This has been the case with regard to comparable discoveries in Egypt throughout the twentieth century, such as the Chester Beatty Biblical Papyri, the Medinet Madi (Manichaean) texts, the Toura (patristic) texts, and the Nag Hammadi (gnostic) Codices.

—2—

Bodmer Papyri in the Chester Beatty Library

The library of Sir A. Chester Beatty has been famous since the early 1930s for *The Chester Beatty Biblical Papyri*, a dozen early Greek papyri that were the sensational biblical discovery of that generation.[1] For the Chester Beatty Biblical Papyri I (P^{45}, the Gospels and Acts), II (P^{46}, the Pauline Epistles) and III (P^{47}, the book of Revelation) traced the text of

1. Kenyon, *Chester Beatty Biblical Papyri*, plus a few irregular volumes: 1. *General Introduction*, 1933; 2. *Gospels and Acts* [Chester Beatty Biblical Papyrus I = P^{45}, first half of the third century]: *Text*, 1933; *Plates*, 1934; 3. *Pauline Epistles* [Chester Beatty Biblical Papyrus II = P^{46}, third century] *Revelation* [Chester Beatty Biblical Papyrus III = P^{47}, late third century]: *Text*, 1934; and *Revelation: Plates*, 1936; *Supplement: Pauline Epistles: Text*, 1936; *Supplement: Pauline Epistles: Plates*, 1937; 4. *Genesis* [Chester Beatty Biblical Papyrus IV = Ra(hlfs) 961, early fourth century; Chester Beatty Biblical Papyrus V = Ra 962, late third century]: *Text*, 1934; (Pap. IV) *Plates*, 1935; *(Pap. V) Plates*, 1936; 5. *Numbers and Deuteronomy* [Chester Beatty Biblical Papyrus VI = Ra 963, first half of the second century]: *Text*, 1935; 6. *Isaiah* [Chester Beatty Biblical Papyrus VII = Ra 965, first half third century], *Jeremiah* [Chester Beatty Biblical Papyrus VIII = Ra 966, late third century], *Ecclesiasticus* [Chester Beatty Biblical Papyrus XI = Ra 964, fourth century]: *Text*, 1937; Hayes, *Plates of Chester Beatty Biblical Papyri*; 7. *Ezekiel* [Chester Beatty Biblical Papyrus IX = Ra 967, late third century]; *Daniel* [Chester Beatty Biblical Papyrus X = Ra 967, first half third century], *Esther* [Chester Beatty Biblical Papyrus IX = Ra 967, late third century]: *Text*, 1937; *Plates*, 1938; 8. *Enoch and Melito* [Chester Beatty Biblical Papyrus XII, fourth or possibly fifth century]: *Plates*, 1941; *Text*: Bonner, *Last Chapters of Enoch in Greek*; Bonner, *Homily on the Passion*.

the New Testament back behind the great fourth-century uncial manuscripts Sinaiticus and Vaticanus, which had seemed, a century ago, to be as far back as one could reasonably hope to go. For P^{45-47} went back to the third century, behind the Diocletianic persecutions, which included in the imperial decree *traditio codicum*, the "turning in" of Christian books for destruction. One had hardly dared to hope to recover biblical manuscripts older than this book-burning holocaust. But now Beatty seems again to have made an important acquisition, this time in 1956, consisting of a number of Bodmer Papyri (in the broader sense of the term).

Beatty had been acquiring papyri and other antiquities from Phocion J. Tano for a number of years. A letter from "Ph. John Tano" dated September 2, 1943, bears on its letterhead "House Founded 1879: Nicolas Tano." Tano gave as his address for correspondence: "Phocion John Tanos, care of Joannides and Ackers, 35 Liperta [e?] Street, Nicosia, Cyprus." On September 8, 1947, the Chester Beatty Library paid Tano £24 for four leaves from a codex, care of the Ottoman Bank, Famagusta, Cyprus. On April 16, 1948, Tano sent Beatty four wooden tablets through the good offices of his brother-in-law, William Acker, an officer in the RAF. In 1950, Beatty ordered on approval Coptic materials offered by Tano for £235. That year Tano wrote Beatty from New York not to involve his American-based nephew, Frank J. Tano, in any transactions, but to remit directly to the Ottoman or Barkley Banks of Famagusta, Cyprus. On September 12, 1951, Tano wrote Beatty's secretary, John Marsh, in London: "I asked to a friend in Paris to forward threw [*sic*] you for Mr. Chester Beatty a collection of Coptic parchemains [*sic*]. Please wen [*sic*] you receive them, kindly forward the parcel to Mr. Chester Beatty's address."

On March 25, 1954, Beatty's secretary John Wooderson recorded in a memorandum: "Mr. A. Chester Beatty asked John Wooderson to see Mr. Tano and find out if he had any Coptic writing or vellum or pages of papyri in Greek; and if so, what they would cost, and if they could be examined in London . . . Mr. Tano said he had no stock in Cairo or Cyprus at present but that he would write later if he found anything interesting."

Thus business relationships were well established long before 1956. It is not necessary, therefore, to seek to correlate acquisitions with trips by Beatty or an agent of his to Egypt. If Tano, for example, had sent the bulk of his manuscript collection to Cyprus in the summers of 1955 and

1956, and not just those intended for the Bibliothèque Bodmer, or if some sent or taken to Geneva on approval had not been acquired there, Tano could have corresponded with Beatty freely from Cyprus while there for the summers, and he could have sent the material and received payment without either party to the negotiations leaving his home.

Beatty had his main residence in London until 1950, when he moved to Dublin. Actually, he had customarily wintered at Mena House in Giza near Cairo. But this habit came to an end in 1950, when the move to Dublin took place. He had both a home in Dublin itself and an estate out of town, as well as the property at 20 Shrewsbury Road for the Library, where a home for the librarian, J. V. S. Wilkinson, was also built. The first public building was constructed in 1952–53. Then a second building at the rear was constructed in 1955–56 and opened as a gallery for the public in 1957, making possible a display of previously undisplayed papyri.[2]

In 1957, Sir Chester Beatty opened the new wing of his celebrated library in Dublin, and this extension gave him a long-awaited opportunity for setting out and arranging various sections of his manuscript collections, including a number of papyri that had been acquired at various times during the past twenty or thirty years, and which could now for the first time be examined in detail.

In 1975 it was enlarged by the adding of a second story and an extension on the front with a new glass facade. The sign at the entrance to the property read: "The Chester Beatty Library and Gallery of Oriental Art." The reading room for those studying manuscripts was the Garden Library, a large room in the first building extending into the garden that separates it from the newer Gallery. The manuscripts were stored in a "Strong Room," a walk-in vault.[3]

2. Skeat, "Papyri from Panopolis," 194. See the earlier guide booklet by the Librarian, R. J. Hayes, *The Chester Beatty Library, Dublin*, 5:

> The collections were housed for years in Baroda House, Kensington Palace Gardens, London, until 1953, having moved his residence to Dublin, he built a special library building to hold the wonderful collections of Oriental and Western printed books and manuscripts which he had brought together during the previous forty years. In 1957 an additional large exhibition gallery was added to enable more of the treasures to be displayed. These buildings are situated in a pleasant suburban setting in Shrewsbury Road, Dublin.

3. Orlandi, "Les Manuscrits coptes de Dublin," 326.

During the interval, while the Gallery was being built, many manuscripts were put on display at Trinity College in Dublin, and some more recent acquisitions were sent to the British Museum to be conserved. T. C. Skeat of the staff of the British Museum submitted on July 4, 1956, a report to the Chester Beatty Library on material that must have been previously supplied to him for conservation and identification. The report describes what was to become Accession Number 1499, edited by Alfons Wouters, and P. Beatty Panop. (which received no Accession Number), which Skeat himself was to edit. When Skeat announced in 1958 the acquisition of P. Beatty Panop., he wrote of its restoration at the British Museum as follows:

> As this writing [on two rolls secondarily pasted face to face and then cut into sheets to produce the quire of a codex] promised to be of much greater interest than the tax receipts [inscribed in the resultant codex], I suggested, and Sir Chester readily agreed, that the codex should be taken to pieces. This delicate operation, which could be effected only by prolonged soaking of the papyrus, was successfully carried out by Mr. Stanley Baker, of the Egyptian Department in the British Museum, and the results exceeded all expectations.[4]

In the *editio princeps* of P. Beatty Panop., Skeat then reported in a preface dated October 1963: "that on completion of the publication, the papyri themselves, hitherto deposited for my use in the British Museum, will be transferred to the Chester Beatty Library."[5] It may have been this late return of P. Beatty Panop. to Dublin that accounts for it not having been entered in the Registry of Accessions; by the time it came back, it may have been assumed to have been accessioned before being sent to the British Museum.

Skeat's unpublished report of June 4, 1956, went on:

> In addition to the above [Accession Number 1499 and P. Beatty Panop.] are two small folders of papyrus fragments. One of these, marked X, contains a small fragment of a leaf of a papyrus codex of the 3rd cent. A.D., containing parts of John XIX. 26–27, 31–32; this may be from the John codex recently acquired by M. Bodmer [P. Bodmer II], and I should be grateful for permission to inform M. Bodmer of its whereabouts. Some of the other

4. Skeat, "Papyri from Panopolis," 194.

5. Skeat, *Papyri*, iv.

> fragments come from Codex B above [P. Beatty Panop.]. There are also 3 or 4 small fragments of what appears to be a Gospel narrative (late 2nd cent. A.D.), and some Coptic pieces."

Skeat has informed Wouters "that in June 1956 he was asked by Sir Chester Beatty to write a report on a group of papyri, acquired by him during that same year."[6] The reference to June must derive from the June 4 date on the document, rather than literally to the date at which the request was made, unless the request was met with remarkable speed. Hence, the acquisition would seem to have been made in May at the latest, if the material had to move from Dublin to the British Museum in time for the report to be completed by June 4. Thus it can hardly be the same acquisition as one referred to in the volume of the Library's Registry of Accessions titled "Chester Beatty Library Acquisitions from April 1956," which reports at Accession Number 1389 that this manuscript was acquired "summer 1956 with ac. 1390 and 2 boxes of loose leaves." Rather one must assume two acquisitions of papyri in 1956. This is confirmed by other considerations. For Accession Number 1499 and P. Beatty Panop. are surely too extensive to be referred to merely as the "2 boxes of loose leaves" acquired in the summer of 1956. And whereas Accession Number 1390 also refers explicitly to having been acquired "with ac. 1389 and 2 boxes of loose leaves," there is no reference at Accession Numbers 1389 or 1390 to Accession Number 1499, nor at Accession Number 1499 is there any reference back to Accession Numbers 1389 and 1390.

The presence of the fragment of P. Bodmer II among these materials indicates that the acquisition of May 1956 or earlier came at least in part from the discovery here under investigation. On the other hand the fragments of a Gospel narrative and the Coptic pieces are too imprecisely described to be readily identified. The former are presumably in Greek, since they might otherwise have been lumped together with the Coptic

6. In a letter of February 24, 1981, from Alfons Wouters. The quotation is from the typescript of his *Chester Beatty Ac. 1499*, 4. Wouters (n. 20) rightly prefers Skeat's date of 1956 for the acquisition to the date given by Lowe, *Codices Latini Antiquiores*, 5, item 1683: "Acquired by A. Chester Beatty in 1958." For Skeat's typed report on file at the Chester Beatty Library is dated June 4, 1956. 1958 may be the date when it was sent from the British Museum and entered into the Registry of Accessions. The Registry of Accessions has at 1499 a penciled note: "1953 Greek–Latin dictionary," which as a secondarily added comment (the Registry of Accessions itself is dated from April 1956 on), also seems less reliable than Skeat's dating of the acquisition of 1956.

pieces. In fact Skeat's identifications seem to have been limited to Greek material. The fragment of P. Bodmer XX glassed with that of P. Bodmer II seems to be another of his identifications. For according to the *editio princeps*, it "has been discovered by Mr. T. C. Skeat among the papyri of the Chester Beatty collection. We are indebted to his courtesy for the communication of the text of this fragment that happily completes this page."[7] At the Bibliothèque Bodmer photographs of the Chester Beatty fragment are glassed with this Bodmer leaf in the lacuna. Thus, though Skeat's report does not mention it, he presumably communicated to Bodmer the existence of this fragment as well as that of P. Bodmer II. Probably the fragment of P. Bodmer XX was so small as not to be initially identifiable in 1956, before P. Bodmer XX was published (1964).

On December 16, 1956, Beatty wrote to I. E. S. Edwards of the staff of the British Museum to the effect that he was sending him six papyri plus a little tin box and on vellum what appeared to be a Coptic sermon. Much of the present task is to seek to identify these, and the earlier vague references, in terms of identifications that could only be made once the material was at the British Museum being restored—identifications then passed on in typescript to the Chester Beatty Library and preserved there. For example, the vellum with "what appeared to be a Coptic sermon" would seem to be what became Accession Number 1486, subsequently identified as the Pachomian Abbot Theodore's Letter 2. For in the Registry of Accessions it is described as "another homily," a description that is no doubt derived from A. F. Shore's appended report: "Text of obscure import, apparently a letter or sermon of reproof. The author quotes from the Old and New Testament and mention is made of the 'remission of debts' (OUHT) at the New Year, probably an allusion to the custom of the Pachomian monastic settlements to gather at this time to order their finances."

This is, in retrospect, indeed a remarkably accurate description of Theodore's Letter 2 (see chapter 4 below).

A. F. Shore, the editor of Accession Number 1389 (the Chester Beatty Library's part of P. Bodmer XXI), reported also about the British Museum's conservation work: "The skilled work of separating the leaves and the necessary conservation was undertaken by Mr. S. Baker, Senior Museum Assistant in the Department of Egyptian Antiquities at

7. *Papyrus Bodmer* XX, 34.

the British Museum . . . I am particularly indebted to Mr. I. E. S. Edwards who first drew my attention to the antiquity and importance of the manuscript."[8]

The Registry of Accessions reports on this item that it "was mounted and framed at the British Museum under the superintendence of Mr. I. E. S. Edwards." Since it is in Coptic, it could have been among the "Coptic pieces" to which Skeat's report referred, but the reference to Edwards may suggest it was among the group of six papyri sent to him for this purpose at the British Museum at the end of 1956. Similar though briefer notes are recorded with other items in the Registry of Accessions. At Accession Number 1486 one reads: "Brought from the British Museum, summer, 1957." Accession Number 1500: "Mounted by Mr. Baker of the British Museum. Found in a box of miscellaneous fragments, mainly papyri, summer, 1957, and returned to the library, August, 1958."[9] At Accession Number 1501 there is a comment that is in substance the same.

These reports make it clear that at least some items acquired at each of the two occasions in 1956 are from the same discovery as are the Bodmer Papyri, two from the first acquisition and one from the second.

1. A fragment from P. Bodmer II, 139/140 (John 19:25–28, 30–32). This fragment is not listed in the Registry of Accessions and has no Accession Number, but is mentioned in Skeat's report of July 4, 1956, and is currently in the Library.

2. A fragment[10] from P. Bodmer XX, including pp. 135, 13–16 / 136, 14–17. This fragment is not listed in the Registry of Accessions and has no Accession Number, nor is it mentioned in Skeat's report of June 4, 1956.

8. Shore, *Joshua I–VI*, 8–9, 16.

9. This item is described as "Vellum codex. 8 vellum leaves containing a collection of traditions. 3rd century or earlier." The leaves are in Arabic, so that the dating poses a problem. When on August 8, 1984, I drew this to the attention of David James, Curator of Arabic materials, he suggested that the dating may be Arabic, and in hypothesis would make the item probably too late to have been part of the shared provenience. Nothing in Arabic is known to have come from this discovery. Furthermore, the presence of eight vellum leaves from a codex "in a box of miscellaneous fragments" that can nonetheless be described as "mainly papyri" seems to raise the question as to whether the material is correctly identified.

10. Haelst, *Catalogue*, 259, item 710, refers to "tiny fragments at Dublin, Chester Beatty Museum," but only one, which is hardly "tiny," is conserved there and published in *Papyrus Bodmer* XX. Of course it may have been assembled from smaller fragments.

But it is currently in the Library, glassed with the fragment of P. Bodmer II; and Skeat is credited by the *editio princeps* with identifying it.

3. The leather cover and about two-thirds of the leaves of P. Bodmer XXI, Chester Beatty Library Accession Number 1389 (acquired in the summer of 1956).

The part of P. Bodmer XXI acquired by the Chester Beatty Library in the summer of 1956 was given the Accession Number 1389. An item from the earlier acquisition and shipment to the British Museum was given the accession number 1499. Hence one might conjecture that the numbers intervening between 1389 and 1499 in the Registry of Accessions could well be part of these two acquisitions. But an examination of the Registry of Accessions makes it apparent that things are not so simple, since many intervening items are modern books. And some are Merton Papyri: Accession Number 1391 are the Merton Papyri acquired from W. Merton in 1957; Accession Numbers 1488 and 1492 are gifts from Merton in 1958; and Accession Number 1496, dated September 1958, was acquired from the Merton bequest. Thus the numeration in the Registry of Accessions is not immediately intelligible.

A broader examination of the Registry of Accessions permits some inductive inferences as to how the sequence in the Registry is to be interpreted: Most of the Accession Numbers intervening between the Merton Papyri of 1957 and the bequest of 1958, numbered on the one hand 1391 and on the other 1496, reflect a largely chronological sequence (as do the Merton items themselves), from Accession Number 1392, dated February 1958, to Accession Number 1485, dated August 1958. The entry at Accession Number 1489 may indicate what the standard practice was: The right hand page reports, "Bought in June, 1955," while the left-hand page, usually left blank to be available for additional information, reports: "Repaired . . . and entered only in August, 1958, on this account." Thus the sequence in the numeration system may reflect more nearly that of the conservation than that of the acquisition.

If such practices may be assumed to hold true also for the material here under investigation, one may interpret the Registry of Accessions as follows: When at Accession Numbers 1389 and 1390 one reads: "Bought . . . summer 1956," one may suspect this information was not recorded in 1956, to be followed by only one Accession Number 1391 ("acquired from Mr. W. Merton, 1957") between summer 1956 and February 1958, the date of Accession Number 1392. Rather, the Accession Numbers

1389 and 1390 may have been assigned and recorded only when the material was returned from the British Museum, before February 1958, perhaps in the summer of 1957 along with Accession Number 1486 (see below). Such an inference would seem to be confirmed by the reference at Accession Number 1389 to "12 glasses," which presupposes the material had already been conserved when it was recorded. The recording on the left-hand page at Accession Numbers 1389 and 1390 must have taken place the following year, since it presupposes Shore's report of July 1958, in listing them as "item no. 1 [2] on Mr. Shore's list." Accession Number 1486, though the entry on the right-hand page reads: "Brought from the British Museum, Summer 1957," was apparently not registered before August 1958, the date of Accession Number 1485; the entry on the left-hand page at Accession Number 1486 contains an excerpt identified as a "Note by Mr. Shore of the British Museum, July 1958." Accession Number 1487 is then dated as bought August 1958. In the case of Accession Number 1493, the entry on the right-hand page is identical with Shore's report of July 1958, indicating that its registration took place only after that time, as one would expect, since it is recorded after Accession Number 1487 acquired in August 1958. At Accession Numbers 1500 and 1501 there is reference on the right-hand page to their being "found in a box of miscellaneous fragments . . . summer, 1957," "and returned to the Library, August, 1958." It was hence the return of some material in the summer of 1957 that led to the recording of a part of it as Accession Numbers 1389 and 1390 on the right-hand page in 1957. But it was only the return of more material in August 1958, along with Shore's report of July 1958, that led to the registering in August 1958 of what had not yet been registered from the material returned the preceding summer, along with the material only recently returned, as well as to the adding of new information from Shore's report to the material that had been registered a year earlier. The fact that only at Accession Numbers 1389 and 1390 does one find reference to the acquisition itself would seem to be due to their being the only items registered in the summer of 1957. For those registered the summer of 1958, even Accession Number 1486 that had been returned in the summer of 1957, and Accession Number 1499, known to have been part of the first acquisition of 1956, been no reference in the Registry of Accessions to their acquisition.

A copy of Shore's report of July 1958, which is a list of Coptic manuscripts, is extant both as a typescript at the Chester Beatty Library and secondarily as cited in the Registry of Accessions. The list includes the following Accession Numbers: 1, 1389; 2, 1390; 3, 1493; 4, 1494; 5, 1486; 6ff [?].

A sifting through the Accession Numbers between 1389 (number 1 on Shore's list, the bulk of P. Bodmer XXI) and 1499 (known to have been acquired with P. Bodmer II) thus points most clearly to Accession Numbers 1390 (Shore 2), 1486 (Shore 5), 1493 (Shore 3), 1494 (Shore 4), and 1495 as probably part of the material acquired in 1956. But just as Accession Numbers between these two poles do not in every case indicate the same acquisition, just so Accession Numbers outside (though near) these limits may on occasion come from the same acquisition. For the Accession Numbers 1389 and 1499 were not chosen as extreme limits but only as items identified as from the same acquisitions as those known to involve Bodmer Papyri. Thus Accession Number 1501 may come into consideration, as perhaps the item with the highest Accession Number that might come from one of the same acquisitions. To be sure, each item that comes in question must be associated with the shared provenience on grounds other than simply its position in the sequence in the Registry of Accessions, though this numeration has proven to be of some relevance. One must also consider items without Accession Numbers, such as the fragments of P. Bodmer II and P. Bodmer XX; P. Beatty Panop., acquired along with these fragments; and W 145 and No. 54, both involving Pachomius's letters. It is all these items that now need to be considered one by one. Since W. 145, No. 54, and Accession Numbers 1486, 1494 and 1495 belong to the Pachomian corpus, they will be discussed in Chapter 4 below. Thus we investigate here only Accession Numbers 1390, 1493, 1499, and 1501, as well as P. Beatty Panop.

4. Accession Number 1390. This item was acquired along with Accession Number 1389 (from P. Bodmer XXI), according to the Registry at Accession Number 1389: "Bought from Phocion J. Tano, 53 Sharia Ibrahim Pasha, Cairo, summer 1956, with acquisition 1390 and two boxes of loose leaves, £835." Accession Number 1390: the Registry of Accessions records in substance the same information. But in addition there is stapled to the left-hand page at Accession Number 1390 a carbon copy of a typescript probably emanating from Tano himself: "Small Village DESHNA just after NAGHI HAMADI about 2 hours before LUXOR by train. Probably from a Library of a Monastery. Found in a Jar in a cemetery."

A. F. Shore assumed not only that Accession Numbers 1389 and 1390 were from the same acquisition, but also that they were from the same discovery. For he appealed to Accession Number 1390 to strengthen his argument (from the Sub-Achmimic corruption of the Sahidic of Accession Number 1389) for a provenience of Accession Number 1389 "from Middle Egypt, perhaps from the region of Achmim (Panopolis)." For here he appends the footnote:[11] "It is perhaps significant that Sir Chester Beatty acquired at the same time [as Accession Number 1389] part of a papyrus codex containing passages from the Gospel of John written in a cursive hand in the Subachmimic dialect, of fourth-century date [Accession Number 1390]."

According to the registry, Accession Number 1390, it is conserved in "five glasses." There is reference to "also one separate glass of Greek text of a school exercise and a leaf cojoined to the text of St. John." The total of six glasses contains eight leaves, since in two cases conjugate leaves are in the same glass. The eight leaves, identified on the labels of each glass pane, are as follows:

Leaf 1 = extant pp. 1/2: | "Greek text (School ↑ exercise)" / → "Greek text (School exercise)."

Leaf 2 = extant pp. 3/4: | "Greek text (School ↑ exercise)" / → [the conclusion of the Greek text and] "Continuation of Gospel of John. Subachmimic. 1. John x 8-18."

Leaf 3 = extant pp. 5/6: | "2. John x 18–36" / → "3. ↑ John x 36–xi 12";

Leaf 4 = extant pp. 7/8: → "4. John xi 12–28" / | "5. ↑ John xi 28–43." Since Leaves 3 and 4 are conjugate and are conserved together, this sheet consisting of Leaves 3 and 4 is presumably the center of the quire.

Leaf 5 = extant pp. 9/10: → "6. John xi 43–55" / | ↑ "7. John xi 55–xii 14." Leaf 5 is conjugate with Leaf 2, with which it is conserved.

Leaf 6 = extant pp. 11/12: → "8. John xii 14-27" / | ↑ "9. John xii 27–39." Leaves 1 and 6 are probably conjugate, to judge by the horizontal fibres discernable on the photographs, but a kollesis on the inner margin of Leaf 6 makes this somewhat less obvious, which may be why the two leaves are not conserved together.

11. Shore, *Joshua I–VI*, 12, n. 2.

Shore's report does refer to three bifolios, of which this would be the third. If the text of the School exercise is continuous from Leaf 1 to Leaf 2, about which Shore was uncertain, Leaf 1 should be conjugate with Leaf 6.

Leaf 7 = extant pp. 13/14: → "10. John xii 40–xiii 2" / | "11. John xiii 2–12."

Leaf 8 = extant pp. 15/16 (actually three fragments of a leaf): → 12. "John xiii 14 . . . 18 . . . 23–6" / | "13. John xiii 28 . . . 31 . . . 35–8."

Shore's typed report of July 1958 states regarding this codex that there are "12 leaves or fragments of leaves (6 folios and 3 bifolios)." But the Registry of Accessions lists five glasses for John and one for the School exercise. Since two of the five glasses contain sheets (bifolios), a total of eight leaves are included in what is recorded in the Registry of Accessions, and they are readily identified in the Library's holdings. Thus, Shore's report of "12 leaves or fragments of leaves" must have been made before it was determined that some of the fragments on Leaves 6–8 (probably from among those that do not touch) nonetheless belong to the same leaf. Indeed, Shore's report states that the text extends from John 10:8 only to 12:14, which indicates that the last three leaves had not yet been identified in terms of their position in the Gospel of John, since these leaves extend the text to John 13:38.[12]

Shore's report remarks regarding the two leaves with the Greek text (leaves 1–2 = extant pp. 1/2–3/4): "It is uncertain whether these leaves are continuous." But the continuity of text on the conjugate leaves (leaves 5–6 = extant pages 9/10–11/12), once the continuation of the text of the Gospel of John has been identified here, makes it clear that the Greek text should also be continuous. It should also be possible to confirm this codicologically by an examination of the originals in terms of the continuity of horizontal fibers from one sheet to the next (from extant

12. Orlandi, "Les Manuscrits coptes de Dublin," 326, speaks of "12 leaves," and adds "on this *recto*, mathematical exercises in Greek." This is presumably an abbreviation of Shore's report rather than an inventory of material as actually glassed and available for examination at the Library. This is also suggested by the use of Shore's term *recto* for the side of a leaf with vertical fibers, but the first side inscribed. For this terminology is made clearer by Shore's addition, omitted by Orlandi, "and half the *verso*." Thus, it is clear that the side with vertical fibers was inscribed first, then the Greek text completed at the top of the side with horizontal fibers, then the Coptic text begun on the side with horizontal fibers.

pp. 4 + 6, the horizontal-fibered side of the sheet next to that which is at the center of the quire, on to extant pages 2 + 11, the horizontal-fibered size of the next sheet still further from the center of the quire).

As one moves beyond this manuscript that the Registry of Accessions clearly ascribes to the Dishnā discovery, it becomes much more difficult to identify further items in the Registry from this discovery. For one must seek to correlate what was recorded in the Registry after the material was conserved and identified at the British Museum with the all too vague references that were made to it near the time of acquisition but before the individual items had been sorted out. Skeat's report of June 4, 1956, refers to "two small folders of papyrus fragments," of which he left unidentified "3 or 4 small fragments of what appears to be a Gospel narrative (late 2nd cent. A.D.), and some Coptic pieces." The second acquisition of 1956 also involved material mentioned all too vaguely. At Accession Numbers 1389–90 it is recorded that they were accompanied in the acquisition from Tano by "two boxes of loose leaves," which are not further identified. On December 16, 1956, "six papyri" plus a "little tin box" were sent to the British Museum for conservation, again without further identification, according to the accompanying letter. But the "little tin box" may be one of the two boxes from Tano, since he is known to have used small tin boxes to protect manuscripts from the elements and from rodents. The Coptic Museum in Cairo has retained these boxes even after their contents were conserved. And Tano supplied Riyāḍ Jirjis Fām, the main middleman of the Bodmer Papyri, with such a tin box for material that Riyāḍ still kept in hiding. This then strengthens the assumption that the box sent at the end of 1956 was one acquired from Tano in the summer of 1956. One can conjecture that the six papyri mentioned at the end of 1956 were Accession Numbers 1389 and 1390, plus four derived from the two boxes of loose leaves. For by a "papyrus" one does not necessarily mean a single sheet of papyrus; for example, the Bodmer Papyri are referred to singly as Papyrus Number so-and-so, which thus can refer to as much as a whole codex. Since sheets are often broken in two at the spine, and the leather cover is often missing, the modest remains of a codex could be included in a reference to loose leaves. The separating out of four "papyri" from two boxes of "loose leaves" could thus have reduced the residue of miscellaneous material to the contents of one box. As a result, only one box is subsequently mentioned. Only at one other place does the Registry of Accessions refer to what may be correlated with the initially vague references. For Accession Numbers 1500 and 1501 report that they were "found [at the British Museum] in a box of miscellaneous fragments, mainly papyri, summer, 1957." This is presumably a reference to the box sent at the end of 1956. But such references, vague though they are, do indicate that the items known to come from the shared provenience (parts of P. Bodmer II, XX, and XXI in the first acquisition, and Accession Number 1390 in the second) were accompanied by others from the same acquisition and hence, at least in some cases, probably from the same provenience. The problem is thus to seek to identify the unidentified items among the "Coptic pieces" of the first shipment and the "two boxes of loose leaves" of the second acquisition, which presumably contain four of the "six papyri," and the contents of the "little tin box" of the second shipment.

5. Accession Number 1493.[13] This is item 3 on Shore's list. It could be one of the "Coptic pieces" of the first shipment to the British Museum or one of the "six papyri" of the second shipment. The entry, based on Shore's list, reads: "Apocalypse of Elias. Coptic Papyrus Codex. 10 leaves of a Sahidic version of the Apocalypse of Elias, numbered A–[K] [1–[20]], carelessly written on poor papyrus in single column in an uncial hand, and to be dated on palaeographical grounds to the end of the ivth / beginning of the vth century. The first five leaves are practically complete; the others, built up from fragments, give a fairly connected text. The leaves form, apparently, a single quire of five bifolios."

It is conserved in ten glasses and one glass of fragments. It was published in 1981 by Albert Pietersma and Susan Turner Comstock with Harold W. Attridge under the title *The Apocalypse of Elijah based on P. Chester Beatty 2018*.[14] The reason for the introduction of the numeration 2018 is obscure, since this numeration is not recorded at the Chester Beatty Library itself.

The association of this manuscript with the shared provenience is largely circumstantial: Its inclusion on Shore's list suggests it is from the material sent in two shipments to the British Museum in 1956. Its position in the Registry of Accessions is among the cluster of material

13. Ibid. inaccurately gives the Accession Number as 1443.

14. Reference to this text prior to its publication is found in Rosenstiehl, *L'Apocalypse d'Elie*, 10: "It remains for us to express a regret: In spite of all our efforts, we have not been able to get to know the Sahidic fragments of the *Apocalypse of Elijah* that are in the Chester Beatty collection."

here under investigation regarding the shared provenience, which was returned to the Chester Beatty Library in August of 1958 (Accession Numbers 1486, 1494, 1495, 1499, 1501). It is associated with the item that the Registry of Accessions explicitly attributes to the Dishnā discovery (Accession Number 1390), following directly upon it in the numeration of Shore's list. It is directly followed on that list and in the Registry of Acquisitions by two letters from the Pachomian archive: Accession Numbers 1494 and 1495, which apparently also come from the shared provenience (see chapter 4 below). The dating (fourth or fifth century) is typical of the Coptic material in the discovery. The nature of the text also fits the assumed monastic context. The poor quality of the manuscript is a trait shared with a number of the other manuscripts of the shared provenience, especially among these later Coptic pieces:[15]

> The Chester Beatty *Apocalypse of Elijah* was written on what Mr. Shore described as papyrus of a poor quality. Certainly quality leaves a good deal to be desired. Frequently one finds patches of twisted, chipped and missing fibers, and in spots the manuscript was left blank due to its inferior state . . .
>
> On the whole P. Chester Beatty 2018 was carelessly written, and a considerable number of errors escaped detection by the copyist . . .
>
> It is surprising that the Chester Beatty manuscript ends abruptly in the middle of the speech of "the lawless one," and the line fillers on the concluding line of page 20 suggest that the abrupt termination is not due to the vicissitudes of survival. At least the immediate *Vorlage* of our manuscript must likewise have lacked the concluding pages of the *Apocalypse.*

6. Accession Number 1499. This could be one of the "six papyri" of the second shipment. The Registry of Accessions reports: "Greek–Latin Dictionary. Papyrus codex. 5th century. 4 quires intact, mounted between glass. Binding and papyrus quires in brown box."[16] Actually, sixteen leaves are glassed, two leaves per glass (usually not conjugate leaves).[17]

15. Pietersma et al., *Apocalypse of Elijah*, 4, 6.

16. Wouters, *Chester Beatty Codex Ac. 1499* typescript, 10, n. 8, reports that the uninscribed leaves are still kept "in the same brown box."

17. Ibid., 5: "Seven leaves of the codex which contained writing had been mounted by him [Baker] in the British museum." Apparently, he means seven pairs of sheets, glassed in seven containers. For he goes on to report (ibid., n. 22) that he received photographs from the British Museum except for the glass containing leaves 9 and 14.

The Registry of Accessions reads as if it assumed that four leaves comprise a quire, resulting in four quires in the eight glass containers. But van Regemorter[18] reported: "This notebook is formed of several quires, most of which have four double leaves, i.e., 16 pages."

Wouters[19] has constructed hypothetically one such quire of leaves 1–8. Thus it is probable that what is glassed is actually two quires of this size or one quire of this size and more than one smaller quire or parts of quires. Of the thirty-two glassed pages, only twenty-three have writing on them. Three leaves are uninscribed on both sides, three are inscribed on one side only, and ten on both sides.[20]

The reference that follows in the Registry of Accessions to "papyrus quires in brown box" would seem to refer to quires in addition to what was "mounted between glass," i.e., to the material not glassed but stored with the cover in the brown box in connection with which they are mentioned. The leaves not glassed were presumably uninscribed. For in his report of June 4, 1956, Skeat described Accession Number 1499 as "a papyrus codex, of which at least 37 leaves are blank." The number of uninscribed leaves may actually be thirty-eight. For E. A. Lowe described the manuscript as follows: "Foll. 51 of a papyrus codex, of which only 13 contain writing."[21] One may conjecture that three uninscribed leaves were glassed because they were part of quires that were in part inscribed and hence were sent to the British Museum for conservation, whereas quires with no inscribed pages were not sent for conservation. Wouters reports: "35 blank leaves of the original codex are kept in the reserve of the CBL, among them 3 complete quires. Of one further quire two (written) leaves have apparently been put between glass. Finally there are 3 separate leaves."[22]

Lowe dated the Latin hand to the last half of the fifth century, but Wouters, following E. G. Turner, prefers the fourth.[23] Lowe also commented: "There is some resemblance to the Barcelona papyrus (our No.

18. Van Regemorter, "Le Papetier-Libraire," 29.

19. Wouters, *Chester Beatty Codex Ac. 1499*, typescript, 7–8.

20. Ibid.

21. Lowe, *Codices Latinis Antiquiores*, 5 (item 1683) and 32 (item 1782).

22. Wouters, *Chester Beatty Codex Ac. 1499*, typescript, 10. He comments (n. 8) that the figure 35 is a correction of an earlier publication of the figure 36. ("Unedited Papyrus Codex in the Chester Beatty Library," 98.) For he had subsequently determined that one leaf in the brown box is not from Accession Number 1499.

23. Wouters, *Chester Beatty Codex Ac. 1499*, 21.

1782)." No. 1782 is "Barcelona, Fundacio Sant Lluc Evangelista Pap. Barc. (foll. 149v-153)," dated by Lowe to the second half of the fourth century. Number. 1782 is the *Psalmus Responsorius*, which is itself part of a codex that probably belongs to the shared provenience, since fragments from it emerged at the Bibliothèque Bodmer and the University of Mississippi (see below). In addition to the script, the lack of familiarity with Latin would seem to be a shared trait between the Dublin and Barcelona codices. Accession Number 1499 contains a Greek-Latin lexicon to the Pauline Epistles and Greek verb paradigms. Lowe has observed: "The Latin seems influenced by the Greek, the scribe apparently more at home with Greek than with Latin." He comments similarly about the *Psalmus Responsorius*: "The unusual word-division and the lack of familiarity with the normal forms of the Nomina Sacra suggest that the scribe was unused to copying Latin."

Berthe van Regemorter has reported:[24] "I examined this little notebook several years ago, when it was still easy to take account of its fabrication. Since then, unfortunately, the back has broken and its particularities are less apparent."

"Several years ago" in reference to 1960 is difficult to date. But one may observe that van Regemorter published in 1958 a study of early bindings in the Chester Beatty Library.[25] In the preface dated September 1957, she acknowledged "the late Librarian of the Chester Beatty Library, Mr. J. V. S. Wilkinson, who, with great kindness, took the trouble to revise the greater part of the text." Since Wilkinson died in 1957, her work on the covers published in that book must have been prior to 1957. If her examination of Accession Number 1599 took place at the same time as she was preparing her book, it would have been before the codex was sent to the British Museum. It was obviously before the book was disassembled for conservation. This apparently took place before it left Dublin. For Wouters has observed: "Apparently the binding was not sent to London, as neither Mr. Baker, nor T. C. Skeat can remember having seen it and it has not been photographed in the Museum."[26]

Since the uninscribed leaves were not glassed, and were being kept with the cover in the brown box when recorded in the Registry of

24. Van Regemorter, "Le Papetier-Libraire," 279.

25. See van Regemorter, *Some Early Bindings*.

26. Wouters, *Chester Beatty Codex Ac. 1499*, typescript, 7.

Accessions, they presumably also were not sent to the British Museum.[27] If the inscribed leaves were hence removed in Dublin when it was to be sent to London, that would account for the breaking of the back and the obscuring of the codicological evidence after van Regemorter examined it.[28]

7. Accession Number 1501. This could be one of the "six papyri" of the second shipment. The Registry of Accessions records: "9 leaves (4 bifolios and 1 folio) of a papyrus codex of Psalms." It has been published in 1978 by Albert Pietersma as P. Chester Beaty XIII and XIV under the title *Two Manuscripts of the Greek Psalter.* Presumably the numeration used in this publication is intended to continue that of *The Chester Beatty Biblical Papyri* published a generation earlier, which involved a numeration of I–XII. P. Chester Beatty XIII consists of four sheets from a codex containing (in the numeration of the Septuagint) Psalms 72:6–23; 72:25—76:1; 77:1–18; 77:20—81:7; 82:2—84:14; 85:2—88:2. It has been assigned the number 2149 in the numeration system of Greek Psalms manuscripts begun by A. Rahlfs and continued by the Septuaginta-Unternehmen of Göttingen. P. Chester Beatty XIV is a leaf from a completely different manuscript, perhaps an amulet, containing Psalms 31:8–11; 26:1–6, 8–14; 2:1–8 (in that order). It has been given the number 2150. Both date from the fourth century. The Registry of Accessions records: "Found in a box of miscellaneous fragments of papyri, Summer, 1957. Mounted at B. M. and returned to Library, August, 1958." Thus these two vestiges of Psalms manuscripts may well be part of the shared provenience, in terms of dating, though there is no further confirmation of such a hypothesis. To be sure, one may point to a textual variant shared (but not exclusively) with P. Bodmer XXIV: At Psalm 76:1, instead of the usual reading ΤΩ ΑΣΑΦ ΨΑΛΜΟΣ, both read ΨΑΛΜΟΣ ΤΩ ΑΣΑΦ. This same reading, in Coptic, is also attested on the wall of cave 8 at the Jabal al-Tarif a few hundred meters

27. Wouters, "Unedited Papyrus Codex in the Chester Beatty Library," 98: "At a certain moment the unwritten leaves had apparently been removed from the damaged papyrus book. At the same time the written leaves had been put between glass."

28. Lowe's comment, *Codices Latini Antiquiores*, 5, item 1683, "acquired by A. Chester Beatty in 1958," must refer to the time the glassed material was returned from the British Museum, since it can hardly refer to the actual time of the acquisition, which was 1956. Then it is even more apparent that van Regemorter examined it before it was sent to the British Museum. For 1958 is hardly "several years ago" in relation to a publication date of 1960.

from the site of the discovery of the Nag Hammadi codices and some five kilometers from Phbow, ten from Dishnā.[29]

Psalms manuscripts are already known to be represented more than once among the Bodmer Papyri, in addition to Accession Number 1501: P. Bodmer IX (Ps 33–34) and P. Bodmer XXIV. Just as P. Bodmer XX (the *Acts of Phileas*) is followed by P. Bodmer IX, P. Chester Beatty XV (the *Acts [Apology] of Phileas*) is followed by vestiges of Psalms 1–4. (Whether this manuscript may belong also to the shared provenience will be discussed below.) It would not be surprising if a Psalms manuscript at the Beinecke Library of Yale University were also from the shared provenience, P. Yale 1179.[30] Its physical similarity to the Pachomian letters will be discussed in chapter 4 below. One may recall the Pachomian requirement that Psalms be memorized by persons applying for admission to a monastery:

> Rule 49: . . . He shall remain outside at the door a few days and be taught the Lord's prayer and as many psalms as he can learn. Rule 139: Whoever enters the monastery uninstructed shall be taught first what he must observe; and when, so taught, he has consented to it all, they shall give him twenty psalms or two of the Apostle's epistles, or some other part of the Scripture.
>
> And if he is illiterate, he shall go at the first, third, and sixth hours to someone who can teach and has been appointed for him. He shall stand before him and learn very studiously with all gratitude. Then the fundamentals of a syllable, the verbs, and nouns shall be written for him, and even if he does not want to, he shall be compelled to read. Rule 140: There shall be no one whatever in the monastery who does not learn to read and does not memorize something of the Scriptures. [One should learn by heart] at least the New Testament and the Psalter.[31]

The inscription in cave 8 may reflect this situation, in that it provides only the opening line of each of a series of psalms, apparently to aid in the transition from one recitation to the next. The opening of Psalm 77 on the wall of cave 8 presents a Coptic text identical with that of

29. Bucher, "Les Commencements des Psaumes LI à XCIII," 157–60.

30. Vergote and Parássoglou, "Les Psaumes 76 et 77 en Copte-Sahidique," 531–41.

31. Veilleux, *Pachomian Koinonia* 2:153 (Rule 49); 2:166 (Rules 139–40). See also Veilleux, *Pachomian Koinonia* 2:187 (note 2 to Rule 49): "'As many psalms as he can learn' may be a gloss of Jerome. The Greek *Excerpta* have simply 'psalms.'"

P. Yale Inv. 1179.[32] To be sure, Psalms manuscripts are the most common manuscripts from the Old Testament, so that it is not surprising that they occur frequently in the holdings of the Chester Beatty Library. But the Pachomian context of some of these holdings would make the presence of Psalms manuscripts among those of the Pachomian provenience especially intelligible.

The *Acts of Phileas* followed by Psalms 1–4 (assigned the Rahlfs numeration 2151), published in 1984 (edited by Albert Pietersma) as *The Acts of Phileas Bishop of Thmuis (including Fragments of the Greek Psalter): P. Chester Beatty XV (With a New Edition of P. Bodmer XX, and Halkin's Latin Acta)*, is what is left of another Greek papyrus codex of the fourth century at the Chester Beatty Library. It has no Accession Number. If too fragmentary to be one of the "six papyri," it could have been within the box sent to the British Museum. But since it seems not to have been conserved there, it may not have been sent at all.

> P. Chester Beatty XV comprises a total of seventeen frames of fragments which apparently belonged to a quire of seven bifolios . . . , or fourteen folios, equalling twenty-eight pages in all. Though the right half of the quire has unfortunately been lost almost in its entirety, much of the left half has survived, be it in fragmentary form.
>
> Pages 1–14 of the reconstructed quire (no original pagination is extant) contain a Martyrdom known from other sources as the *Acts of Phileas*, while the second half, pages 15ff., apparently included at least the first four Psalms of the Greek Psalter . . . [33]

32. The one apparent divergence is actually in a lacuna, where the Yale manuscript is restored NAS[AF], with the Greek letter *F.* presumably on the basis of the editors' collation base, British Museum Ms. or. 5000, whereas Bucher read the text of cave 8 with the Coptic letter *F.* But that part of the inscription of cave 8 is now lacking, and hence Bucher's reading cannot be confirmed. But at Psalms 81 and 82 on that inscription Bucher read NASAF with the Coptic rather than the Greek letter, whereas the inscription actually uses in both instances the Greek letter. At Psalms 73, 74, 77, and 79 Bucher also read the Coptic *F.* These places are now all missing except in 79, where the letter in question is too obscure to be read. At Psalm 78, Bucher also filled a lacuna with the Coptic *F.* In view of not infrequent minor inaccuracies in Bucher's transcription, it would be hazardous to follow him in assuming, without the ability to confirm the reading, a divergence that would have involved the Coptic translator or scribe in changing to the Coptic *F*, away from the Greek *F* of the translation base, such as is found for example in the Greek of P. Chester Beatty XIII at Psalm 75:1. (Psalm 76:1 has a lacuna here.)

33. Pietersma, *Acts of Phileas Bishop of Thmuis*, 11.

A further unfortunate fact is that the provenance of the fragments as well as their initial place of framing is wrapped in mystery. Suffice it to say here that they had been mounted poorly with many edges left folded and fragments on top of each other. In some cases fragments framed together were upside down in relation one to the other.

P. Beatty Panop. This is an unbound quire, without Accession Number, acquired early in 1956 along with Accession Number 1499 and the fragments of P. Bodmer II and XX. It was compiled by T. C. Skeat and published in 1964 with the title *Papyri from Panopolis in the Chester Beatty Library Dublin*. For it consists of a quire cannibalized from "two long rolls containing official correspondence of the Strategus of the Panopolite nome, and dating from A.D. 298 and A.D. 300 respectively."[34] The resultant quire was "largely blank, but containing here and there a few tax-receipts bearing dates between A.D. 339 and 345, issued to a certain Besas Antoninus Alopex of Panopolis, and to members of his family."[35]

Skeat inferred that the quire not only was produced in Panopolis but was also discovered there, which would of course eliminate it from the shared provenience under investigation here. However the inscription of the text on the two rolls and the resultant quire at Panopolis does not eliminate the possibility of its burial near Dishnā rather than at Panopolis. Not only is there a precedent for records of one city being discovered at another place, to which they had e.g. been taken when the official in question retired to that place. Actually the nome of Panopolis extended on the right bank upstream well beyond the headquarters monastery of the Pachomian Order at Fāw Qiblī and the nearby site of the discovery of the "Dishnā papers," indeed to Qinā, some sixty kilometers beyond.[36]

Another consideration also tends to relativize the tension between the Panopolitan origin of the documents and the possibility of their discovery near Dishnā: The Pachomian order extended as far downstream as Panopolis. Indeed there seems to have been a northern branch of the order centered at Panopolis, with monasteries of Tbe-we, Tse-, S-mi-n and Tesmi-ne, under Petronius, a person of means (who turned them

34. Skeat, *Papyri*, viii.

35. Ibid., vii. These receipts have been published by Youtie et al., "Urkunden aus Panopolis II," 214–34.

36. Ibid., xix, xxxiv, and xxxvi.

over to the order) as the general Abbot of this group, who in turn was subordinate to Pachomius as General Abbot of the whole order.[37] Given the Pachomian practice of convening all the monks from the different Pachomian monasteries in August of each year at the headquarters monastery Pabau near Dishnā to go over their accounts and receive new monastery assignments, it would be easy to explain the transportation of writing material that originated in or near Panopolis to Pabau, where it could have been deposited and later buried nearby.

The situation is somewhat similar with the remains of the two rolls at the Bibliothèque Bodmer containing Homer's *Iliad*, books 3 and 4, in that the recto contains documents of Panopolis (P. Bodmer L), and the verso contains Homer's *Iliad*, published as P. Bodmer I. For this is responsible for the early suggestions that the Bodmer Papyri were discovered at Panopolis and/or that P. Bodmer I was not part of the main discovery responsible for the bulk of the Bodmer Papyri. But the emergence of further fragments of the *Iliad* (P. Bodmer XLVIII) and the *Odyssey* (P. Bodmer XLIX) among the residue of the other Bodmer Papyri suggests that P. Bodmer I/L is part of the same discovery near Dishnā as is the bulk of the Bodmer Papyri. The emergence in 1976 at the Institut für Altertumskunde at the University of Cologne of fragments of Homer's *Odyssey*, books 3 and 4, (Inventory Number 902 = P. Köln 40), which it had acquired along with a fragment of P. Bodmer XXVI, would also strengthen the tie of the Homeric materials with the bulk of the Bodmer Papyri, especially if a comparison of the Cologne fragments with P. Bodmer I, XLVIII, and especially XLIX reveals any connecting links between them (see below).

Of course the information that P. Beatty Panop. is from the same acquisition as fragments of P. Bodmer II and XXVI does not carry with it the assurance that it is from the same discovery. For the antiquities dealer could very well have sold at the same time materials he had acquired from different discoveries. Skeat emphasized this possibility in a letter of July 10, 1981. Indeed he points out that the Institut für Altertumskunde of the University of Cologne has materials from the same Panopolitan archive.[38] Yet in view of the fact that Cologne is one

37. Horn, "'Da berief er alle Vorsteher der Klöster ein,'" paper presented at the Third International Congress of Coptic Studies in Warsaw, August 24, 1984.

38. Youtie et al., "Urkunden aus Panopolis I," 1–40; Youtie et al., "Urkunden aus Panopolis II," 207–34; Youtie et al., "Urkunden aus Panopolis III," 101–70.

of the repositories of material from the shared provenience (see below), the sharing with the Chester Beatty Library of the Panopolitan documentary papyri, much like its sharing with the Chester Beatty Library of the Pachomian materials, is not in itself an adequate reason to assume a different provenience.

Yet the substantive issue posed by Skeat has to do with the documentary nature of this material, which would be of no relevance to a monastery library. But another consideration may indicate the reverse, namely the status of this codex as an unbound quire of second-hand papyrus with a scattering of receipts on some of the pages, making the whole hardly usable for literary purposes. Skeat's typescript dated June 4, 1956, had characterized it as follows:

> Papyrus codex, made up of waste papyrus, i.e. documents or rolls written on one side only, the written sides being pasted together so as to form a blank "book." . . . The book so constructed was used, over a period about 338–345 A.D., for inserting a number of receipts for various taxes paid by "the sons of Antonius Besas, son of Alopex," but the number of receipts so entered is small in proportion to the size of the "book," most of which remained blank.

Berthe van Regemorter had reported:

> I examined this piece, which it would be appropriate to call a blank book, long before it had been studied from the point of view of the text. One could tell that there was a text, but it was hidden at the interior of the leaves that were double. It was not a codex, but a bundle of sheets of papyrus ready to be sold *as the client's order required*. This large packet of leaves of the same dimension did not have the slightest trace of stitching, no needle holes, no little strips of parchment to consolidate the quires, nothing. It was a large bundle of sheets of papyrus, all of the same dimension, simply folded in two.[39]

Van Regemorter had already associated P. Beatty Panop. with Accession Number 1499 as another illustration of the bookseller producing uninscribed codices for sale. She described it as follows:

> This notebook is formed of several quires, the most of which have four conjugate leaves, hence sixteen pages. It must have been of use to a student. There is little text: The blank leaves are followed by several pages of quadruple lists of words in Greek, what one

39. Van Regemorter, "Le Papetier-Libraire," 280.

> commonly calls a dictionary. There are more blank pages than pages of text. The text is interspersed with blank pages in the second half of the little volume. On the last page there is at the top a single line of text, an alphabet in Roman capitals, very carefully drawn.[40]

It is somewhat striking that the first acquisition by Sir Chester Beatty early in 1956 consisted primarily of two uninscribed books. When one recalls Bodmer's rather idealistic definition of "world literature" that would comprise his library, one recognizes that this is the kind of material he would not acquire. And when one recalls that he had at his disposal in Cairo the expert advice of Father Doutreleau, one recognizes that these are the kinds of items that would hardly be recommended to him to purchase. It is not hard to imagine these being the main items that Bodmer had not acquired from the material offered him in 1955, which makes the presence among it of fragments of P. Bodmer II and XX all the more poignant; indeed fragments of P. Bodmer II were promised Bodmer in 1956 and arrived only between October 1 and 19 of 1956, too late for inclusion in the *editio princeps*. Chester Beatty Accession Number 1389 (the book of Joshua in Sahidic) would seem to be the major instance of Sir Chester Beatty securing what Bodmer would not have rejected, since it is the cover and two-thirds of the leaves of P. Bodmer XXI. Yet Father Doutreleau at times had to resort to special pleading with Bodmer on behalf of the Coptic material, since the Greek material was more immediately appealing as "world literature."

Indicative of the situation may be the information recorded at Chester Beatty Accession Number 1933, manuscript 820: "Coptic vellum manuscript, ix or xth century A.D., 20 pages, 5 bifolios . . . containing a sermon attributed to Theophilus, Patriarch of Alexandria, 402–430 A.D. . . . Acquired from Tano, Cairo, and brought from Bodmer Library, Geneva, to Dublin. April 1958. 350 Cyprus L."

This acquisition, not of the shared provenience, to judge by the date, must have been sent to Bodmer on approval, and after his negative decision forwarded on to Beatty. This does not mean that Bodmer had discontinued acquisitions, but that such a relatively late ecclesiastical manuscript in Coptic did not have interest for him in the way that further leaves of Menander obviously did.

40. Ibid., 279.

In general, one may say that the Chester Beatty Library's part is much more fragmentary and less literary than the material at the Bibliothèque Bodmer. For although the Bilbliothèque Bodmer does contain much material of inferior quality, it contains a large quantity of relatively intact codices, whereas the two relatively intact codices at the Chester Beatty Library are largely uninscribed and lack any literary value. The fact that only one item from the Pachomian Archive was acquired by Bodmer but the bulk by Beatty (and somewhat less by Cologne) is also indicative of Bodmer's literary orientation. In spite of the quantity of Coptic material acquired by Bodmer, one should not lose sight of the much higher ratio of Coptic to Greek among the Beatty acquisitions, such as Accession Number 1493. The Greek material was either a quantity of fragments, as in the case of Accession Number 1501, or in very bad condition, as in the case of P. Chester Beatty XV:[41] "The state of preservation of P. Chester Beatty XV must be described as poor. As is obvious from the Plates, many fragments are not only worm-eaten but badly torn. In some places the surface has totally disintegrated, in others it was stripped . . . No complete page has survived . . . The most complete page is 5, which has been built up from three fragments . . ." [42]

One may recall Shore's typed report of July 1958 on Accession Number 1390:

> 12 leaves or fragments of leaves (6 folios and 3 bifolios) of a papyrus codex containing Greek mathematical exercises and an incomplete Coptic version of John x, 8—xii, 14 in the Subachmimic dialect. The leaves come apparently from a school exercise book or private notebook. The Greek text occupies one leaf, and the recto and half the verso of a second. It is uncertain whether these leaves are continuous. Beneath the Greek exercises on the verso of the second leaf a line has been drawn across the page and the remaining text is in Coptic, written in a darker ink, and beginning in the middle of a sentence.

Here one can envisage a monk copying John either from a copy that was defective and began in the middle of a sentence, or on a series of inadequate writing surfaces, most of which are lost, but one of which was a quire that had been spoiled by a schoolboy's exercises. The surviving quire in any case gives an indication of the low quality of material

41. Pietersma, *Acts of Phileas*, 11–12.

42. Ibid.

available for monastic use, reminiscent of the second-hand of P. Beatty Panop.

The Suez Crisis of October 1956 broke communication with Geneva, and no doubt with Dublin as well. Yet, futile attempts on the part of the Bibliothèque Bodmer to secure more at the beginning of 1957 may indicate that Tano had not retained what Bodmer had passed over but had sold out to Beatty. In 1958 Tano showed Doutreleau about nine leaves of Menander that he had on consignment, which would suggest that his own holdings had indeed been sold out completely. Bodmer of course ordered this material, but by the end of 1959, Doutreleau was informed by the Bibliothèque Bodmer that it was no longer in the market for papyri. The fact that the Chester Beatty Library was able to acquire as late as 1962 a new fragment of Accession Number 1494, Horsiesios's *Letter 3*, suggests that business with Sir Chester Beatty had continued.

From this survey, it is apparent that the Chester Beatty Library made important acquisitions of Bodmer Papyri. In addition to the Library's parts of P. Bodmer II, XX, and XXI (Accession Number 1389), also P. Beatty Panop. and accession 1499 came from the same acquisition early in 1956, as did P. Bodmer II. Accession Number 1390, explicitly attributed to Dishnā as its provenience, was acquired in the summer of 1956 from Tano, along with P. Bodmer XXI (Accession Number 1389), as well as two boxes of fragments including apparently the two manuscripts with Psalms (Accession Number 1501). Indeed, the involvement of the Chester Beatty Library is considerably larger than what has been indicated thus far, in that Pachomian materials treated in chapter 4 below have been omitted here, except when they incidentally bear upon matters being discussed.

When one comes to correlating the evidence of chapters 2–4, it will become clear that at least the three parts of Bodmer Papyri I, XX, and XXI, the item said to come from Dishnā (Accession Number 1390), and the five Pachomian items (Accession Numbers 1486, 1484 and 1495, and items W 145 and No. 54) in all probability come from the same Pachomian discovery near Dishnā as do the Bodmer Papyri. Other items at the Chester Beatty Library, in various degrees of probability as has been discussed above, may also have come from the shared provenience, such as Accession Numbers 1493 (the *Apocalypse of Elijah*), 1499 (the Greek grammar and a Graeco-Roman lexicon to Pauline epistles), 1501 (two Psalms manuscripts), P. Chester Beatty Papyrus XV (the *Acts of*

Phileas), and P. Beatty Panop. Thus, sixteen separate items of the Chester Beatty Library have come into consideration.

One may compare this with some twenty-six rolls or codices plus one Pachomian item, a total of twenty-seven, (plus fragments of P. Barcin. and of Mississippi Coptic Codex I [the Crosby Codex]) that are known to have been acquired in whole or part by the Bibliothèque Bodmer. Thus in terms of manuscripts represented, the Bodmer collection is some twice the size of the Beatty collection. Of course some of the items at the Chester Beatty Library that have been considered may not be from the shared provenience, just as others not included at all may be from the shared provenience. But the more nuanced discussion of degrees of probability in the case of the items at the Chester Beatty Library has to do in part with the accessibility there of records permitting a discussion item by item, whereas in the case of the Bibliothèque Bodmer such detailed information was not available, and hence degrees of probability are less visible. In any case, it becomes apparent even before turning to the holdings of other repositories that the nomenclature Bodmer Papyri, for all that came from the shared provenience, gives a somewhat misleading impression in quantitative terms. In terms of quality, the designation is more appropriate.

Part Two

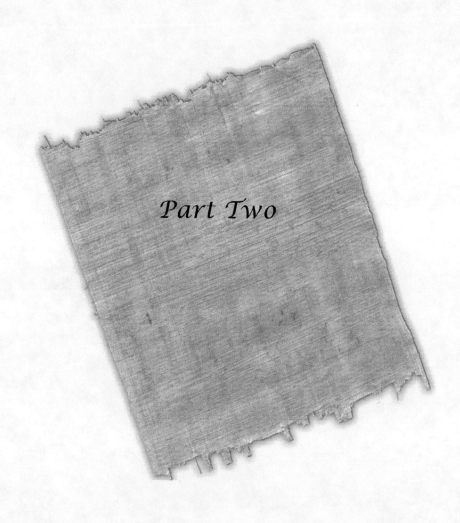

—3—

Mississippi, Cologne, Barcelona

THE UNIVERSITY OF MISSISSIPPI

Two codices were acquired by the University of Mississippi: Mississippi Coptic Codex I (the Crosby Codex), now named the Savery Codex, and Mississippi Coptic Codex II, which is half of P. Bodmer XXII. The acquisition has been narrated both by William H. Willis,[1] then Professor of Classics at the University of Mississippi and at Duke University; and by the proprietor of the Art Gallery Maguid Sameda, 55 Gamhouria Street, Cairo: Maguid's son, Sultan Maguid Sameda.[2]

David M. Robinson, then a professor at the University of Mississippi, visited Sameda's shop in the summer of 1954, at which time he purchased what he took to be all the papyrus then available at this shop.[3] In the

1. Willis, "New Collections of Papyri," 383–89 and Plate V; 389–92 and Plate VI.

2. From an interview of September 18, 1973, with Charles W. Hedrick, whose notes taken at that time were communicated in a letter of March 5, 1985.

3. They are the "third group" in "the Robinson Papyri" bequeathed to the University of Mississippi, as described by Willis, "New Collections of Papyri," 382. Willis in a letter of February 25, 1980, reported that he assumed these papyri are unrelated to those of the shared provenience that concern us here. Yet, two fragments that were inventoried as Robinson Papyri are from the shared provenience, P. Robinson inv. 38 from P. Bodmer XXVI and P. Robinson 201 from P. Barcin. Inventory Number 149–61. And Willis has also joined several with papyri from Cologne that were acquired in the same batch as the fragments of Bodmer Papyri (itemized above).

autumn of 1955, Sameda sent two further packets, one containing two codices. There is nothing to associate the acquisition of 1954 with these two codices acquired late in 1955. But the initial acquisition did establish the necessary working relationship. Sameda reports that Robinson received delivery of the two codices in Switzerland.

Sameda has maintained that he had access to the whole find and could have made the whole of the discovery available to Robinson "if he had been fair." For Robinson offered him only $500, and Sameda had to "pressure" him for a more reasonable price. This sounds like the usual haggling of the Arab marketplace. The deal was finally consummated through negotiations with Willis, for a price that Sameda reports as $9,000. This may well have been his initial asking price.

Willis reports that the University of Mississippi paid $3,000 for Mississippi Coptic Codex I (the Crosby Codex) and $1,500 for Mississippi Coptic Codex II (half of P. Bodmer XXII). The funds were secured through public subscription by the Friends of the Library late in 1955.[4]

The following brief article appeared in the *New York Times*:[5]

> **BIBLE SCRIPTS BOUGHT**
>
> 2 Rare Collections Are Gifts to University of Mississippi
>
> Special to the New York Times.
>
> UNIVERSITY, Miss., Nov 26—Two rare Biblical manuscripts have been acquired by the University of Mississippi. They contain the books of Jeremiah, Lamentations, Jonah, Jude, an Epistle of St. Peter, and the lost treatises on Easter of the second century church father, Bishop Melito of Sardis.
>
> Written in Coptic, the ancient language spoken by the native Egyptians who were converted to Christianity in the second and third centuries, the manuscripts were brought to this country last fall for appraisal by Dr. David M. Robinson.
>
> The manuscripts, which were bought for the university by Friends of the Library, a private organization, will be deposited for exhibit and study in the university library.

A widow provided the funds for the first codex named in honor of her father, an avid student of the Bible, who however had the proclivity of ripping pages out of the Bible if there was "an outrageous tale of mayhem and murder." On being shown the acquisition that her generosity had

4. Willis, "New Collections of Papyri," 381–82.
5. *New York Times*, November 27, 1955, p. 135, col. 2.

made possible, she declared the Crosby Codex to be the "ugliest book I have ever seen."[6]

The acquisition of 1955 involved two packages. One contained late Roman and Byzantine Greek and Coptic papyri.[7] But there was at the time nothing to connect it with the contents of the other packet,[8] which contained the two Coptic codices.

Several months later, another shipment arrived from Sameda with some four hundred small Greek fragments attesting six hands, one fragment from a fourth- or fifth-century codex, and another five from earlier literary rolls, one perhaps an epic, another perhaps Homeric scholia,[9] again without any explicit relation to the two codices.

Both codices have been identified since 1958–1959 as coming from the same provenience as the Bodmer Papyri.[10] Indeed, parts of both were among the material acquired by the Bibliothèque Bodmer:[11]

6. Willis in a letter of July 30, 1984.

7. Willis, "New Collections of Papyri," 382.

8. Willis in a letter of February 25, 1980.

9. Willis, "New Collections of Papyri," 382. It is unclear whether these Homeric scholia fragments are from the same roll as the Cologne Homeric scholia fragments published by Henricks, "Schoia Minora zu Homer III," 1–3 and plates 1–2.

10. Willis, "New Collections of Papyri," 383, n. 1:

> Professor Martin, from a photograph seen at the Oslo Congress [August 1958], was the first to observe the similarity of hand and format between Mississippi Codex I and codices in the Bodmer collection. His observation has subsequently been confirmed by Pastor Rodolphe Kasser, editor of the Bodmer Coptic codices, upon reading an advance copy of this paper with its plates. "The comparison of the photographs with the Bodmer manuscripts does not leave me in any doubt: Mississippi Codex I (the Crosby Codex) presents characteristics shared with numerous Bodmer codices," wrote M. Kasser on January 21, 1959. "But it is the Mississippi Codex II that provides us the proof we sought: it contains quires V, VI, VII, VIII and 2 detached leaves of quire X of a codex of which the Bibliothèque Bodmer possesses quires I, II, III, IV and IX complete . . . The Mississippi codices come hence from the same batch as the Bodmer Papyri."

Kasser, *Papyrus Bodmer* XIX 17, n.2 reaffirms that Mississippi Coptic Codex I (the Crosby Codex), is "of the same origin as the Bodmer Papyri" and points out that it "is also written in two columns" (except for the last tractate). Similarly with regard to Mississippi Coptic Codex II, Michel Testuz, *Papyrus Bodmer* XIII, 11: "It seems to us interesting to underline that the format of this manuscript [Mississippi Coptic Codex II] seems identical to that of our codex. Do both of them come from the same scriptorium? Would they have been discovered at the same place? Two questions that will probably remain forever unanswered."

11. Michel Testuz, *Papyrus Bodmer* XIII, 12: "One must also note that there are

- Fragments from Mississippi Coptic Codex I (the Crosby Codex), now the Savery Codex, were subsequently identified at the Bibliothèque Bodmer, and are now reported to be at Duke University in Durham, North Carolina.
- Mississippi Coptic Codex II consists of pages 61–124, 143–46 and a back flyleaf, that is to say, sixty-eight inscribed and two uninscribed pages, a total of seventy pages or thirty-five leaves, from a codex that originally consisted of 80 leaves or 160 pages. Most of the rest of the leaves are in the Bibliothèque Bodmer, as P. Bodmer XXII: pp. 1–60 and 125–42, a total of 78 pages or 39 leaves. Missing are the cover, two postulated unnumbered front flyleaves, and two postulated back flyleaves. Thus the codex is rather evenly divided between the two repositories.

At first Willis sought to trade the half of this codex belonging to the University of Mississippi to the Bibliothèque Bodmer for another codex:[12]

> The Mississippi half was never at the Bodmeriana; Kasser learned of it from sample photos I had given Victor Martin in 1958 at our Congress in Oslo, and wrote in January 1959 to confirm that Bodmer had the first half. Thereafter began long and painful negotiations with Bodmer (through Kasser), whereby I sought to exchange our half for some other text in Bodmer's possession. At first he wouldn't listen, but by 1961 he tentatively agreed to offer us his Matthew [P. Bodmer XIX] for it; by then, however, the University of Mississippi administrators refused to go along, for fear of offending our donors. So all that was left was for us to exchange photos, and we gave Bodmer permission to publish the whole codex as XXII.

at the Bibliothèque Bodmer some small fragments, in Coptic, of the same sermon 'Concerning the Passover,' which were mixed with a whole batch of diverse parcels, most of which one has not yet been able to identify. Do these fragments originally belong to the manuscript that is currently at the University of Mississippi?" Kilpatrick, "Bodmer and Mississippi Collection," 36, refers to "the Coptic text [of Melito 'Concerning the Passover'] at the University of Mississippi with some fragments at Geneva." Willis has reported in letters of July 8, 1980, and July 30, 1984, that these fragments are now at Duke University. He has made photographs of the fragments available; and to the extent they have been identified, they have been integrated into the transcription. Fifty inscribed fragments ranging in size up to 8 by 2 or 6 by 3 cm have thus been made accessible to the *editio princeps*.

12. Willis, in a letter of July 8, 1980.

The preface to *Papyrus Bodmer* XXII reports as follows about the publication of the codex acquired in part by Bodmer and in part by the University of Mississippi:[13]

> We have, today, the great satisfaction of being able to present to the learned world, in a single publication, a very fine codex of parchment, all but complete, of which the fragments, no doubt dismembered shortly after its discovery, have finally arrived either at the Bibliothèque Bodmer or at the University of Mississippi (U.S.A.). Thanks to the largeness of spirit evidenced by the interested parties, not only photocopies of the document could be exchanged, but it was even decided that the two parties would authorize each other to publish the whole of the document, one of the editions being in the French language, the other in the English language. The first beneficiaries of this agreement will be Coptologists and specialists in the biblical text, who will have the advantage of finding in a single book the totality of a text that is extremely important for them . . .
>
> In concluding this preamble, we wish to thank those who, through their friendly collaboration and their enlightened counsels, have contributed to the successful completion of this work. We have in mind particularly Professor W. H. Willis of the University of Mississippi (U.S.A.), who, through his objective and comprehensive spirit, has in large measure facilitated the realization of our common project. It is to him that will come the honor of preparing for the English language world the parallel edition to the one presented here.

The Savery Codex is a single-quire papyrus codex in Sahidic, dated by William H. Willis to the third century[14] or to the second half of the second century;[15] by Colin H. Roberts to the late second or early third century;[16] by Allen Cabaniss to around 300 AD;[17] and by E. G. Turner to the "Third or Fourth" century.[18]

13. Kasser, *Papyrus Bodmer* XXII, 5.
14. Willis, "New Collections of Papyri," 389.
15. Willis, in a letter of July 30, 1984.
16. According to Willis, in a letter of July 30, 1984.
17. Cabaniss, "University of Mississippi Coptic Papyrus," 71: "circa A.D. 300."
18. Turner, *Typology*, 137.

The contents of the Savery Codex are as follows (according to a modern numeration introduced to simplify the several Coptic pagination systems in the codex):

- Pages 1–6 are missing, with only the inner margin surviving. Perhaps they contained a front flyleaf (pages 1–2) and a brief first tractate (pages 3–6).
- Pages 7–51 contain what the subscript title (51, column 2, lines 3–4) refers to as "On the Passover of Melito." Only with page 15 do vestiges of letters at the inner margin occur, and only with page 23 does one actually find substantive parts of the text extant. But since the length of this text is known from other manuscripts, it can be postulated that it began on page 7.
- The next tractate begins at the top of page 52 with the superscript title "The Jewish Martyrs who were in the time of Antiochus the King" (column 1, lines 1–3), and ends with a colophon "The Jewish Martyrs" at the bottom of page 74 (column 1, lines 13–14).
- The next tractate is 1 Peter, with a superscript title on 75, column 1, lines 1–2, and a subscript title on 107, column 2, lines 6–7, each reading "The Epistle of Peter."
- The next tractate begins with a superscript title at 107, column 2, line 8 and a subscript title at 124, column 1, lines 8–9, each reading "Jonah the Prophet."
- The last tractate differs from the others in having no superscript title and in employing a single broad column per page rather than the usual two (or at the end of the tractates sometimes only one) narrow columns. It has been thought to be a homily, perhaps for Easter morning,[19] or a hymn.[20] It begins on 124,10, but is extant only as two lines on page 124 and twelve lines each on pages 125–26 (and a very few letters on pages 127–28). One may postulate this tractate ended on page 134, followed by an unscribed back flyleaf, though only uninscribed inner margins are extant on pages 129–34.

19. Willis, "New Collection of Papyri," 386.

20. In letters of July 8, 1980, and December 4, 1984, Willis has accepted the identification of this tractate with the Sahidic "non-biblical Hymn" listed among unpublished Bodmer Papyri by Kasser, *Compléments au Dictionnaire copte de Crum*, xv.

The contents of P. Bodmer XXII + Mississippi Coptic Codex II, and their position in the codex, is as follows:

- Jeremiah 40:3—51:22 = pages 1–60 was acquired by the Bibliothèque Bodmer.
- Jeremiah 51:22—52:34 = pages 61–72 was acquired by the University of Mississippi.
- Lamentations = pages 72–102 was acquired by the University of Mississippi.
- Epistle of Jeremy = Baruch 6 = pages 102–18 was acquired by the University of Mississippi.
- Baruch 1:1—2:2 = pages 118–24 was acquired by the University of Mississippi.
- Baruch 2:2—4:23 = pages 125–42 was acquired by the Bibliothèque Bodmer.
- Baruch 4:23—5:5 = pages 143–46 was acquired by the University of Mississippi.
- Baruch 5:6–9 is conjectured to have been on the front of the first of the three postulated back flyleaves, and Jeremiah 40:1–2 (preceded, since these two verses are so brief, by "a rather voluminous title") on the back of the second of the two postulated front flyleaves. An uninscribed leaf acquired by the University of Mississippi is conjectured by Kasser to be the second back flyleaf.[21]

There was a further fragment in the 1954–1955 Robinson Papyri of the University of Mississippi that shows how interrelated various repositories were in materials from the shared provenience. In 1984 the Library of Duke University acquired from the University of Mississippi what had been previously inventoried as P. Rob. inv. 38. William H. Willis identified it as a sliver of P. Bodmer XXVI that immediately joins

21. Kasser, *Papyrus Bodmer* XXII, 8, especially notes 1 and 2. It is not always the case with the material of the shared provenience that a text is complete. Chester Beatty acc. 1390 begins its text of the Gospel of John in the middle of a sentence at 10:7. Thus the conjecture of missing text in P. Bodmer XXII + Mississippi Coptic Codex II, though reasonable, is not at all certain. Since flyleaves do on occasion include such inscriptions, as in the case of Nag Hammadi Codices III and XI, and P. Bodmer XXIII, the conjecture of second, completely uninscribed flyleaves seems to go too far into pure speculation.

the Cologne fragment of that codex, P. Köln 4 = inv. 904.[22] It is thus clear that Mississippi and Cologne each acquired part of the fragmentary remains of the Bodmer Papyri. There may be other instances, for Willis has effected other joins between Robinson Papyri and those of Cologne:

- P. Rob. inv. 32 joins P. Cologne inv. 906 (scholia to *Odyssey* 1)[23]
- P. Rob. inv. 35 joins P. Cologne inv. 901 (Achilleus Tatios)
- P. Rob. inv. 37 joins P. Cologne inv. 903 (a piece of ethnography or a philosophical treatise)
- P. Rob. inv. 43 joins P. Cologne inv. 902 (*Odyssey* 3–4).

Furthermore, documentary papyri among the Robinson Papyri have been identified by Willis as having the same hand as documentary papyri from the Cologne papyri within the lot numbered inv. 901 through inv. 924. But is has not been permitted for any of this material shared between the Robinson Papyri and Cologne to be compared with unpublished material at the Bibliothèque Bodmer, such as the *Odyssey* fragments (P. Bodmer XLIX), to see if we have to do with the same manuscripts.

What had been inventoried as P. Robinson inv. 201 is a fragment of Cicero's *in Catilinam* 1–2 from the codex P. Barcin. Inventory Numbers 149–61 at the Fundacio Sant Lluc Evangelista of Barcelona (see below), which was found tucked inside Mississippi Coptic Codex I.[24] It now belongs to the Library of Duke University, where it bears the designation "P. Duke. inv. L 1 (ex P. Rob. inv. 201)."[25] Other fragments of the same copy of Cicero's *in Catilinam* were at the Bibliothèque Bodmer until Bodmer gave them to the Fundacio Sant Lluc Evangelista (see below).

It is hard to avoid the inference from these varied interlocking relationships that Mississippi acquired, in addition to one codex and half

22. Willis, in a letter of July 30, 1984: "P. Rob. inv. 38 is a sliver of leaf 55/56 of P. Bodmer XXVI (Menander's *Aspis* lines 487–98, 524–32) which immediately adjoins P. Köln inv. 904 (*ZPE* 1 [1967] 103–4 and pl. II)."

23. Willis, "New Collections of Papyri," 382, lists, in the acquisition "several months later" than that of the two codices, a fragment or fragments of "perhaps Homeric scholia."

24. Willis, "Papyrus Fragment of Cicero," 324.

25. Willis, in a letter of July 30, 1984.

of another, also fragments stemming from the same discovery as that in which Cologne, Barcelona, and Geneva were also involved.

Although the codex has remained unpublished, various persons have worked on it over the intervening years. Willis himself has prepared a complete and revised transcription of the codex, though the fragments from the Bibliothèque Bodmer had not yet been placed. He has also prepared an apparatus of Coptic variants to 1 Peter.[26]

Carroll D. Osburn, then professor at Harding Graduate School of Religion in Memphis, Tennessee, later of Pepperdine University, studied the material, especially the text of 1 Peter, from time to time during the seventies.[27]

In May 1971 Charles W. Hedrick was permitted by John Sykes Hartin, Director of Libraries of the University of Mississippi, after consultation with Willis, to borrow the photographs of the Savery Codex so as to identify and label them in terms of a single modern pagination (since the codex has several Coptic numeration systems). The photographs were then returned to the University of Mississippi, along with "A Conversion Table of the Crosby Codex Prepared for the University of Mississippi."[28]

Ruth Majercek and Birger A. Pearson, both of the University of California at Santa Barbara, made a draft transcription and translation of "On the Passover of Melito" in July 1978.

Stuart George Hall published his edition of Melito's *On Pascha* in 1979, including "Mississippi Coptic Codex I (the Crosby Codex) . . . cited in his own Latin by the present editor from photographic copy of original."[29] For Hedrick worked out plans with Hall to provide him with a copy of the Institute's copy of the photographs, when they met in my home on August 28, 1972, at the meeting of the Society for New Testament Studies that was part of the International Congress of Learned Societies in the Field of Religion. The copy was made in time enough for Hall to take it back to England with him. In the preface, acknowledgement is made "to Dr. Charles W. Hedrick and Dr. M. Van Esbroeck [who edited

26. Willis, in a letter of May 27, 1980.

27. Osburn, in a letter of February 6, 1985.

28. Hedrick reported in a letter of May 20, 1971, that he had been permitted to borrow the photographs and included with his letter to me a copy of his letter of that same date to John Sykes Hartin, acknowledging the loan.

29. Melito of Sardis, *On Pascha and Fragments*, xlv.

a Georgian text], each of whom made contributions without which the work would have been, if not impossible, then significantly impaired."

With the approval of the university chancellor, the University of Mississippi's Museums Gift and/or Exchange Committee recommended the deacquisition of the two Coptic codices,[30] in order to produce the capital to acquire papers of William Faulkner then on the market.[31] The two codices were offered to H. P. Kraus, the New York dealer of rare books. Carroll Osburn was engaged by Kraus to examine the two codices and specifically to provide a detailed report of the still-unpublished Mississippi Coptic Codex I (the Crosby Codex). This report, submitted April 24, 1981, confirmed that all the material from the two codices that Willis had originally reported as belonging to the University of Mississippi was still present.[32] Kraus acquired the two codices in 1981[33] for a price reported to Willis to be $250,000.[34]

On January 17, 1984, Dr. Braun, Director of the Bibliothèque Bodmer, reported that Kraus had offered Mississippi Coptic Codex II, half of P. Bodmer XXII, to the Bibliothèque Bodmer for SFr300,000 (then about $100,000). Since it is no longer acquiring such materials, the sale was declined. These leaves were put on sale by Kraus for $150,000 (subject to prior sale).[35]

On October 25, 1983, I visited Kraus in his shop in Manhattan. To my inquiry as to who had acquired Mississippi Coptic Codex I (the Crosby Codex), he responded that it was not his policy to divulge the names of his clients. Hence on July 24, 1984, I sent him a letter addressed "to whom it may concern," explaining my interest in the codex and sug-

30. Reported in a letter of July 30, 1984, from Thomas M. Verich, University Archivist.

31. Willis, in a letter of July 30, 1984. An article in the *Los Angeles Times* of January 27, 1985, reports the publication by the University of Alabama of previously unpublished poems "recently donated to the University of Mississippi by Leila and Douglas Wynn of Oxford, Miss." Douglas Wynn gave them to his wife Leila Wynn in 1984, so the gift to the University of Mississippi must have been in the course of 1984. This then would seem not to be part of the Faulkner collection, acquired with the proceeds from the sale of the two Coptic codices.

32. I am indebted to Carroll D. Osburn for providing a copy of his report of April 24, 1981, to Kraus.

33. Kraus, in a letter of July 3, 1984.

34. Willis, in a letter of July 30, 1984.

35. Item number 26 in Kraus catalogue *Cimelia* (1983) 126.

gesting that the information I had would be of interest to the owner. I sent it to Kraus with the request that he forward it to the owner.

On August 6, 1984, Winsor T. Savery telephoned me, identifying himself as the current owner the Pax ex Innovatione Foundation he had set up (though its headquarters are in Vaduz, Liechtenstein). He has since renamed the codex the Savery Codex. Thus, in order to make clear the identity of the codex, it should perhaps be fully cited in academic circles as Mississippi Coptic Codex I (the Crosby Codex) = the Savery Codex. Mr. Savery has expressed considerable interest both in the investigation in which I was involved and in the possibility of the Institute for Antiquity and Christianity exhibiting and editing the codex. On July 31, 1985, he visited the Institute and prepared a document authorizing the exhibit and edition. On August 12, 1985, the codex arrived at the Institute. After receiving approval from Savery, preliminary reconservation—involving the cleaning of the glasses, the placement of fragments, and the centering and attaching of the sheets to the lower plexiglass pane—was carried out with the assistance of Tova Meltzer, Jeff Meizels, and Sterling Bjorndahl on the evenings of September 23, 26, 27, and 30, 1985, as well as on October 3, 1985, preparatory to photography on October 5, 1985.

On September 26, 1985, William H. Willis agreed to participate fully in the edition, in making his photographs, transcription, collation of 1 Peter, and related notes available to the edition. James Goehring assumed responsibility as volume editor, sharing with Willis the completion of the Melito text. Edmund Meltzer assumed responsibility for editing the segment from 2 Maccabees, with Hans-Gebhard Bethge assisting with the Greek manuscript evidence in the critical apparatus. Willis retained responsibility for completing 1 Peter. Charles W. Hedrick assumed responsibility for editing Jonah. Goehring assumed responsibility for editing the last unidentified text.

INSTITUT FÜR ALTERTUMSKUNDE OF THE UNIVERSITY OF COLOGNE

In 1967 Reinhold Merkelbach published a fragment (inv. 904 = P. Köln 3) from Menander's *Aspis*, acquired by the Institut für Altertumskunde of the University of Cologne in the spring of 1956. This was the same spring when Chester Beatty made his first purchase of Bodmer Papyri.

It was then identified as part of P. Bodmer XXVI once the *editio princeps* was published in 1969. Hence it is evident that the Institut für Altertumskunde of the University of Cologne had acquired some of the material from the same discovery as did the Bibliothèque Bodmer. This poses the question as to whether other materials in the Cologne collection stem from the same discovery, especially materials from the same acquisition early in 1956, including items numbered from inv. 901 through inv. 924. Some of these are documentary, and some of the hands have been identified in part with hands of documentary papyri among the Robinson Papyri of the University of Mississippi (see above). Others are literary and have in several cases in addition to inv. 904 been identified with fragments among the Robinson Papyri.

The most significant item within this spectrum of inventory numbers that seems most likely to have come from the shared provenience is inv. 902 = P. Köln 40. It is a group of fragments of the *Odyssey*, book 3: 87–94; 460–72; 489–96; and book 4: 18; 20; 21; 106–11; 135; 138–40; 164–77; 199–206; 230; 257–64; 339–42; 344; 346–54. For when it was published in 1976, striking similarities of the hand with that of P. Bodmer I were noted: "Similarity with the hand of P. Bodmer I . . . , for which Martin proposes the span of time from 350 to 450, is very great. In certain ligatures of letters, e.g. in *alla* and *kai*, hardly any difference can be observed . . . The Cologne papyrus also agrees with the Geneva piece in that (apart from the diaeresis and the apostrophe) no signs of any kind have been employed."[36] There are other similarities as well. The dating of the two collections around 400 CE is the same. And the date of acquisition is much the same, especially if one takes into consideration unpublished fragments of Homer at the Bibliothèque Bodmer: In the case of P. Bodmer I, the acquisition was presumably early in the 1960s, with the date of publication in 1964 the *terminus ad quem*. But since in that initial publication no mention was made of further fragments from the *Iliad* and the *Odyssey* at the Bibliothèque Bodmer, one may assume that such fragments that the Bibliothèque Bodmer planed to publish as P. Bodmer XLVIII (the *Iliad*) and P. Bodmer XLIX (the *Odyssey*) arrived in Geneva only later, presumably among the bulk of the shipments, which clustered around 1955–1956. Now it was in the spring of 1956 that Cologne acquired its fragments.

36. Kramer, "Odyssee," 89–97.

In fact, the bulk of the Homeric material at both repositories consists of fragments. Even in the case of P. Bodmer I (the *Iliad*) only the last half of book 5 retained its original form as a roll, whereas what is left of the first half of book 5 and all that is left of book 6 were in the form of fragments. Fragments can be readily distanced from the manuscript from which they came and be associated with other manuscripts, and along with other such manuscripts may turn up at other repositories. Thus there is a rather widespread scattering among the various repositories of fragments of materials from the shared provenience: Fragments of manuscripts in Geneva have been located in Dublin (from P. Bodmer II and P. Bodmer XX), in the acquisitions of the University of Mississippi (P. Rob. inv. 38 from P. Bodmer XXVI), in Cologne (inv. 903 = P. Köln 3 from P. Bodmer XXVI), and at the Fundacio Sant Luc Evangelista in Barcelona (a fragment of P. Bodmer XXV which was released to the Bibliothèque Bodmer). And fragments from manuscripts located at one of these other repositories have been located at other of the repositories: Fragments from the Savery Codex emerged in Geneva (and were released to William H. Willis, who was then in charge of the Savery Codex); fragments from P. Barcin. inv. 149–61 of Barcelona emerged at the University of Mississippi and at Geneva (the latter were released to Barcelona); three fragments from Chester Beatty Manuscript W. 145 emerged at Cologne (see chapter 5 below); and Willis has made several joins of Mississippi fragments with Cologne materials (see below). Thus it would not be at all surprising if the fragmentary remains of a set of Homeric rolls ultimately emerged at two of the repositories of material from the same discovery.

There are, of course, also differences between P. Bodmer I and Cologne inv. 902 = P. Köln 40. P. Bodmer I is written on a roll of documentary papyrus that was cut in two to serve for inscribing on the back book 5 and book 6 of the *Iliad*, whereas the fragments of books 3 and 4 of the *Odyssey* at Cologne are written on the front of what apparently was a single roll. And the measurements diverge: Whereas the roll used for book 5 of the *Iliad* was 450 centimeters long and that used for book 6 was 210 centimeters long, that used for the *Odyssey* books 3–4 was 321 centimeters long. Both book 5 and book 6 of the *Iliad* were on rolls 31 centimeters high (since these two rolls had been cut from the same larger roll), but books 3–4 of the *Odyssey* were on a roll 17.5 centimeters high. In the *Iliad*, book 5, the columns of writing are 18 centimeters high, but in book 6, they are 24 centimeters high; in the case of the *Odyssey*, books 3–4, the height is 14.5 centimeters. In the *Iliad*, the two books have similar distances from the beginning of one column to the beginning of the next, from 13 to 17 centimeters, averaging 15 centimeters, whereas for the *Odyssey*, 3–4, the measurement is about 7 centimeters.

However, these divergent measurements do not function to disassociate the Cologne Homer from the Geneva Homer once one has taken into account the wide fluctuation between the measurements of book 5 and book 6 of the *Iliad* and especially the same scribe's treatment of the writing surface of book 5 and book 6, in spite of the height of the roll being the same:

> The difference in the height of the columns in the two books corroborates, we think, the hypothesis of independent copies. But, as one will see, still other indications speak in the same direction.
>
> There results from the observations that have just been made that the two books of the Iliad represented here constitute, from the point of view of the construction of books, distinct unities . . . In fact, considered as "books," these two papyri present marked differences. The disposition of the text on the surface that supports it is not the same. The writing, on the other hand, is identical. A single hand transcribed the two books but adopted for each a different principle for dividing the text in columns.[37]

Given this much fluctuation by the same scribe within rolls of the same height, the divergence in the case of the much shorter roll of the *Odyssey* 3–4, such as the narrower columns, is not surprising.

Of course, no final decision concerning the relation of the Homeric material in Cologne to that in Geneva can be made until the material in Geneva becomes available either through the publication of P. Bodmer XLVIII–XLIX or through the Bibliothèque Bodmer making the material available prior to publication for comparison with the published Cologne fragments. But on the basis of the information available, it would seem probable that the Homeric material in Cologne is part of the same collection as that in Geneva.

The possibility that the Homer fragments of Cologne and Geneva may come from the same Homeric set is strengthened by the observation that there is a join between a Cologne fragment of Homer and a fragment at the University of Mississippi, P. Rob. inv. 43. For since Mississippi

37. Martin, *Papyrus Bodmer* I, 8–9.

Coptic Codices I and II are apparently from the shared provenience, as well as the Mississippi fragments P. Rob. inv. 38 (which is part of P. Bodmer XXVI) and P. Duke. inv. L 1 (ex P. Rob. inv. 201) (which is part of P. Barcin. 149–61, see below), it may be that other fragments acquired by the University of Mississippi from the same dealer at about the same time (such as the Homer fragment here under discussion) may be from the same discovery.

Indeed, there are other joins between Cologne and Mississippi fragments that might reflect the shared provenience with which we have to do here.[38] The most tempting such item, in terms of the text involved, may be Cologne inv. 906, two small fragments containing scholia to *Odyssey*, book 1, lines 67–69 and lines 79–116, from the third century CE, written (as is P. Bodmer I) on the back of a roll of documentary papyrus.[39] These two fragments join with a fragment of the same text among the acquisitions of the University of Mississippi, P. Rob. inv. 32, which apparently derives from the acquisition "several months later" than that of the two Mississippi codices.

P. Cologne inv. 901 (Achilleus Tatios III 17,5—24,1) joins with P. Rob. inv. 35. P. Cologne 903 joins with P. Rob. inv. 37. Thus, among the literary texts acquired by Cologne, in the same batch as the fragment of P. Bodmer XXVI, there are a number that have joins with texts acquired by the University of Mississippi, in connection with that University's acquisition of material from the same discovery as the Bodmer Papyri. This would tend to strengthen the probability that not only are P. Cologne inv. 901–4, 905–6 (where such joins have been identified) from the same discovery, but also that other literary texts between P. Cologne inv. 907 and 924 may be from the shared provenience. But thus far no joins have been made that would support this assumption.

In 1968, two small rolls containing Pachomius's letters 8 and 10–11a in Coptic were published from the same Cologne collection, inv. 3287 and inv. 3286. They were identified as Pachomian by Hans Quecke in 1973 in connection with his preparations to edit the Chester Beatty Glass Container No. 54 and the Chester Beatty Manuscript W. 145, containing respectively Pachomius's letters in Coptic and Greek. Although Quecke

38. These joins were effected by William H. Willis. My attention was drawn to them by Ludwig Koenen on a visit to Claremont April 22, 1985, and a subsequent letter from him of May 5, 1985.

39. Henrichs, "Scholia Minora zu Homer," 1–3; plates 1–2.

assumed the Pachomian materials originated from the same discovery, this was only conclusively demonstrated when in 1982 Cornelia Römer published Cologne inv. 3288 = P. Köln 174, three small fragments of Chester Beatty Manuscript W. 145 that were in the Cologne collection. Cologne's in-house record concerning accessions of 1963–1964 reports the following concerning inv. 3286–88: "Two Coptic and three smaller Greek parchments. These parchments come from the region of Nag Hammadi in Upper Egypt, where also the famous Gnostic papyri were found by fellahin. In spite of the difference of the material and the amazing occurrence of the Greek language, these parchments could have belonged to the same monastic community as the Gnostic papyri. But in that region monastery stood next to monastery, and the scholarly analysis will have to try to reach clarity here." This record is a striking confirmation of the hypothesis, which had already been worked out on the basis of the circumstantial evidence, and that the Pachomian material emerged at the same time and places as did the Bodmer Papyri, that the Pachomian material is of the same provenience (see chapter 5 below). For, as has been seen in the case of Doutreleau's report from Tano, it was Tano's custom in talking to foreigners to refer to Nag Hammadi, the larger and better known town in the region, rather than the nearby town, Dishnā, to designate the discovery known in Upper Egypt as the "Dishnā papers" (see chapter 4 below). Although Cologne did not itself acquire its material from Tano, the reports by Bongard and Doutreleau, those from Dublin and Cologne, as well as that of Kasser, all no doubt originate with Tano. To this extent they are hardly independent witnesses that would tend to strengthen Tano's story. But Tano was sufficiently familiar with the site of the discovery, whose subsequent clandestine excavation he financed, that his report can be taken at face value (see chapter 4 below). Rather, these various reports of material emanating from the region between Dishnā and Nag Hammadi and variously designated by one name or the other serve to associate still further these various materials with the same provenience.

Cologne inv. 1240–59, 1370–74, and 1695–1701 comprise a collection of documentary papyri largely from the first half of the fourth century CE that contain many references to the same family. This family also figures in the Dublin tax receipts written here and there on an otherwise largely uninscribed and unbound quire made from two inscribed rolls published by T. C. Skeat as P. Beatty Panop. (see chapter 2 above).[40] If it were the case that P. Beatty Panop., though doubtless written in Panopolis, was buried near Dishnā with the other materials here under investigation, then the same might be true of the Cologne materials. Acquisitions of the spring of 1962 begin with inv. 1400, which would suggest that the documentary papyri in question were either acquired on more than one occasion or were introduced into the inventory at different times. A further list of acquisitions from 1962–1963 begins with inv. 1745, so that the year 1962 would presumably be the *terminus ad quem* for the acquisition of these documentary papyri. If, as we have seen, inventory numbers in the early 900s were acquired in 1956, and those in the 3000s in 1963–1964, involving in both cases material from the shared provenience, then the intervening numbers given to these documentary papyri seem to indicate they were acquired during the time when material from the shared provenience was still available.

TWO BARCELONA REPOSITORIES

The Fundacio Sant Lluc Evangelista

This foundation acquired a fragment of P. Bodmer XXV that it has presented to the Bibliothèque Bodmer in exchange for fragments of Cicero's *In Catilinam* belonging to its Codes Miscellani. These fragments, acquired originally by the Bibliothèque Bodmer, link that Barcelona codex to the same provenience as the Bodmer Papyri. A further fragment from the Codex Miscellani now at Duke University was also found inside Mississippi Coptic Codex I (the Crosby Codex). E. A. Lowe cites this codex as "1782.—Barcelona, Fundacio Sant Lluc Evangelista Pap. Barc. (foll. 149v-153)," dated to the last half of the fourth century:

> Five papyrus leaves, the fifth a mere strip, from a codex containing Latin and Greek texts; ours opens on the verso of the first folio, the recto being the end of Cicero's Second Catilinarian oration (probably belonging to the Duke University fragment of Cicero's First Catilinarian oration—C.L.A., XI. 1650 . . . Origin uncertain, probably Egypt. The unusual word-division and the

40. Hagedorn, "Papyri aus Panopolis, 207–11; Youtie et al., "Urkunden aus Panopolis I," 1–40; Youtie et al., "Urkunden aus Panopolis II," 207–34; Youtie et al., "Urkunden aus Panopolis III," 101–70. This publication also contains the tax receipts from the otherwise uninscribed quire of P. Beatty Panop. Other documentary papyri from Panopolis with Cologne Inventory Numbers 4532–33 were presumably acquired too late to come into consideration here. Browne, "Panegyrist from Panopolis," 29–33.

> lack of familiarity with the normal forms of the Nomina Sacra suggest that the scribe was unused to copying Latin.[41]

This lack of experience in copying Latin might well be what one would expect of a Pachomian monastery and in this regard may be compared with Chester Beatty Library Ac. 1499, the Greek–Latin lexicon for the Pauline Epistles, where again insufficient Latin seems documented.

The Palau Ribes Collection of the Papyrological Seminar of the Theological Faculty of the University of Barcelona

In the Palau Ribes Collection of the Papyrological Seminar of the Theological Faculty of Barcelona there is a parchment Coptic codex from the early fifth century in Sahidic: Papyrus Palau Ribes 181–183. It contains Luke, John and Mark (in that order) from the early fifth century, which have been published by Hans Quecke,[42] included in a series edited by the Spanish scholar Father José O'Callaghan. Hans Quecke has drawn attention to one affinity with the Bodmer Papyri: "The cover of P. Palau Rib. Inv. Nr. 181/18[3] reminds me very much of that of P. Bodmer XIX."

Rodolphe Kasser has pointed out that P. Palau Ribes 181–183 is in almost perfect condition, whereas all the Bodmer Papyri display serious rotting. Yet there is a striking divergence in the state of preservation among the Bodmer Papyri themselves, from the earliest, which survive as no more than relics rebound in late antiquity in such a way that they could no longer be used, to the predominantly fourth-century manuscripts that are in relatively good condition, often more comparable in condition to P. Palau Ribes 181–183 than to the third-century codices among the Bodmer Papyri. Since P. Palau Ribes 181–183 is dated to the fifth century, its deterioration prior to burial might be expected to be less extensive than is the case with the bulk of the Bodmer Papyri that are earlier. Just as no clear distinction in the deterioration of the manuscripts has usually been made between what was caused prior to burial and what was caused during burial, no clear distinction has been made between what was caused prior to the discovery and subsequent to the discovery. When one considers that some of the material was reburied

41. Lowe, *Codices Latinis Antiquiores*.

42. Quecke, *Das Lukasevangelium saïdisch*; Quecke, *Das Markusevangelium saïdisch*; Quecke, *Das Johannesevangelium saïdisch*.

and retrieved some months later soaked by the inundation of the Nile, then one must reckon with the probability that the deterioration of what was reburied would be greater than in the case of what was not reburied. Of course, the length of time that the material stayed reburied was much less than the length of time during which the material was originally buried, just as the time the manuscripts were in existence prior to their burial was less than the time they spent buried. Yet, these differences in the lengths of time may to a considerable degree be counterbalanced by the place where the materials reposed during such periods of time. The dryness in the desert at the site of the burial may stand in quite sharp contrast to the dampness of a Pachomian monastery near the river (indeed an area surrounded by water during the annual inundation such as at Phbow), and to the dampness of modern Dishnā near the river prior to the final termination of the inundations as a result of the High Dam. A fragmentary parchment sheet of a relatively recent Ethiopic manuscript photographed in November 1975 at Qina had acquired a further hole through each leaf, eliminating a couple of square centimeters, when examined again in December 1980 at al-Qasr. Qina and al-Qasr are both locations quite comparable to, and on each side of, Dishnā.

Information from Egypt to the effect that Father O'Callaghan was involved with material from the same discovery as the Bodmer Papyri may be more relevant with regard to the relation of P. Palau Bib. Inv.-Nr. 181–183 to the Bodmer Papyri than is the present state of its preservation. But the relation of the P. Palau 181–183 codex to the shared provenience remains no more than a good possibility.

OTHER POSSIBILITIES

In addition to Chester Beatty Accession No. 1499, P. Beatty Panop., and Mississippi Coptic Codex I (the Crosby Codex), there are other codices that, though not located at repositories known to have directly acquired materials of the same provenience as the Bodmer Papyri, may nonetheless be investigated as to whether they may be from the same discovery. For they too fall within the Coptic biblical category to which a plurality of the Bodmer Papyri belong, have been dated in the fourth and fifth centuries to which the bulk of the Bodmer Papyri have been dated (see chapter 4 below), and have emerged since the mid-1950s as did the Bodmer Papyri.

There are other manuscripts of the Coptic period that have come to attention in recent years and that may be here mentioned but that for the time being lack sufficient supporting evidence to be included in the group of manuscripts that are under consideration as Bodmer Papyri.

The Bohairic codex of the Minor Prophets at the Vatican Library: This codex was presented for sale for £E 50,000 by its two purported owners at a private showing late in September 1973 in the Art Gallery Maguid Sameda, 55 Gamhouria Street, Cairo, by Sultan Sameda, the son and successor of the antiquities dealer Maguid Sameda, who had sold Mississippi Coptic Codices I and II to David M. Robinson in 1954.[43] That showing is documented by photographs, made at the time, of the stack of leaves and of a page containing Hosea 12:2–11 and another containing Zephaniah 3:16–20 followed by Haggai 1:1. At some juncture, it was offered to the Bibliothèque Bodmer, which commissioned Bruno Urio to prepare an expertise. Had it been acquired by the Bibliothèque Bodmer, it would no doubt have been included in the assumption of a shared provenience. Hence, this irregularity in the market and its relatively recent appearance on the market should not exclude it from consideration here.

In 1954, Paul Kahle discussed a newly identified dialect that he designated Middle Egyptian (also called today Oxyrhynchite), known then on the basis of six manuscripts only.[44] Since that time, three codices have emerged,[45] one having been offered for sale to the Bibliothèque Bodmer during the same years that the Bodmer Papyri were being acquired,[46] and two having been acquired in May 1961 by H. P. Kraus of New York City.[47] Had the sale to the Bibliothèque Bodmer been effected, that codex would have been automatically included here among the Bodmer Papyri, and indeed it (and perhaps the other two) may well be of the same provenience, as Rodolphe Kasser has suggested. One of these, a papyrus codex of the Pauline Epistles, was published in 1974.[48] It is there

43. Willis, "Papyrus Fragment of Cicero," 324.

44. Kahle, *Bala'izah* 1, 220.

45. Kasser, "Prolégomènes," 83, n. 8, states that Kahle's description took place "avant la decouverte des trois grands manuscrits M aujourd'hui connus."

46. Reported in a letter of April 16, 1981, by Rodolphe Kasser.

47. Petersen, "Early Coptic Manuscript of Acts," 225.

48. Orlandi and Quecke, *Lettere di San Paolo in Copto-Ossirinchita*

reported by Tito Orlandi to be of unknown provenience,[49] and dated to the fourth or early fifth century by Guglielmo Cavallo.[50] The other two are described by Petersen as follows: "One of these contained the complete text of the *Gospel of St. Matthew*, the other the first half of the *Acts of the Apostles*. Both were written on fine parchment and are well preserved with their original bindings and wooden covers intact. The *Matthew* codex numbers 238 leaves, the *Acts* codex 107 leaves. Both codices measure 12.5 by 10.5 cm . . . The date of the two manuscripts is judged by competent authorities in paleography as of the fourth or early fifth century."[51]

Kasser had in 1966 made the following reference to his access to the two parchment codices: "this dialect is now represented not only by the few manuscripts that are more or less Fayyumic know to Paul Kahle (cf. *Balaʾizah* I, pp. 220–27), *but also by the two important manuscirpts already cited by us*."[52]

In a note, he refers to his acknowledgement earlier on the page to Julius Assfalg of Munich and Theodore C. Peterson of Washington, "who have made us the photocopies (or copies) of unpublished texts that they are preparing for publication, and have permitted us to make use of them." They were apparently still unpublished.[53]

The three Middle-Egyptian (Oxyrhynchite) codices: One was offered to but not acquired by the Bibliothèque Bodmer during the period when that library was acquiring the Bodmer Papyri. This may have been the papyrus codex of the Pauline Epistles acquired by Milan at the beginning of the 1970s, since Hans Quecke had received a photograph of a page to produce an expertise for the University of Heidelberg a year or so earlier. The other two were acquired in May 1961[54] and resold on the

49. Ibid., 1.

50. Ibid., 13.

51. Petersen, "Early Coptic Manuscript of Acts," 225. The conclusion of the codex containing the first half of Acts leads to this conjecture on page 226, n. 3: "One may conclude from this that there was a companion volume 2 of the *Acts* and that this volume may still be in hiding and may some day make its appearance unless it is destroyed and lost."

52. Kasser, "Compléments morphologiques," 20.

53. Kasser, "Prolégomènes," 83, n. 8.

54. Petersen, "Early Coptic Manuscript of the Acts," 225: "In May 1961 two recently discovered early biblical manuscripts came into the possession of Mr. H. P. Kraus of New York City. One of these contained the complete text of the *Gospel of St. Matthew*, the other

bibliophile market by Hans Peter Kraus of New York, the parchment codex of the first half of Acts to William S. Glazier[55] (now in the Pierpont Morgan Library), the parchment codex of Matthew to William H. Scheide[56] (now in the Scheide Library in Princeton). Hans Quecke[57] has raised the question whether the codices in this dialect, which is relatively well localized, would have been found so far from its place of origin. But in view of the fact that the Bodmer Papyri include Coptic materials in Sahidic, Bohairic, and Proto-Sahidic as well as texts in Greek and Latin, while the nearby Nag Hammadi Codices include Sub-Achmimic as well as Sahidic, no rigid correlation of the location of the discoveries with the location of the dialects is to be expected.

The following is a preliminary inventory of the ancient books that are to be investigated in terms of a shared provenience (omitting P. Bodmer XVII, since it is clearly of a different provenience): There are represented, though in a few cases quite fragmentarily, thirty-two ancient books: Three papyrus Greek rolls and twenty-nine codices, twenty-two made of papyrus, and five of parchment. (Two unpublished texts at the Bibliothèque Bodmer have not been identified in terms of the writing material.) Twelve papyrus codices are in Greek, six in Coptic, two in Latin (both of which are partially in Greek). All five parchment codices are in Coptic. In Greek are only the twelve papyrus codices (two

---

the first half of the *Acts of the Apostles*. Both were written on fine parchment and are well preserved with their original bindings and wooden covers intact. The *Matthew* codex numbers 238 leaves, the *Acts* codex 107 leaves. Both codices measure 12.5 by 10.5 cm."

55. Kraus, *Rare Book Saga*, 214:

> Another, probably his most important purchase, was a complete codex on vellum of the *Acts of the Apostles* in Coptic from the 4th century. This is an unbelievably early date for a manuscript. (See Plate 12) The script is similar to that of the famous *Codex Sinaiticus*. The original binding is preserved—wooden boards, morocco back with blind stamped decorations—and the last page is decorated with a full-page miniature of an ankh, or Egyptian cross, between two peacocks. That is, according to scholars, the earliest miniature in a Christian Codex (for details see the two chapters in my Festschrift, *Homage to a Bookman*, 1967).

56. Ibid., 313–14: "I also sold him a manuscript of top importance: the complete *Gospel of St. Matthew* in Coptic on vellum from the 4th or 5th century, in a hand similar to the *Codex Sinaiticus*. It also contains the Great Doxology in two languages, Greek and Coptic, the earliest manuscript of this text. I remarked recently that this is certainly the greatest book in his collection."

57. In a letter of July 11, 1981, from Hans Quecke.

of which are partially in Latin). In Coptic are the five parchment codices and ten papyrus codices, plus the two whose writing surface is unknown, a total of seventeen Coptic codices. In Latin are two papyrus codices (both of which are partially in Greek). Non-Christian are, in addition to the three papyrus rolls, one Greek codex as well as a part of two more (one Greek and one Latin and Greek); there is also one in Greek with documentary contents. Codices that are (at least predominantly) Christian are ten Greek codices (two of which are largely in Latin) and all seventeen Coptic codices, a total of twenty-seven codices. The Old Testament is represented in five Greek and ten Coptic codices, a total of fifteen codices. The New Testament is represented in three Greek and five Coptic codices, a total of nine codices. Three of these codices contain material from both Testaments, so that the Bible is represented in a total of only twenty-one codices. Thus there are six non-canonical Christian codices.

Such raw statistics may have no apparent significance beyond a numerical impression of what is involved in the discovery. However, some trends may be apparent. Rolls are all non-Christian, but non-Christian material is rare among the codices. The papyrus codices are predominantly Greek, but with a visible minority in Coptic. The parchment codices are all in Coptic. (Latin is rare, confined to papyrus codices that also have some Greek.) Rolls are all papyrus. They and the papyrus codices tend to be early, parchment codices to be late. Greek tends to be early (second to fourth centuries), Coptic late (perhaps third but predominantly fourth to fifth centuries). These trends are not surprising but either reflect what is typical or are based on too limited a quantity to be very relevant. For an itemization of the inventory, one may be referred to the appended essay, "The Pachomian Monastic Library at the Chester Beatty Library and the Bibliothèque Bodmer."

Whether there are more manuscripts that can be reasonably assumed to have been part of this discovery is an open question. In the case of the Bibliothèque Bodmer, the reticence to divulge information concerning unpublished materials and the hesitancy to make the holdings available for study suggest that only time (the time it takes to publish or to modify a policy) will tell whether there are other materials from the same discovery that are not included in the present survey. The same may not be the case with some of the other repositories. The Chester Beatty Library permits full access to the material and information there.

Only in the case of the University of Mississippi does one have some specific reason to think that no other materials of the same provenience were acquired.[58]

There are other manuscripts that have emerged during the past generation that may be from the same discovery, although no explicit link has yet been identified. A papyrus codex of the Pauline Epistles in the rare Middle-Egyptian (Oxyrhynchite) dialect of Coptic of the fourth or fifth century has been published by Tito Orlandi in Milan, where the codex is at the Universita degli Studi di Milano.[59] A parchment codex of Matthew in the same dialect from the fifth century at the Scheide Library in Princeton has been published by Hans-Martin Schenke,[60] who also published the codex of the first half of the book of Acts of the same period in this same dialect, acquired by William S. Glazier and on deposit at the Pierpont Morgan Library (formerly assigned to Paulinus Bellet for publication).[61] A fourth-century papyrus codex of the Minor Prophets in the Bohairic dialect, which I saw in Cairo in 1975, in the same antiquities shop of Sameda from which the Mississippi codices came, arrived in 1980 in the Vatican Library,[62] where it is edited by Hans Quecke.[63] There has been on the market, at unrealistically high prices, a collection consisting of a gnostic papyrus codex in Sahidic dialect of the fourth century containing copies of the *First Apocalypse of James* and the *Letter of Peter to Philip* (both previously known only from Nag Hammadi: Codices V, 3 and VIII, 2 respectively), as well as a previously unknown dialogue of the Resurrected with his disciples. Also up for sale were fragments of a fifth-century Sahidic papyrus codex of Pauline

58. William H. Willis wrote in a letter of February 15, 1980: "As for the 1955 purchase for Mississippi, there was nothing to connect the two codices with the miscellaneous Greek and Coptic documents which Sameda sent at the same time (autumn 1955) in a separate package. Most of these latter are of a III-cent. date or earlier, but some are early Byzantine. Sameda gave no hint of the provenience of any."

59. Orlandi and Quecke, *Lettere di San Paolo*.

60. Schenke, *Das Matthäus-Evangelium im mittelägyptischen Dialekt*.

61. Petersen, "Early Coptic Manuscript of Acts," 225–41; Kebabian, "Binding of the Glazier Manuscript," 25–29; Bober, "On the Illumination of the Glazier Codex," 31–49; Plummer, *Glazier Collection*, 7–8.

62. Tito Orlandi reported in an interview of August 24, 1981, that the Prefect of the Vatican Library reported to him in June of 1980 that the codex had been presented to Pope John Paul II earlier that same year.

63. According to a letter of July 11, 1981, from Hans Quecke.

Epistles, a codex of Exodus in Greek, and Greek metrodological fragments. Whether this is just a (no doubt partial) list of what has emerged in the apparently steady stream of clandestine excavation and marketing of papyri in Egypt, or whether there are here materials from the same discovery as the Bodmer Papyri is hard to ascertain. Such material should be kept in view, even if it is not at present to be included in the survey of what in the broader sense may be called the Bodmer Papyri.

—4—

The Dishnā Papers

ABŪ MANĀʿ

Ḥasan Muḥammad al-Sammān,[64] a tall, dull peasant, and Muḥammad Khalīl al-ʿAzzūzī, an ignorant one-eyed peasant perhaps in family origin from the hamlet Naj Azzūz seven kilometers to the southwest of Abū Manāʿ [so Fatḥallāh Dāʾūd], both from the hamlet Abū Manāʿ "Bahri," found a jar containing books about 300 meters out from the foot of the Jabal Abū Manāʿ, at al-Qurnah, "the corner" of the cliff. According to popular Coptic etymology the ancient name of the mountain was Abū Mina, named after St. Mina, a name gradually corrupted into the modern Arabic name of Abū Manāʿ.

The hamlet of Abū Manāʿ nearby is on the right bank of the Nile in a segment of the valley where the river flows from east to west. Though the hamlet is on the right bank, it is not near the river, but rather some four kilometers from the river's edge, near the outer limit of arable land, five kilometers northeast of Fāw Qiblī and five and a half kilometers northwest of Dishnā. Some four kilometers of dirt road separating it from the main asphalt highway was due to be paved. Rural electrification reached Naj al-Ramlah, the section of the hamlet where Ḥasan lives, toward the end of 1980. Thus Abū Manāʿ lies apart from the bustling

64. Interviewed at Naj al-Ramlah behind Abū Manāʿ on August 11, 1981.

mainstream of Egyptian life along the Nile, the railroad and the highway, which make of Dishnā, with its railroad station, the local center. Hence Dishnā, which earlier in the century was considerably larger than Nag Hammadi twenty-four kilometers downstream, plays a similar role as does Nag Hammadi in the case of the gnostic codices—as the main town after which the discovery is named, though in neither case actually being the nearest hamlet to the site. As a result the two discoveries, which took place twelve kilometers apart at the Jabal al-Tārif and the Jabal Abū Manāᶜ, or, in terms of the nearest hamlets, ten kilometers apart at Hamrah Dūm and Abū Manāᶜ, are usually named in terms of the relevant centers along the trunk route, as the Nag Hammadi codices and the Dishnā papers.[1]

Ḥasan found the jar buried a couple of meters deep when he was digging *sabakh* to fertilize the fields. He called over to Muḥammad al-ᶜAzzūzī "to see what the poor find." Then Ḥasan broke the jar with his mattock and left the pieces where they lay. Then he pulled out the books from the jar and put them in the skirt of his *jallabīyah*. Some that were torn and in very bad condition were burned on the spot. As Ḥasan was carrying the rest home, he gave away some to passersby, since he was told that they were the books of giants, which aroused fear in him. There was also in the jar a square mirror some twenty centimeters across with a wooden back; Muḥammad Khalīl al-ᶜAzzūzī took it. Ḥasan did not actually have a chance to look at it until after it had been confiscated by the police.

The date of the discovery was toward the end of the year of the coup that deposed King Farouk and ultimately brought Nasser into power. The date of that event, July 26, 1952, is for Egypt what the Fourth of July is for the U.S.A. and the Quatorze Juillet is for France—an unforgettable date after which, in this Egyptian case, a main street of Cairo was

1. Baedeker, *Egypt and the Sudan*, 222, gives the population of Dishnā as 10,386, Fāw as 15,448, and Nag Hammadi as 3,867. Elston, *Traveller's Handbook for Egypt and the Sudan*, 225, lists the population of Farshut, 8 kilometers southwest of Nag Hammadi, as "over 17,000." This may account for the relatively low population listed for Nag Hammadi by Baedeker, who does not list a population for Farshut, whereas Elston does not list a population for Nag Hammadi. Baud and Parisot, *Egypte*, 289, refers to Farshut as a "large village," with more prominence given to Nag Hammadi, whose size is however not indicated. Hogarth et al., *Egypt*, 409, omit Farshut completely. None mention Abū Manāᶜ or Hamrah Dūm.

renamed. With the help of this reference point, the discovery may be dated with some confidence late in 1952.

The books were taken to the house where Ḥasan lived, which was the family home of his wife, presided over by her father ʿUmar al-ʿAbbādī, and inhabited also by the latter's two sons. The books were kept in a large jar which the middlemen of Dishnā took to be the jar in which the books had been discovered. The jar was hidden under chaff used as cattle fodder lying in the patio. A few books would be taken out at a time and offered as barter in exchange for sugar, but without success, whereupon they would be returned to the jar. Ḥasan and his brother-in-law ʿAbd al-ʿĀl ʿUmar al-ʿAbbādī[2] crushed up the leaves of a very large papyrus book without its cover and used it as tinder to light their water pipe, presumably before the Dishnā market revealed the value of the books. When parchment was lit on fire it burnt like an oil lamp.

A nephew of ʿUmar al-ʿĀbbadī's wife, and thus a first cousin of Ḥasan's wife, ʿAbd al-Raḥīm Abū al-Hājj, was a village barber of Abū Manāʿ who went from house to house plying his trade, as well as a sharecropper working fields belonging to a powerful goldsmith of Dishnā, Riyāḍ Jirjis Fām (b. 1906).[3] Riyāḍ came from a very primitive background. His father had been very poor, and had made a living by weaving baskets out of the reeds growing at the edge of the Nile. Though the daily wage at the time was as low as a piaster, Riyāḍ himself boasts of having made as much as £E 100 a day at various enterprises: a goldsmith's trade, a chicken factory, the sale of beans and antiquities. ʿAbd al-Raḥīm told Riyāḍ [on December 13, 1980], of the discovery and suggested that the latter come to Abū Manāʿ to see the books. For the people of Abū Manāʿ would be afraid to take the books to Dishnā to show, but would trust Riyāḍ in their own village. This was about a fortnight after the discovery. Riyāḍ took with him Mūsā Fikrī Ashʿiyah,[4] a friend and fellow goldsmith of Dishnā, who often sat with him in his shop. They visited ʿAbd al-Rāḥīm, but he did not want to receive into his house Mūsā Fikrī, a complete stranger, so he sent them away empty-handed. They returned a second time, but in front of ʿAbd al-Rāḥīm's house, which was near the police station, Mūsā Fikrī lost his nerve and turned back. Riyāḍ obtained

2. Interviewed at Naj al-Ramlah behind Abū Manāʿ on August 11, 1981.

3. Interviewed in his home at Heliopolis.

4. Interviewed in his home in Dishnā and in his goldsmith's shop there.

nothing. But on a third trip alone to the house of ʿAbd al-Rāḥīm, the latter Riyāḍ went and brought three or four books, which Riyāḍ bought for some £E 1,000 and took home to Dishnā.

Mūsā Fikrī recalls ʿAbd al-Rāḥīm telling him that Riyāḍ had bought from him one book for £E 40 and three for a total of £E 750. This might suggest two transactions separated by an inflation in the market value. But since Riyāḍ on occasion mentioned having given ʿAbd al-Rāḥīm £E 1000 after having sold all the books, so as to keep his friendship (since he was convinced ʿAbd al-Rāḥīm had more books), the larger sum may not reflect a second acquisition but only a final payment commensurate with the enormous profits.

ʿAbd al-Rāḥīm had himself acquired one very good book, a Greek papyrus codex with a leather cover. Riyāḍ asked him to sell it, but he would not. But they made a pact, ʿAbd al-Rāḥīm swearing on the Koran, and Riyāḍ on the Bible, according to which ʿAbd al-Rāḥīm promised to sell to no one except Riyāḍ. The latter in turn gave ʿAbd al-Rāḥīm a gold necklace and land he owned at Abū Manāʿ, as well as a metal box lined with cotton to hold the book. The box was buried in the patio where the water buffalo stays at night. Each year ʿAbd al-Rāḥīm paid money to Riyāḍ.

Ḥasan's brother-in-law ʿAbd al-ʿAl, though living in Abū Manāʿ, worked in a jewelry shop of Dishnā together with Ṣubḥī Quṣtandī Dimyan (deceased), to whom he sold a book for £E 15. Ṣubḥī Quṣtandī Dimyān showed his book to the Dishnā priest "al-Qummuṣ" Manqaryūs (deceased about 1966) to inquire if it were as valuable as the Ḥamrah Dūm books (the Nag Hammadi codices), for "al-Qummuṣ" Manqaryūs was born at al-Qaṣr, the home of Muḥammad Ali al-Sammān, the discoverer of the Nag Hammadi codices. Indeed "al-Qummuṣ" Manqaryūs's family home in the Coptic quarter of al-Qaṣr is across the street from that of "al-Qummuṣ" Basīlyūs ʿAbd al-Masīḥ, in whose home Nag Hammadi Codex III had been stored. In fact, the two priests were cousins: the mother of "al-Qummuṣ" Manqaryūs, Astir, and the father of "al-Qummuṣ" Basīlyūs, "al-Qummuṣ" ʿAbd al-Masīḥ, were sister and brother. The families were also related through the mother of "al-Qummuṣ" Basīlyūs. Rāghib Andarāwus "al-Qiss" ʿAbd al-Sayyid, the brother-in-law of "al-Qummuṣ" Basīlyūs ʿAbd al-Masīḥ, but at the time living at Dishnā where he taught in the Coptic parochial school, had acquired

Nag Hammadi Codex III from his brother-in-law, taken it to Dishnā, and sold it to the Coptic Museum in 1946 for £E 250. Jirjis, the son of Ṣubḥi Quṣtandi Dimyan, then also a teacher in Dishnā (later a medical doctor in Alexandria), took the Dishnā book to the Coptic Museum in Cairo. The Museum demanded the other Dishnā papers, threatening to put Jirjis in jail. But he appealed to a powerful friend, who persuaded the Museum to return the book to Jirjis and not to turn him in. He then sold the book to Zakī Ghālī, an antiquities dealer in Luxor, for £E 400. Zakī Ghālī was the first antiquities dealer to obtain any of the Dishnā papers.

Fatḥallāh Daʾūd has a somewhat different version as to the relations among the first middlemen than that of Riyāḍ, reported above. Knowing the book to be valuable, "al-Qummuṣ" Manqaryūs nonetheless told Ṣubḥī it was worthless, hoping in this way to be able to acquire it for himself. Then "al-Qummuṣ" Manqaryūs sent Riyāḍ to Abū Manāʿ to find the identity of the owner of the rest, not divulged by Ṣubḥī, and acquire the books for themselves, whereupon they would divide the profit. Mūsā Fikrī and Shafīq Ghubrīyāl, who together operated another goldsmith shop, were brought into the partnership. But Riyāḍ ultimately cut the others out of their fair share of the profit.

Since bad relations later emerged, apparently due to Riyāḍ's not fully honoring such a partnership (see below), one may well assume some such loose agreement must have existed as that reported by Fatḥallāh Daʾūd, who himself got entangled in those bad relations (see below). Riyāḍ's version of the story seems slanted to provide him a more independent claim to the profit, in that he acknowledged no indebtedness to the others. And Riyāḍ's insistence that Mūsā Fikrī accompanied him to Abū Manāʿ only as a friend, just for the ride, seems on the face of it to be less than the full story. The recurrence of "al-Qummuṣ" Manqaryūs, Mūsā Fikrī, and Shafīq Ghubrīyāl at various points in the subsequent story (including the conviction of Mūsā Fikrī) would be much more intelligible if they were not merely bystanders. One may hence conjecture that each of the four partners had something to contribute: presumably the priest provided the expertise, the strongman offered the acquisition and disposal of the books, and the goldsmiths provided, perhaps, needed capital.

Danyal Manqaryūs had been the first person from Dishnā to have seen the books, according to his son Isḥāq, but had been afraid to acquire them. Riyāḍ learned from him that the books were in the home of ʿAbd al-ʿĀl, who happened to be a friend of Riyāḍ. The latter played down their value so as to avoid having to compete with Danyal Manqaryūs for this acquisition.

The day after acquiring the four books in the house of ʿAbd al-Rāḥīm, Riyāḍ returned to Abū Manāʿ, accompanied only by his son Nuṣḥī, then about twelve years old. But this time, he went directly to the house of ʿUmar al-ʿAbbādī, and acquired the jar with all it contained for £E 200. When Riyāḍ left ʿUmar al-ʿAbbādī's house, villagers threatened to rob him, so he retreated back to ʿUmar al-ʿAbbādī's house. The latter sent his sons, both armed, to escort Riyāḍ and his son Nuṣḥī out of the hamlet as far as the paved highway.

Shakir Bahnam, mayor of Dishnā (d. ca. 1965), went to Abū Manāʿ to visit a friend, Muḥammad al-Kabir ("the giant"), who was of the tough Hawwarah tribe.[5] Ḥasan feared that the mayor might have come to turn them in to the police, so he burnt the remaining evidence, minor quantities of material that were not in the jar when Riyāḍ had bought it.

Dishnā

Riyāḍ went directly from the home of ʿUmar al-ʿAbbādī' in Abū Manāʿ to "al-Qummuṣ" Manqaryūs in Dishnā. Riyāḍ's son Nuṣḥī carried the jar on his shoulder into the priest's house. There Riyāḍ counted out to "al-Qummuṣ" Manqaryūs one by one thirty-three books (an oft-repeated figure also used for the quantity of books in the discovery, a figure which, in the present context, actually includes the four books already acquired from ʿAbd al-Rāḥīm), plus three or four rolls some twenty-five centimeters or more in height, plus two to four roughly triangular-shaped leaves about fifteen centimeters high, and about ten small rolls the size of one's finger, later said by Tano to be letters.

5. Farshut was a stronghold of the Hawwarah. Elston, *Traveller's Handbook for Egypt and the Sudan*, 226, reports:

> [Farshut] was at one time the residence of a powerful Arab chieftain. Its inhabitants are supposed to be descendants of the Hawara tribe of Arabs, who were famous for their skill in the breeding and managing of horses. Their dogs were also noted from all other breeds of the country.

Baud and Parisot, *Egypte*, 289, report: "[Farshut] was for a long time the center of the tribe of the Hawwarah, subdued by Muḥammad ʿAlī after a long resistance.

Hamrah Dūm was also a Hawwarah stronghold, which explains to a large extent the incessant feuds surrounding that hamlet at the site of the discovery of the Nag Hammadi codices.

"Al-Qummuṣ" Manqaryūs, fearing the police, had his son, also named Nuṣḥī, throw into the toilet a large cloth some two meters long and twenty-five centimeters wide in which a thick parchment codex with a wooden cover had been wrapped. The cream-colored cloth was like silk in that it reflected different colors in the sunlight. It was a loose weave like a net and had on it a picture, some thirty centimeters high, of a man, under which something was written in Coptic. Riyāḍ broke the lid of the jar and threw it also into the toilet. Nuṣḥī "al-Qummuṣ" Manqaryūs recalls taking the jar to the nearby Coptic church and breaking it there, to throw the shards into the toilet of the church (though Riyāḍ recalls the pieces having been thrown into the toilet in the home of "al-Qummuṣ" Manqaryūs).

Nuṣḥī "al-Qummuṣ" Manqaryūs recalls one parchment book was pressed so hard into the bottom of the jar that it had become misshapen into the contours of the pointed bottom. One may correlate this codex with the codex broken into two parts and hence known as P. Bodmer XXII and Mississippi Coptic Codex II, in that the same misshapen contour is reported of both (see chapter 2 above).

At first the books were kept at the home of "al-Qummuṣ" Manqaryūs, since the partners were sure that the house of Riyāḍ would be searched if the police became suspicious (as in fact it was). But the partners assumed the police would not search the house of a priest. The books were in a wooden box that was hidden at times under the floor, at times in the ceiling behind the rafters. But at one time (see below), there was fear that even the priest's home might be searched. Hence, "al-Qummuṣ" Manqaryūs hid the books in a cupboard beneath the cushions of a divan. He then went to his neighbor Saʿīd Diryās Ḥabashi, and asked permission to sun the divan in the latter's sunny patio, explaining that the divan was infested with fleas that a good sunning might expel, but that there was no sunny patio in the priest's own home where such a sunning could be done. Once the fear of a police search had proven to be unfounded, "al-Qummuṣ" Manqaryūs retrieved the divan, only to find that the best book was missing. He accused Saʿīd Diryās of taking it. But Saʿīd Diryās maintains that "al-Qummuṣ" Manqaryūs had not told him that the books were in the divan, and he was quite unaware of the risk he had taken. Had he known there were precious books there, he has said somewhat humorously, he would not have taken just one, as he was falsely accused of doing, but he would have taken them all. Fatḥallāh

Daʾūd has also affirmed that Saʿīd Diryās, who on his day off is indeed usually to be found in the Coptic church of Dishnā, is above suspicion. For his father was at the time already deceased, his mother was deaf, and he himself was not at home when the divan was brought in. Yet Riyāḍ, who initiated a private investigation, determined that Saʿīd Diryās had sold the book to Fāris, a tailor of Dishnā (deceased), for only £E 30, whereupon Fāris sold it for £E 700 to Tano, who showed it to Riyāḍ.

"Prof. José O'Callaghan Martinus of Barcelona (passport number 95912)" was in residence at the Franciscan Church adjoining the Sugar Factory near Nag Hammadi from November 14–20, 1964 (and again beginning February 1, 1965), having come "to look for papers," according to the parish diary of the Franciscan Church.[6] He obtained some three leaves from a priest of Dishnā.[7] Saʿīd Diryās has reported that a Spanish priest obtained in about 1966 some material from "al-Qummuṣ" Tānyūs (born at al-Qaṣr in 1914, died at Dishnā on August 7, 1970), the son of "al-Qummuṣ" Manqaryūs. Professor ʿAziz S. ʿAṭīyah (see below) has recalled "al-Qummuṣ" Tānyūs having brought a small fragment as a sample to show him in Maadi and then having disappeared. The widow of "al-Qummuṣ" Manqaryūs has recalled that there were a couple of leaves from the discovery lying among the priestly books in the home, but a hurried search on her part failed to locate them.[8] Thus O'Callaghan may well have acquired the stray leaves that had still been in the home of "al-Qummuṣ" Manqaryūs long after the books had, in principle, been disposed of. The antiquities dealer of Alexandria, Tawfīq Saʿd (see below), brought a foreigner in priestly attire dressed in black with a little beard to the home of Riyāḍ in Heliopolis, wishing to see the books. But whether this was a follow-up visit on the part of O'Callaghan has not been determined.

Hardly more than a month after the discovery, Muḥammad al-ʿAzzūzī was angered at having been excluded from the profits that had

6. This information was recorded by Father Rafael (deceased). The parish diary was consulted with the help of Father Hanna on January 10, 1975.

7. According to Milad Sidra, a third order Franciscan priest of Nag Hammadi who accompanied Father O'Callaghan during his visit. Milad Sidra was interviewed by Klaus Koschorke at the buffet of the Nag Hammadi train station on December 11, 1974, and again by me at Nag Hammadi on January 10, 1975.

8. The widow of "al-Qummuṣ" Tānyūs "al-Qummuṣ" Manqaryūs was interviewed in her home in Dishnā on December 18, 1976.

been made by the family of ʿUmar al-ʿAbbādī so he broke the story to the police. They found the first concrete evidence with Maṣri ʿAbd al-Masiḥ Nuḥ of Abū Manāʿ (later living at Kom Ombo south of Luxor), who had acquired from ʿUmar al-ʿAbbādī a wooden board found in the jar, on which was inscribed in black ink a list by number and title in Coptic and Greek, but not in Arabic, of forty-three items, taken to be an inventory of the contents of the jar. The Dishnā police had raided Maṣrī's house, confiscated the board and a gun for which he had no license, and taken him in. Fatḥallāh Daʾūd had friends among the police and was visiting them at the police station when Maṣrī was brought in. There he saw the board, which he thought (rightly?) to be a front or back cover from a codex. The board and some fragments that the authorities had also seized were sent to Cairo to the Minister of Culture and National Guidance, at that time Egypt's blind poet, Taha Hussein, who recognized the unusual importance of the discovery. Police and representatives of the Service des antiquites were sent to search the site of the discovery.

Maṣrī implicated Riyāḍ, Mūsā Fikrī, Shafīq Ghubrīyāl, and "al-Qummuṣ" Manqaryūs. Although charges were not brought against "al-Qummuṣ" Manqaryūs, no doubt only because he was a priest, this must have been the occasion when he transferred the books to the home of Saʿīd Diryās. But the others were charged and arrested, except for Shafīq Ghubrīyāl, who was spared by a case of mistaken identity. For he was familiarly called by the name of his mother, Rihannah, rather than by that of his father, Ghubrīyāl. The police did not recognize the reference to Shafīq Rihannah as referring to Shafīq Ghubrīyāl, but mistook it as referring to Shafīq Muḥārib Bisharun (deceased), who was arrested and prosecuted with the others. The police also arrested three more in Abū Manāʿ: Ḥasan; the brother of ʿAbd al-ʿAl; and Abū al-Wafā Aḥmad Ismāʿīl, who had acquired a single parchment leaf roughly triangular in shape. After a night in jail, they were released pending trial.

It was about three years after the arrest that the trial took place. The house of Riyāḍ had been searched without finding incriminating evidence. But Mūsā Fikrī and other defendants told Riyāḍ Jirgis Fām that in their effort to exonerate themselves, they were going to identify him as the one who had the books. He retorted that if they did, he would kill them when he was released from jail. He gave Mūsā Fikrī £E 300 not to testify against him. He also bribed those at Abū Manāʿ whom the prosecution had planned to use as witnesses against him: Abū al-Wafā (£E 300), the mayor (£E 500) and the sheriff. The defense lawyer, Hilmī Bandarī, argued that it was not against the law to own antiquities, that such villagers knew neither the authenticity nor the value of such things, and that there was a lack of incriminating evidence. Nonetheless, the presiding judge, Rabāᶜ Tawfīq, a native of the Fayyum, found all guilty of unlicensed trafficking in illegally excavated antiquities, and sentenced each to a year in jail.

Riyāḍ paid the judge £E 20 per defendant for the privilege of appealing the case. He hired a former minister of the government from Cairo, Aḥmad ᶜAlī Allūbā "Pasha," as attorney for the defense. The case came to court at Qinā about a year and a half after the initial conviction. Six were acquitted, but Ḥasan and Maṣrī ᶜAbd al-Masīḥ Nuḥ were found guilty—no doubt because the evidence of their trafficking one with another was in the possession of the authorities—and given six-month sentences, which in the case of Maṣrī was suspended, no doubt for having cooperated with the authorities. Only Ḥasan served a prison term. This may be the ultimate authentification of his role as discoverer and, hence, illegal trafficker in the antiquities. But as the most ignorant and least enriched by the whole transaction, Ḥasan least deserved serving time.

Riyāḍ had first seen the books only some fortnight after the discovery, a couple of months before his arrest. But it was about six months after the arrest that he actually began to market the material he had acquired. This was not a simple procedure but involved rather complex arrangements. For during the period from the initial arrest to the final acquittal (a period of about five years) Riyāḍ was kept under a kind of house arrest. He was not permitted to go to Cairo, and could leave town for up to ten hours (traveling as far away as Luxor or Sohag) only with a pass from the secret police, two of whom were assigned to guard his house by night and day.

It is this situation of relative house arrest that may explain the role of Fatḥallāh Daʾūd, a longtime friend of Riyāḍ. For Riyāḍ had gone on pilgrimage to Jerusalem in 1944 and then returned on a second pilgrimage, accompanied by Fatḥallāh Daʾūd, a year later, as tatooing on the inside of their arms attests. On the basis of such a close friendship, Fatḥallāh Daʾūd could be trusted with what seems to have been a largely disinterested role. For he was neither an owner of books nor a partner in the arrangement but only a porter of books for Riyāḍ to market in Cairo. There he would stay at the Abas Hotel on Klut Bey Street between Ramses Station and Opera Square, supporting himself at least ostensibly by selling animal fodder he would bring from Dishnā. Riyāḍ instructed him to report back to "al-Qummuṣ" Manqaryūs, Mūsā Fikrī, and Shafīq Ghubrīyāl a lower price than he actually received for his book sales. The assumption of this arrangement was that they, as partners, expected a share of the profits, profits diminished to the advantage of Riyāḍ by such understatement. Yet Fatḥallāh Daʾūd reported to them the actual amount obtained. Although Saʿīd Diryās reported that Fatḥallāh Daʾūd sold books to Tawfīq Saʿd in Alexandria, Fatḥallāh Daʾūd has denied ever having met Tawfīq Saʿd. Fatḥallāh also has reported that although Riyāḍ had said he would introduce Phoqué to him, Fatḥallāh never actually met Phoqué.

Riyāḍ was determined to extricate from Fatḥallāh Daʾūd for himself the resultant diminution of income. So he approached neighbors of Fatḥallāh Daʾūd whom he knew to be on bad terms with him—the Abū Baḥbuḥ family, and engaged them to kidnap and to hold for the appropriate ransom the small son of Fatḥallāh Daʾūd. They stole into the house by the dark of night and, in the obscurity, seized by mistake a somewhat less valuable commodity, his daughter Sūsū.

Fatḥallāh Daʾūd refused to pay the ransom but rather turned to the police, accusing Riyāḍ and the Abū Baḥbuḥ family of kidnapping. Riyāḍ told the officer in charge of the investigation that he would kill him if the officer made difficulties for him. The officer retorted that as a result of such a threat, he would be all the harder on Riyāḍ. Riyāḍ was indeed put in jail. But other policemen warned the officer in charge that Riyāḍ was the strong man of town with underworld toughs at his command. So Riyāḍ was released.

Yet Fatḥallāh Daʾūd, along with other concerned Copts of Dishnā, had sent a battery of telegrams to Egyptian President Nasser appealing to him to intervene. Police were in fact sent from Cairo to investigate. The investigators asked Riyāḍ Jirjis Fām if he had bribed his way free from the local officer who had imprisoned him. Though he now maintains he had not done so, Riyāḍ Jirjis Fām stated at the time that he had paid a £E 400 bribe, saying this just to make trouble for the officer, who was in fact removed from office. The authorities effected the release of

Sūsū after about a week of captivity without the payment of the ransom. Sūsū is now married and has children of her own; she lives in Aswan.

Charges were not pressed against Riyāḍ. When, some years later, he was fighting with a neighbor who was jealous over the profits he had made from the books, his son Waṣfī, who had heart trouble, was struck with a blow and died of a heart attack. Fatḥallāh Daʾūd considers this sufficient retribution for the crime, though he had to wait about eleven years for it to come: the kidnapping took place in about 1957, but the revenge only in 1968.

Riyāḍ has a somewhat different version of the kidnapping than that of Fatḥallāh Daʾūd reported above, a version that tends to put Riyāḍ in a somewhat better, or at least less bad, light. Fatḥallāh Daʾūd owed him £E 2,000, but had refused to pay his debt, on the grounds that Riyāḍ had received so much from the sale of the books that he had no need to press his claim. Hence Riyāḍ persuaded three men, who were already planning to kill Fatḥallāh Daʾūd, that it would be better to settle their score by kidnapping the child. Since Fatḥallāh Daʾūd laid out £E 3,000 in expenses related to getting Sūsū back, he obviously was in a financial position such that he could have paid his debts if he had wished. To this version of the story Fatḥallāh Daʾūd has retorted that he never owed Riyāḍ £E 2,000. His family had not been lacking in funds since the time of his grandfather, from whom he and his relatives inherited land in Dishnā reaching from the train station to the Nile River.

Concern for the safety of his family after the death of his son led Riyāḍ to decide to sell his home in Dishnā and move to the Cairo suburb Heliopolis, where his four brothers as well as sisters had already moved, and where he had stayed on trips to Cairo up to that time. He bought a large, modern, multistoried apartment house duplex, were he subsequently lived. Rāghib Andarāwus "al-Qiss" ʿAbd al-Sayyid has spoken with great envy of the two "palaces" Riyāḍ bought with the profit from the books. But Riyāḍ states that what he made on the books was used for living expenses, and that he bought the building with money he earned by the sweat of his brow as a goldsmith, a profession from which he retired only in 1970.

Phoqué

The Crypriote antiquities dealer of Cairo, Phokion J. Tano, is referred to in Arabic as "Phoqué," a frenchified version of his first name but also a recognizable Arabic name. This is in conformity with the Arab practice that each person normally has only a single name, followed by the name of one's father and grandfather (or tribe).

People from Dishnā often brought antiquities to Phoqué's shop. It is from them he heard of the manuscript discovery. Since a trip by Riyāḍ to Cairo was difficult, Phoqué flew to Luxor, from which he sent a government employee as a messenger to Dishnā to ask Riyāḍ to come to Luxor to show what he had to sell. Riyāḍ took a leaf to Luxor to show to Phoqué, who entertained him sumptuously at the Luxor Hotel. Phoqué told him he should bring all the books, but Riyāḍ explained that the police surveillance made this impossible. Phoqué offered to go to Dishnā to see them, but Riyāḍ pointed out that this too might compromise him. Finally, Riyāḍ offered to bring a book to Cairo, and Phoqué returned to Cairo.

Before returning to Dishnā, Riyāḍ showed the leaf at the Chicago House, where a man told him that though it was a very good leaf, customs inspection meant that he could not acquire and export it. This may have been Charles Nims. For he reported on March 3, 1966, that, years earlier, he had been shown an interesting manuscript there. Indeed, he had been sufficiently interested to write Ernest Cadman Colwell, whom he knew to have been interested in manuscripts when president of the University of Chicago, though he was no longer there. For Colwell had been at Emory University from 1951 to 1957, from which Nims recalls him replying that no funds were available. At the time Colwell was director of the International Greek New Testament Project, which was amassing manuscript evidence on the Gospel of Luke, of which P^{75}, owned by Riyāḍ, was to become by far the most important witness. The International Greek New Testament Project planned to move next to the Gospel of John, of which P^{66} and P^{75}, both owned by Riyāḍ, were also to become by far the most important witnesses.

A week later Saʿīd-Allah, an antiquities dealer of Baliana (74 kilometers downstream from Dishnā), who regularly circulated through Dishnā, visited Riyāḍ there. He made an arrangement with Riyāḍ to take one of the books to Cairo, sell it for him there, and bring him the money. About a month later, he returned with the report that he had sold it for £E 300. Riyāḍ demanded £E 1000 or the return of the book, threatening to shoot Saʿīd-Allah with his gun right there in his house. Saʿīd-Allah made a new offer of £E 700, which was also refused, whereupon he returned the book. Though Saʿīd-Allah often returned, at times with clients, Riyāḍ never sold to him.

Meanwhile Phoqué, noting that Riyāḍ had not arrived in Cairo, made inquiries about relatives in Cairo and succeeded in locating one of his brothers, Fahim. Phoqué persuaded Fahim Jirjis Fām to take him to Riyāḍ's home in Dishnā, arriving and departing under cover of darkness. Riyāḍ showed Phoqué the book that he had retrieved from Saʿd-Allah. Phoqué gave Riyāḍ his home address in Cairo and persuaded him to bring him the book there. Riyāḍ took the book on the night train and received £E 1100 for it in Phoqué's home.

Riyāḍ made this trip by means of a procedure he developed so as to circumvent the police surveillance. For he made friends with the guards and would ply them with alcohol on Saturday nights until they fell into a drunken stupor in time for him to catch the 11 p.m. train to Cairo. Since his shop was normally closed on Sundays, his absence would not have been observed until Monday. But he would take the train from Cairo back Sunday night and be home before dawn Monday so as to open his shop at the normal time.

A fortnight later Phoqué returned to Dishnā but was unable to acquire more from Riyāḍ. However, Riyāḍ returned to Cairo with another book in about a fortnight and received £E 1500 from Phoqué for it. Again in a fortnight, Riyāḍ went to Cairo and sold a third book to Phoqué for £E 5,000. A fortnight later he took a very large book, as large as from the elbow to the tip of the fingers, for which he obtained £E 7000. On the fifth trip he took a parchment codex, which Phoqué considered less good and hence acquired for only £E 3,000. In all, Phoqué acquired about a dozen books, about half papyrus, half parchment. Riyāḍ sold, for £E 100 each, some ten rolls, each of which was as long as one's finger and had a stamp on it. Phoqué told him they were letters. Riyāḍ finally sold Phoqué a box with the remaining fragmentary materials for £E 200.

The relationship between Riyāḍ and Phoqué was not nearly as cut and dried as this summary might seem to suggest. Various anecdotes recalled by Riyāḍ reflect the actual procedure.

Phoqué brought to his shop a Russian who taught in Cairo to appraise a papyrus book and a parchment book. He affirmed they were very good books and encouraged Riyāḍ to bring the rest. Phoqué paid the appraiser £E 300 for his expertise.

Phoqué advised Riyāḍ how to protect the books. He told him to have made for each a metal box lined with cotton, and gave him £E 50 for this purpose. He explained to him that in turning the leaves of a book one should not use one's fingers but rather should slip a knife under a leaf and turn it over, one leaf at a time. If the leaves of a book were stuck together, one should put them in the steam rising from boiling water so that they would come apart without damage. Phoqué emphasized the importance of even the smallest fragment. For when a fragment the size of a fingernail fell on the floor, Phoqué would dampen his finger and touch it down onto the fragment, thus lifting it up so it would not be damaged or lost.

Riyāḍ experimented in the case of the one long papyrus roll he owned. In order to count the leaves (*sic*!), he tried to unroll it but saw that it was breaking. Hence, he dipped the whole roll in warm water. He was then able to unroll it. It consisted of some thirty leaves (columns?), the bottom part of each uninscribed. He noted a signature (subscript titles?). The ink did not run; indeed, the script when wet was even more beautiful. In about five minutes, the stack of leaves coiled back up of its own accord.

Phoqué showered Riyāḍ with gifts. After Phoqué had first met him in Luxor and urged him to come to Cairo (although, then Riyāḍ had in fact not come), Phoqué returned to Luxor and sent for him a second time. When asked why he had not come to Cairo, Riyāḍ replied that he was afraid. Thereupon Phoqué offered him £E 1500 as a gift, which he declined. But when Riyāḍ would come to Cairo, with or without a book, Phoqué would take him out on the town, give him £E 70 or £E 100 and in general function as his host to the pleasures of big-city life. This continued even after Riyāḍ had sold all the books that he possessed. He has estimated, somewhat expansively, these gifts as totaling £E 12,000. Fatḥallāh Daʾūd and Zakī Basṭā, the antiquities dealer of Qinā, reported that Riyāḍ built the apartment house he owned in Heliopolis from his profit on the books; but Riyāḍ maintains he lived off of the profit and bought the apartment house with what he earned as a goldsmith, a job from which he retired in 1970.

Phoqué offered to take Riyāḍ to see an important person from America who had acquired a book and who was interested in meeting with him, but Riyāḍ was not willing to go.

In about 1955–1956, Phoqué engaged Riyāḍ to undertake clandestine excavations at the site of the discovery, for which purpose he provided £E 500. Neither of the two of them was actually present at the work, which continued for about a month and produced only cloth. The police came upon the diggers, who maintained that they were only digging for *sabakh*. The authorities erected a sign forbidding digging and posted a guard to prevent it. In about 1962, Bedouin camping nearby found gold and papyrus inscribed with hieroglyphs, which they sold at Luxor.

Phoqué explained to Riyāḍ how he exported the books from Egypt: The director of the Alexandria customs office was a close friend and often a houseguest in Cairo. Phoqué would pay him to clear the material through customs for export to Cyprus, where Phoqué's family home is located.

Riyāḍ reported that next in the sequence of buyers after Phoqué came ʿAzīz Suryāl, who at the time in question lived in the high-class Cairo suburb of Maadi. Riyāḍ has reported this relationship as follows:

ʿAzīz Suryāl heard of Riyāḍ having ancient books, and sent a messenger to him to come to visit him. On that first visit ʿAzīz Suryāl photographed the books Riyāḍ had brought but then returned the books, calling upon him to bring others. Actually Riyāḍ visited ʿAzīz Suryāl several times, bringing a few books each time. But each time ʿAzīz Suryāl would say that this was not what he wanted, but when he would find what he wanted, he would buy it. ʿAzīz Suryāl continued to make a photographic record of the books he had seen but not purchased, with a number on each photograph. On occasion Riyāḍ was accompanied by Fatḥallāh Daʾūd and Mūsā Fikrī, although they had nothing to do with the books—a view already suspected of being tendentious. ʿAzīz Suryāl showed Riyāḍ a book in his library that referred to Fāw Qiblī and told him this was the provenience of the books.

ʿAzīz Suryāl kept one book he said was the best of all the books. It had a picture of a soldier holding in his left hand the head of a crowned king and in his right hand a knife or sword. He was looking downward. On his heels were spurs and under each foot a gazelle. It was like St. George and the dragon. Beneath the picture was half a page of writing. The book consisted of about one hundred papyrus leaves, with a thick papyrus cover. Though small in dimensions, estimated at about 17 by

10 centimeters, it was very thick. ʿAzīz Suryāl offered £E 1,000 for the book. Riyāḍ asked for more. ʿAzīz Suryāl said he did not at the time have much money, but he would take the books to America and sell them there. On his return, he would give Riyāḍ seventy percent of what he received and keep only thirty percent for himself. He swore on the Bible by "my Jesus" that he was honest and could be believed. Riyāḍ recalls the date as around 1955. ʿAzīz Suryāl asked Riyāḍ to give him a supply of the beans (*ful*) that are the staple of the Egyptian peasants' menu to take to America. When Riyāḍ delivered the book, he also brought him twenty kilograms of *ful* and twenty kilograms of *az* (small peas). But ʿAzīz Suryāl did not return from America to pay him.

Once, after Riyāḍ had gone to ʿAzīz Suryāl's villa in Maadi accompanied by Fatḥallāh Daʾūd and Mūsā Fikrī, ʿAziz Suryāl took them back to Riyāḍ's residence in Heliopolis in his car. The police stopped all traffic for an official motorcade of dignitaries. But the automobile of ʿAzīz Suryāl was permitted to pass through, since it had a flag flying on the hood to indicate his status. Riyāḍ thus recalls ʿAzīz Suryāl and his wife as important persons in the eyes of the government.

Reports of ʿAzīz Suryāl acquiring Dishnā papers have come from all sides. Rāghib Andarāwus "al-Qiss" ʿAbd al-Sayyid, who had sold Nag Hammadi Codex III to the Coptic Museum, noticed in the Coptic church of Fāw Qiblī a former pupil, Misakin Andarāwus, and interviewed him concerning the Dishnā papers.[9] Misakin Andarāwus reported that a person in Maadi, who had been in America, obtained some of the books. Saʿīd Diryās Ḥabashī reported that ʿAzīz Suryāl, a professor of history who had lived in Maadi but was now in America, had bought two of the Dishnā books from Riyāḍ in Cairo.[10] He later reported having heard that ʿAzīz Suryāl took all the books out of Egypt. Mūsā Fikrī also reported that he knew of ʿAzīz Suryāl, who is now in America,[11] obtaining one roll

9. Interviewed in Claremont, California, in November 1978.

10. Interviewed in his home at Qina on December 23, 1976.

11. ʿAtīyah, *History of Eastern Christianity*, 120:

> The first demonstration of a spontaneous approach toward the Christian West took place when the Copts decided to send a delegation of three members to represent the Coptic Church officially in the World Council of Churches held at Evanston, Illinois, in the summer of 1954.

ʿAtīyah's footnote 1 on p. 120 lists the three delegates, the third being designated simply as "the writer of these pages."

not from Fatḥallāh Daʾūd but perhaps from Riyāḍ. The son of the deceased antiquities dealer Tawfīq Saʿd, Émile Saʿd, "Bijoutier Antiquaire" according to his card, proprietor of the jewelry shop Tewfik Saad et Fils, 19 Rue de France, Alexandria, reported to me in his sumptuous home that Dr. ʿAzīz Suryāl, identified as a Copt now in America, had bought two of the Dishnā books from his father, who had sold all six of the Dishnā books.

Fatḥallāh Daʾūd has on two occasions confirmed that ʿAzīz Suryāl had acquired a book, though the details vary in the two narrations. On January 4, 1980, he reported that he had witnessed Riyāḍ sell ʿAzīz Suryāl one papyrus book with the picture of a man with a bow and arrow. (Nashi Riyāḍ also remembered the illumination as portraying an archer with drawn bow and arrow on a chariot.) On the facing page was another picture, which, however, was very mutilated. After the transaction, ʿAzīz Suryāl took them all to church in his car. On an earlier occasion, Fatḥallāh Daʾūd had reported what may be an alternate version of the same event: Riyāḍ took Fatḥallāh Daʾūd to church at Mar Jirjis at Gizeh. Riyāḍ saw ʿAzīz Suryāl in church and pointed him out to Fatḥallāh Daʾūd as the person to whom Riyāḍ had sold a book. After church, ʿAzīz Suryāl took them to his home for coffee. Riyāḍ told Fatḥallāh Daʾūd not to tell anyone that ʿAzīz Suryāl had acquired a book.

ʿAzīz Suryāl ʿAtīyah, Distinguished Professor of History at the University of Utah, has a rather divergent version of these events. The most prominent difference is that he did not actually acquire any of the books. His address book still lists together the names of Fatḥallāh Daʾūd, Riyāḍ Jirjis, and Mūsā Fikrī. But he never met the latter two—their names had merely been given to him by Fatḥallāh Daʾūd. Fatḥallāh Daʾūd had come to his home in Maadi some time between 1951 and 1954. This timing was reconstructed in view of the fact that ʿAtīyah was in Evanston at the second meeting of the World Council of Churches in the summer of 1954, returned to Maadi for the winter of 1954–1955, was on the beach at Alexandria in the summer of 1955, and left permanently for America in September 1955. Fatḥallāh Daʾūd brought two books, one on papyrus, the other (the book of Proverbs) on parchment. He left them with Professor ʿAtīyah and then returned later the same day or the next evening, accompanied by Tawfīq Saʿd, retrieved the books and disappeared.

Zakī Ghālī, antiquities dealer of Luxor, had been the first to acquire a book from Dishnā, sold to him by Jirjis Ṣubḥī Qustandi (see above). Zakī Ghālī followed up this lead: He visited Riyāḍ as a houseguest at Dishnā again and again over a two year period, at times for as long as a week, acquiring a few books at a time. He acquired, in all, ten books for £E 5,000 or £E 6,000, some small, some large, which he sold to Phoqué, in the presence of Riyāḍ, for a profit of £E 12,000.

Zakī Basṭā, the antiquities dealer of Qinā who sold Nag Hammadi Codices II and VII to Tano, has reported that Riyāḍ, accompanied by Pilatus, first went to Cairo, then to the Graeco-Roman Museum in Alexandria, which refused to buy any of their books and instead sent them to Tawfīq Saʿd. Riyāḍ recalls selling three books to Tawfīq Saʿd in Alexandria for £E 3,000 plus a ring, which he sold for £E 500. In the process, he visited Alexandria three or four times, and each time Tawfīq Saʿd spent lots of money entertaining him. Fatḥallāh Daʾūd has reported that he himself never met Tawfīq Saʿd (but see above), though Riyāḍ had told him that he had gone to Alexandria and had sold books to Tawfīq Saʿd.

On one occasion, Zakī Ghālī and Tawfīq Saʿd came together to Dishnā, but not finding Riyāḍ there, they went on to Cairo, where they found him and bought three books for £E 3,000. They were accompanied by a Spaniard who was dressed in black with a little beard and who looked like a priest. This was the last sale, in about 1956, before the proceedings at the appellate court were completed.

Riyāḍ showed a single leaf, in about 1956, to Muḥammad Farag al-Shir of the firm Sons of Farag el Chaer, Antiquity Dealer, Licence No. 116, adjoining the shop of Tano at 53 Gamhouria Street. Muḥammad Farag al Shir brought in a Swiss professor of languages at Cairo University who earned as much as £E 700 a month, to whom Muḥammad Farag al-Shir was indebted for having taken his sick son to Switzerland for treatment. When asked by Muḥammad Farag al-Shir what he could do in return, the Swiss had said he would like a good antique. He paid £E 500 to 700 for the one leaf but said he wanted a book. If Riyāḍ would bring a book for him to Muḥammad Farag al-Shir, he would go to Switzerland and bring back £E 15,000, £E 20,000, or whatever was needed to pay for it. But Riyāḍ had no books left. Riyāḍ recalls having sold some books the first year after the discovery, but then suspending sales for two years due to police surveillance, then selling the rest in 1955.

Various European embassies sent representatives to Riyāḍ to get books, but he had to reply that all were gone. The director for antiquities stationed at Luxor had him come to Luxor and proposed they together sell books and share the profit, but he replied there were no books to sell.

THE DISHNĀ PAPERS AND THE BODMER PAPYRI

Although the two stories (the discoveries of the Bodmer Papyri and the discovery of the Dishnā papers) are not interdependent—one having been worked out exclusively on the basis of interviews in Egypt, the other then belatedly derived from publications and European scholars such as Father Louis Doutreleau—traits relating them to each other have already been mentioned in passing. The first impression from the publications is that hardly anything is known other than inconclusive speculation based on internal evidence. Only as the investigation was far advanced did it become apparent that both at the Bibliothèque Bodmer and at the Chester Beatty Library more was known that the publications would lead one to expect, and this belated information only provided striking confirmation of what had already been established from the interviews in Egypt.

It is the Chester Beatty Library that has made its registry and correspondence available, from which the most striking confirmation has been derived. Chester Beatty Ac. 1389 (Joshua) clearly comes from the same discovery as do the Bodmer Papyri, since it is part of P. Bodmer XXI. In the registry at the Chester Beatty Library titled "Chester Beatty Library Acquisitions from April 1956" there is the annotation at 1389: "Bought from Phocion J. Tano, 53 Sharia Ibrahim Pasha, Cairo, Summer 1956 with acquisition 1390 and two boxes of loose leaves. £ 835." At acquisition 1390 (a school exercise in Greek and part of the Gospel of John in Sub-Achmimic of the fourth century) a typed paper is stapled in the registry that reports: "Small village Deshna just after Naghi Hamadi about 2 hours before Luxor by train. Probably from a library of a monastery. Found in a jar in a cemetery."

Rather than one of the typed notes from A. F. Shore, this seems to be a more crude note, probably from Tano himself. In any case, he would be the ultimate source of this information. This notice is as explicit as one could hope to find by way of confirmation that the remains of this unpublished papyrus codex is one of the "Dishnā papers," which would by implication apply to the other things that were part of the same acquisition, namely part of one of the Bodmer Papyri and two boxes of loose leaves—a tantalizing allusion to hard-to-identify items. It is thus independent confirmation of the reports to the same effect from Geneva, that is to say, an independent report of Tano's information. Unfortunately, the item in the registry was located first on January 19, 1984, when the piecing together of the story was for all practical purposes complete. Indicative of the neglect of such a registry—which in the case of the Nag Hammadi Codices delayed for a generation the unravelling of that story—is the fact that A. F. Shore, in supporting the then-current assumption of Panopolis (Achmim) as the provenience, appealed (in addition to Sub-Achmimic traits in the Sahidic of the text he was publishing, part of P. Bodmer XXI) to the Gospel of John in Sub-Achmimic (Lycopolitan, around Lycopolis = Assiut), precisely the one codex identified in the registry as from Dishnā, as "acquired at the same time."

There are traits shared between reports given in Egypt about the Dishnā papers and those given in Europe and America about the Bodmer Papyri that make it evident that both reports have to do with the same material. The most obvious instance is the three photographs provided by the antiquities dealer of Alexandria of Dishnā papers his father had sold. For they have been identified as from P. Bodmer XXIV (Psalms, LXX, identified by Albert Pietersma) and P. Bodmer XL (the Song of Songs, identified by Marvin Meyer, in Sahidic). But once Albert Pietersma had identified the one photograph as P. Bodmer XXIV, and Hans Quecke had verified the conjecture that the other two are from the unpublished manuscript in the Bibliothèque Bodmer, still other correlations have confirmed this discovery. The timing fits rather well. The discovery was made at the end of 1952, but the legal proceedings, the house arrest, the use of a trusted friend as a middleman, and the clandestine trips to Cairo all point to a considerably longer extension of the marketing than, for example, in the case of the Nag Hammadi Codices, all of which had reached the Cairo market within a year. Thus, the bulk of the acquisitions from 1955 to 1958 is not surprising, and in terms of earliest date, P. Bodmer I published in 1954 is not excluded. The two rolls of the *Iliad* (one intact enough to seem to be a roll, the other more a group of fragments hardly identified as a separate roll), like the other fragments of Homer (P. Bodmer L), could fit well Riyāḍ's report of some three or four rolls, some of which was burnt. The balled-up codex

P. Bodmer XXII = Mississippi Coptic Codex II corresponds to the balled-up book described by Riyāḍ. The general description provided by Riyāḍ and others fits rather well. There were some rolls, some codices, some in papyrus, some in parchment, some in small letters (Greek), some in large (Coptic), the quantity was some thirty books, plus some ten small rolls the size of one's finger.

—5—

The Pachomian Library

ANCIENT LIBRARIES[1]

Although the manuscript holdings of the libraries of pre-Christian antiquity and of medieval monasteries are familiar as major repositories of the heritage of antiquity, knowledge about early Christian monastic libraries is scanty. The Essene monastery at the Wadi Qumran has shown for Judaism what may be involved. The Nag Hammadi codices indicate that gnostic libraries must have existed. The library at the Monastery of Saint John the Theologian on Patmos has continued to modern times, and early catalogues have survived to indicate what a collection of early medieval times could involve. Material accessible to the Venerable Bede also suggests what a monk had available in the early eighth century in England. The monastery of Sankt Gallen in Switzerland became an important repository of books from the ninth century that has survived. The library of the White Monastery of Sohag founded by Shenoute became the major repository of Coptic materials from Upper Egypt. But the bulk of this very large repository is much later, and one may assume (as in the case of the monastery on Patmos) that many of the books in the oldest collection have not survived. Thus, a catalogue fixing the

1. See Irigoin, "Les manuscrits grecs 1931–60"; and Roberts, "Two Oxford Papyri."

collection at a given time may be more relevant as a basis of comparison than the modern survivors of an ancient library.

Perhaps the most relevant comparison in this regard is provided by a splinter of limestone covered with a monastery catalogue discovered in 1888 by Urbaine Bouriant.[2] Though the dealer said he had acquired it at Gournah, Bouriant was sure it came from Qous, whose ruins were being exploited without governmental control at the time. The maximal dimensions of the ostracon are 24 by 18 cm, and it is inscribed on both sides, with two columns on the recto and one on the verso. After an appeal for prayer for the peace of the church (in Greek), there follows the title: "[Catal]ogue of the Holy Books of the Place [i.e., Monastery] of Apa Helias of Tp. . . ." The location of a monastery with this name is not known, but the inclusion of two catechisms of Kos suggests that region. The diocese of Kos extended downstream as far as Chenoboskia. A mutilated date when some books were restored may be 452, which would fit with the date of the death of Shenoute in 451, whose eulogy is included among works acquired later than this restoration, leading Bouriant to propose the last half of the fifth century as the earliest date for the ostracon. W. C. Crum dates it to the sixth or seventh century in view of the lack of a reference to the life of Pesenthius of Kuft, bishop from 601–631, during whose lifetime the ostracon must have been written.[3]

Although the books themselves are unfortunately no longer extant (so far as we know), the catalogue has the advantage over largely extant collections such as that of the White Monastery, in that the White Monastery collection has a preponderant overlay from later centuries and is so scattered among various repositories as to be discussable only after a laborious process of hypothetical reconstitution, to which Stephen Emmel has devoted himself. The catalogue of the monastery of Apa Helias is divided into two parts, in that items 59–80 are books that came into the monastery after the others. Thus, it may be relevant to compare the older and the newer accessions. Within the older collection of fifty-eight books, forty-three are on papyrus, which is subdivided into "old papyrus" (six books), "papyrus" (twenty-five books) and "new [or "cheap"] papyrus" (twelve books). Thirteen documents are on parchment, and for two documents the material is not specified. Among the

2. Bouriant, "Notes de voyage 1," 131–38.

3. Winlock and Crum, *Monastery of Epiphanius*, Vol. 1, *The Archaeological Material.*

twenty-two newer acquisitions, the distribution is as follows: "old papyrus" (two books), "papyrus" (eleven books) "new [or "cheap"] papyrus" (five books), and "parchment" (two books), with two books unspecified. The relative rarity of "old papyrus" may indeed suggest the term is meant chronologically. The quantity of parchment codices declines from almost a fourth to an eleventh, which runs counter to the usual trend for parchment gradually to replace papyrus. Within the older acquisitions there is a distinction of twenty-four that have been restored in 451(?). Here the distribution is two old papyrus documents, eleven papyrus books, nine new (or cheap) papyrus books, and one parchment book, with two unspecified. Here one may note that three-fourths of those on "new" (or "cheap") papyrus were restored, compared to almost none of the parchment books. Only a third of the "old papyrus" is restored, though one of the unspecified items among those restored was written "in an old book."

The catalogue of the monastery of Apa Helias reports that the bulk of the older segment that was not restored consisted mostly of books of the Bible (in basically canonical order). No biblical book was restored, and in the newer collection only three are biblical books. In the older part there are three Pachomian books; in the older part there are four books by Shenoute, in the newer part a eulogy over him. There is in the newer part a book of medicine, the only secular work in the library. There are no titles that suggest gnostic contents.

THE PACHOMIAN LETTERS

Pachomius (died 346) wrote a number of letters. The only language in which he was capable of writing with any ease was Coptic.[4] And there are quotations of these letters in Coptic documents of one of his first successors, Horsesios, and in the writing of the next great monastic founder, Shenoute of the White Monastery of Sohag.[5] Thus, the existence of Coptic letters written by Pachomius seems certain. They must have been translated into Greek during the fourth century. After all, there was at the headquarters monastery at Phbow a Greek House where those who could not speak Coptic were grouped together under

4. Quecke, "Die Briefe Pachoms," 101–2 n. 30; Dummer, "Zum Problem der sprachlichen Verständigung," 48–49.

5. Quecke, *Briefe*, 11–13, 44–52.

a house-father, Theodore, from Alexandria, to translate. Then Jerome produced a Latin translation. In his preface he mentions that "they were [already] translated from Egyptian [i.e., Coptic] into Greek."[6] Jerome also reports that this was the first writing he had been able to get back to, after the death of Paula, a Roman lady of high patrician standing who had accompanied him from Rome to found with him a cloister in Bethlehem, and who died January 26, 404. Hence, this Latin translation is usually dated to 404, or since Jerome reports his inactivity was "long," perhaps 405. These letters, eleven in number (actually thirteen, since 9 and 11 are actually two letters each, distinguished as 9a/9b and 11a/11b), are in a sense disappointing in that generally they have little to say, and in fact contain some passages in a "mystic tongue" that is still not deciphered.

Quecke refers to the Pachomian material: "Only in the most recent time have a few complete letters cropped up also in Coptic and Greek."[7] The possibility of further material becoming available is called "not at all excluded."[8] "It is among the odd accidents that in a very short temporal distance from each other various different fragments of the Coptic text of the letters and a manuscript with the Greek text have emerged."[9]

Letters of Pachomius in Sahidic were early collected and translated into Greek. The Greek was translated into Latin in 404 by Jerome in Bethlehem.[10] Apart from a few quotations in other Coptic monastic texts,[11] the Coptic and Greek texts of Pachomius's letters have been completely lost. But subsequent to the discovery of the Dishnā papers, they have emerged in the same places where the Dishnā papers are known to have emerged. This sudden emergence of the Coptic and Greek texts in just these collections, after missing for a millennium and a half, is such a remarkable coincidence as hardly to be fortuitous. Rather, it seems

6. Ibid., 66, and n. 2.

7 Quecke, "Briefe Pachoms in koptischer Sprache," 655–56.

8. Quecke, *Briefe*, 63.

9. Ibid., 9.

10. Quecke, "Brief Pachoms in koptischer Sprache," 655; Boon, *Pachomania Latina*, lvi.

11. References are given in: Quecke, "Ein neues Fragment," 66, n. 2; Quecke, *Briefe*, 44–52. See also Quecke, "Anhang: Die koptischen Fragmente und Zitate der Pachombriefe," in *Briefe*, 111–18.

probable, on the face of it, that they are of the same provenience,[12] namely that of the Bodmer Papyri that have emerged at the same place in the same period. This in turn would suggest that the provenience of the Bodmer Papyri = Dishnā papers is ultimately Pachomian.

A third ingredient in the story of the Bodmer Papyri is the emergence, in the three main repositories of Bodmer Papyri, of original materials of the Pachomian monastic order. This itself is circumstantial evidence that these Pachomian materials may be part of the "Bodmer Papyri" = "Dishnā papers," and other indications will tend to substantiate this impression. The idea is not wholly new. Already in 1956, Victor Martin had suggested that the provenience might be a third-century monastery (sic!), but this suggestion was not pursued.[13] Odile Bongard also reported a monastic provenience at Dishnā.

Riyād Girgis Fām is from Dishnā, but his mother came from Fāw Qiblī. He reported (December 13, 1980) a legend of Fāw Qiblī to the effect that the monastery of Fāw Qiblī formerly had many monks. The ruler of that time was an idolater, but his wife and son were Christians. The ruler told his son to take soldiers and destroy the monastery. But the son, being a Christian, did not carry out the order. Instead he warned the monks of his father's intention. So the monks hid the books of the monastery at the mountain for safekeeping before the ruler came and destroyed the monastery. He reports that the legend was confirmed to him as true by ʿAzīz Suryāl, who no doubt had in mind the Pachomian monastery of Phbow, modern Fāw Qiblī.

This could be a reference to Justinian and his wife Theodora, whose Monophysite leanings were both notorious and very effective. They did not have a son, and hence to this extent the report would be garbled. But

12. Quecke has assessed the situation in a letter of 29 viii 1990 as follows:

> It seems to me logical to assume that the various Pachomiana of the Chester Beatty Library and P. Bodmer 39 come from the same *discovery*. For one thing it would be highly unusual if the various Pachomiana of the Chester Beatty Library should not come from one discovery, but only accidentally came together in the Chester Beatty Library, even though Chester Beatty had no special interest in Pachomiana. In that it is now proven by P. Bodmer 21 that material of the same provenience landed in the Bodmer Library and the Chester Beatty Library, the inference is close at hand that also the Pachomian material in both libraries is of the same provenience.

13. *Papyrus Bodmer* II.

in other regards, the collapse of the monastery in connection with the Chalcedonian/Monophysite struggle seems probable.

Riyād reported there were some ten small rolls the size of his finger that Tano bought from him for £E 100 each, which he distinguished in size and value from the few large rolls. Riyād said Tano told him they were letters. Some of them may be identified with some of the material under consideration here. P. Bodmer I (*Iliad*, book 5) was a roll 31 cm high, of which both top and bottom margins are in part intact, so that Riyād would have known it as a roll 31 cm long. He spoke of some four rolls of about a quarter of a meter long. It is over against this dimension that he would have spoken of the ten small rolls the length of a finger.[14]

Three items have appeared that are strikingly similar to one another and to Riyād's rule of thumb. One of them is directly linked to the material of the shared provenience, in that it is at one of the major repositories (the Chester Beatty Library) and is a Pachomian text. The other two are less obviously related to the shared provenience. But since one is another copy of the same Pachomian text, and since the other consists of Psalms 76–77 in Coptic, and since both are dated to the appropriate time period, the physical similarity of the three items may be taken seriously as indicative of a shared provenience. One can calculate the approximate size when rolled, though no measurements or photographs in that condition seem to have survived.

Chester Beatty Ac. 1486, Theodore's Letter 2 on the annual remission of debts in *rotuli* form, that is to say, with the lines parallel to the narrow edges of the roll, to be read with the roll hanging down rather than opened from side to side. It is on parchment, is 57 cm high and of fluctuating width, 13.7 cm at the top, narrowing to 8.8 cm between lines 23 and 24 (14 cm from the top), widening then toward the bottom to as much as 13.7 cm eight lines from the bottom (9.7 cm from the bottom), with a maximum width of 15.5 cm.[15] Since the left and right margins are relatively intact and yet present a waving rather than a straight edge of the beginning of the lines, the original piece of skin was itself of irregular shape. It was first folded the length of the text, at right angles to the lines, and then rolled.[16] This vertical fold, visible on plate 42 in Quecke's

14. *Papyrus Bodmer* I, 18.

15. Quecke, "Ein Brief von einem Nachfolger," 427.

16. Ibid., 427, n. 1 remarks that this is the same as the Yale Psalms (Yale 1779).

edition and on the original, becomes a split toward the bottom. At line 1, this fold is 8 cm from the left edge, 5.3 cm from the right; at line 55, it is 8 cm from the left edge, 7.5 cm from the right; at line 83, it is 7.5 cm from the left edge, 5.5 cm from the right. This large sheet when folded and rolled would hence have a maximum length of no more than 8 cm and a width or diameter of the flattened roll of about the same.

Other Pachomian materials have also emerged at two of these same locations. The Letter 2, on the annual remission of debts (on parchment in *rotuli* form of the sixth century at the Chester Beatty Library [Ms. Ac. 1486]), from Pachomius's understudy and successor, Theodore, was published in 1975.[17] It is 57 cm high and of fluctuating width. There is a reference to the annual New Year's reunion just prior to the first of Masore (in August) at Phbow ("Pba[u]") on line 59 (the alpha is uncertain); there is reference to Pachomius (not by name) on lines 49–53, 81–84.

A second copy from a private German collection published in 1981 is quite similar. It is in Sahidic on parchment in *rotuli* form, of the fifth century. The reference to Phbow ("Pbau") is on line 57, the allusion to Pachomius on lines 47–50, 51, and on lines 78–81. Both texts share a scribal trait, a circumflex over a one-vowel qualitative.[18] There are only eleven textual variants between the two copies. The somewhat tattered parchment is of such irregular shape as to suggest to its editor that it came from an animal's leg: 52 cm tall and of varying breadth, 9.4 cm at line 29, to 16.6 cm at line 60.[19] There is a fold from top to bottom for the length of the sheet, from 8 cm (at line 29) to 9 cm (at line 60) from the left edge.[20] This would indicate that the sheet when folded would have measured no more than 9 cm wide. There are major breaks indicating folds at 13.6, 26.5 and 39.5 cm from the top, with minor breaks at 6.5, 20.2 and 33 cm from the top.[21] The presence of the greatest distance between folds at the top (7.1 cm between 6.5 and 13.6 cm from the top) would tend to indicate the roll was rolled from bottom to top. This would suggest that after having been folded down the middle, it was

17. Veilleux. *Pachomian Koinonia* 3:6–7.

18. Quecke, "Eine Handvoll," 221.

19. Krause, "Erlassbrief," 233, n. 4.

20. Ibid., 233 n. 5.

21. Ibid., 233 n. 6.

then rolled, with the roll subsequently pressed into folds that broke more on one side than on the other. The resultant folded roll would be some seven centimeters wide. Thus, the final dimensions would have been 9 by 7 cm.[22] Thus, the dimensions of these two copies of the same text are almost identical, both when unrolled (the narrow waist in each may be due to the knee of an animal) and when rolled and flattened. Thus, although the repository of this roll cannot on other grounds be identified as a place where items from the shared provenience are located, the striking three similarities of these two rolls, not only in such common traits as being both parchment Sahidic scrolls of the fifth [?] century, but in such uncommon traits as the *rotuli* form, the leg-like contours, and the text of Theodore's otherwise unattested [?] Letter 2, whose identity according to the editor [August 25, 1984] may not be divulged, make it very probable that these twins both come from the shared provenience. Both fit admirably Riyād's characterization of some ten rolls that Tano told him were letters of finger length.

The third text in *rotuli* form of similar dimensions is P. Yale Inv. 1779, containing Psalms 76–77 (LXX) in Sahidic on papyrus. It has been dated "to the fourth or the early fifth century A.D."[23]

P. Yale Inv. 1779 is a group of twenty-nine fragments that when placed together form a long sheet measuring 26 by 67 cm. This sheet was folded once vertically at its center, and then twenty-two times horizontally. As the height of the folds decreases steadily from 4 cm at the top to 2 cm at the bottom, the horizontal folding must have commenced at the bottom—the standard practice in antiquity. Some creases have developed into considerable breaks—especially the uppermost ones, as this was the outer part of the folded papyrus and exposed to tear and wear; the three upper left-hand folds have been entirely lost.[24]

Thus, when rolled and flattened, this roll would have been 4 cm wide and some 13.7 cm long, to judge by measurements made on the full-size facsimile in the catalogue, page 28. Though longer than a finger, it may well have been part of a group distinguished from long rolls over 30 cm in length.

22. Krause, "Erlassbrief," n. 8 refers to 1486 and Yale 1779 as of similar size. He also refers to Pachomian letters at Cologne, in Quecke, "Eine Handvoll," 221 and n. 7.

23. Vergote and Parássoglou, "Les Psaumes 76 et 77," 532. Petersen, *Collection,* 41, had already said fourth to fifth century

24. Vergote and Parássoglou, "Les Psaumes 76 et 77," 531.

A third parchment of similar dimensions, though not explicitly Pachomian, was published in facsimile in a book catalogue of circa 1962 and edited in 1974. It is 67 cm high, 26 cm broad. It contains Psalms 76–77 (LXX) in Sahidic. The top is partly missing. The second psalm is completed on the back. Is is in *rotuli* form. It was folded down the middle from top to bottom as much as 13.5 cm from the left edge and then rolled. It was then flattened, causing breaks about every three centimeters. Thus, its appearance would be about 13.5 by 3 cm.[25]

These three Pachomian rolls and the psalms roll, all of approximately the same size,[26] may well be the small rolls Riyāḍ referred to as being the length of his finger, which he sold to Tano for £E 100 each.

Two manuscripts in Cologne with letters of Pachomius have been brought into this comparison by Martin Krause, who, after mentioning them as "parchments of similar size," notes: "compare also the Cologne Pachomius letters."[27] Two parchment sheets, Pap. Colon. Copt. 1 (3287; Pachomius's Letters 10–11) and 2 (3286; Pachomius's Letter 8) measure 50 by 10 cm, and 31 by 11 cm, "and evidently do not come from a codex,"[28] since they are written only on one side (though the first half of Letter 10 is also copied on the back). They are "parchment pieces that perhaps were hardly fit for book production."[29] Kropp says of the larger piece:[30]

> This parchment is very light, well preserved, only damaged on the edges by burning. Breaks due to folding are not present. Thus it may have contributed to its good conservation that the piece was rolled up, along the length, and thus only the edges could be damaged.
>
> The dimensions of the piece are unusual, 10 by 50 cm. Thus it presents itself as trash, and as we shall see its use also correspondents to this . . .
>
> The unusual dimensions of the parchment confirm that this piece was trash, left over from normal parchment leaves. Furthermore the piece is full of holes. The scribe took this into

25. Petersen, *Collection of Papyri*. The frontispiece and the foldout p. 28 present the facsimile; Petersen's description is on p. 29. Cf. Vergote and Parássogou.

26. Krause, "Erlassbrief," 220.

27. Ibid., 220; 223, n. 8.

28. Quecke, "Briefe Pachoms in koptischer Sprache," 656.

29. Ibid., 657.

30. Kropp, "Ein Märchen als Schreibübung," 69, 79.

> consideration. The piece did not come into consideration for clean work, it was at most still usable for practise in penmanship.

Pap. Colon. Copt. 2, Inv. Nr. 3286, is described as follows:[31]

> That here a characteristic side of Coptic monastic life is touched results also from the narrow folding of the leaf, which thus could be carried conveniently by its owner in the pocket.

Its dimensions are 11 by 31 cm. Whether it was first folded down the center of the column before being rolled and pressed flat is not stated, nor is it evident from Plate 3, although the horizontal folds as close together as every other line can in some cases be discerned. Quecke points out that the two leaves "can never have formed with each other or with other leaves a manuscript." Yet "both leaves were in all probability inscribed by one and the same hand."[32]

The Cologne inventory number 3288 (published in P. Köln 4, Nr. 174) contains part of Pachomius's Letter 7. It may well have been one of the small rolls. Whereas the bulk of the Bodmer Papyri (I–XXVI) were published between 1954 and 1969, the Pachomian material has come to light only in the 1970s. Actually, the first part to be published appeared in 1968 but was not yet recognized as Pachomian. It had been acquired in 1962–63 by the Papyrus Collection of the University of Cologne for its Institut für Altertumskunde. It was correctly identified by Hans Quecke in 1972 (the identification was published in 1973 in *Zetesis* q.v.). It includes Pachomius's Letters 8, 10, and 11a in Coptic on two parchment leaves of the fifth or sixth centuries, written by the same scribe.[33] The two leaves are not from a codex, since written only on one side, except for number 1, which bears on the (usually uninscribed) hair side the first half of Letter 10, which the flesh side also begins, apparently as a student's first effort broken off uncompleted. "They never could have formed a manuscript with each other or with other leaves."[34] Quecke conjectures that the whole collection of Pachomios's letters was copied on such loose leaves by the scribe.[35] According to Manfred Weber of the

31. Ibid., 82.

32. Quecke, "Die Briefe Pachoms," 97, but according to n. 7 also in his review, *Or* 38 (1969) 498. In the note, he says Manfred Weber confirmed this view in a letter.

33. Quecke, "Briefe Pachoms in koptischer Sprache," 656.

34. Quecke, "Die Briefe Pachoms," 97.

35. Quecke, "Briefe Pachoms in koptischer Sprache," 657.

Cologne collection, both were acquired from the same dealer[36] (Inv. Nr. 3286 = Pap. Colon. Copt. 2 with Letter 8, 31 by 11 cm, and 3287 = Pap. Colon. Copt. 1 with Letters 10 and 11a, 50 by 10 cm).[37] It was folded.[38] A still further manuscript apparently from the same find, Cologne inventory number 3288, contains part of Pachomius' Letter 7 in Greek.[39]

Chester Beatty Ac. 1494 is another papyrus roll, this time not in *rotuli* form, but in the usual form, with three columns. Yet, it is not in the usual format of columns of reasonable and standard width but has columns of irregular width up to 37 cm in the second column, whereas the column to the left is 28.5 to 30 cm wide and that to the right 17.5 cm. It is of the fifth century A.D. in Sahidic,[40] with Horsiesios's Letter 3. The beginning of the first column is damaged, indicating the roll was rolled from right to left, leaving the left edge exposed to wear and tear. It is 89.5 cm long, 28.7 cm tall. There are horizontal breaks at 10.5 and 23 cm from the top, indicating it was folded twice, and then vertical breaks from 3 cm on the right edge to 5 cm near the left edge, confirming that it was then rolled from right to left and the roll pressed flat, creating creases and ultimately breaks. The folded roll would hence measure some 12.5 by 5 cm.

Chester Beatty Ac. 1495 is a still third papyrus roll in five columns in Sahidic, Horsiesios's Letter 4. It is 117 cm by 29 cm. If there was a first fold, after which the roll was rolled, the length of the roll when rolled would be 16 cm. Orlandi-Cavallo date to the sixth century.

Two letters from Horsiesios (Pachomius's ineffectual successor until Theodore stepped in to assist him), Letters 3 and 4 (Chester Beatty Library Ac. 1494–1495), have also been identified at the Chester Beatty Library in 1972, on papyrus.[41] Letter 4 refers to Pachomius without naming him, and by name to his successors Petronios and Theodore. Ac. 1494 is 47 cm broad, about 28 cm high. There are three columns.

36. Ibid., 656, n. 11.

37. Quecke, *Die Briefe Pachoms*, 41–42. Cf. also Quecke, "Briefe Pachoms in koptischer Sprache," 657–58; Hermann, "Homilie in Sahidischem Dialekt," 82–85; Kropp, "Ein Märchen als Schreibübung," 69–81; Veilleux, *Pachomonian Koinonia* 3:3–4.

38. Krause, "Erlassbrief," 233, n. 8, refers to Quecke "Eine Handvoll," 221 and n. 7

39. Roemer's letter; published in P. Köln 4, Nr. 174.

40. Shore, *Joshua I–VI*, assigns it to the fifth century; Orlandi places it in the seventh century.

41. Typescript by Orlandi in Italian; Veilleux, *Pachomian Koinonia*, 3:8.

The verso is uninscribed except for the title. It has been assigned to the seventh century. Ac. 1495 is 108 cm broad, about 29 cm high, in five columns. It has been assigned to the sixth century.[42]

Chester Beatty W. 145, =129 (Quecke) a parchment roll of Pachomius's letters in Greek in *rotuli* form, 90.5 cm tall (originally ca. 102 cm), by 15.9 cm wide, narrowing to 14 cm toward the bottom. In addition to circa ten centimeters missing at the bottom, a few centimeters are lost on the right edge. Most of the text is on the front, but the end of the text covers almost a third of the back. The roll is composed of five sheets sewn rather crudely together. The text was rolled from the beginning—the top—as can be inferred from the damage at the end of the text that is on the front (that is to say, at the bottom), and from the numerous folds parallel to the lines at the beginning or top, where the rolling was obviously tighter; there are no folds further down the roll.[43] The roll is not glassed (except for the bottom—last of the five sheets at the bottom of the roll) and has not been flattened but retains its supple rounded condition and can be readily rolled and unrolled.

More of the Pachomian material is at the Chester Beatty Library. At about the same time that the identification of the Cologne text was announced, a Chester Beatty text (Manuscript W. 145) was also first made known (in 1972, the announcement published in 1974, and the text published in 1975): A fourth-century Greek (translation of a Coptic original) parchment roll in *rotuli* form (Chester Beatty Manuscript W. 145), containing Pachomius's Letters 1–3, 7, 10, and 11a.[44] This copy presumably did not contain all of Pachomius's letters, but Quecke is uncertain whether this means it is an excerpt from the already established complete collection, or whether it is an early form before the collection had become complete.[45] It is 90.5 cm (originally probably 102 cm) by 15.9 cm (narrowing to 14 cm toward the bottom). In addition to about 10 cm missing at the bottom, a few centimeters are lost on the right edge.

42. Orlandi, "Les manuscrits coptes de Dublin," 323–38, esp. 326, reports he will publish both.

43. Quecke, "Die Briefe Pachoms," 97–98, and n. 12; see also, Quecke, *Die Briefe*, 73–77.

44. The fourth-century date for this parchment is from Skeat, according to his letter of December 17, 1970, and from Quecke, *Die Briefe Pachoms*, 98, with n. 13 reporting Skeat.

45. Quecke, "Briefe Pachoms," 103.

Most of the text is on the front, but the end of the text covers less than a third of the back. The roll is composed of five sheets sewn rather crudely together. T. C. Skeat wrote a report on the roll on December 17, 1970, and the editor Hans Quecke saw it first at the end of 1971.[46] The text was rolled from the beginning, as can be inferred from the damage at the end of the text that is on the front and from the numerous folds at the beginning where the rolling was obviously tighter.[47]

P. Bodmer XXXIX, due to appear in 1984–85, was first identified as Pachomius's Letter 11b on parchment in Coptic by Tito Orlandi at the Bibliothèque Bodmer in 1975.[48]

Thus, one has a group of rolls that in distinction from the familiar scrolls of antiquity were, with one exception, folded before rolling, which hence are characterized by a shortness distinguishing them from the large rolls such as P. Bodmer I (in descending order of length): the papyrus roll Chester Beatty Ac. 1495, 16 cm; or the papyrus roll Chester Beatty Ac. 1494, 12.5 by 5 cm; the papyrus roll P. Yale Inv. 1779, 13.7 by 4 cm; or the two Cologne rolls probably no longer than 10 and 11 cm; and probably the third as well. These, together with the even smaller flattened parchment rolls Chester Beatty 1486, 8 cm; and that in a private German collection, 9 by 7 cm, might well represent the some ten small rolls Riyād described as finger-length in distinction from the larger rolls.

In 1974 four badly damaged but consecutive leaves of a sixth-century Coptic papyrus codex (Chester Beatty Glass Container No. 54) were published, containing Pachomius's Letters 11b, 10, 11a, a cryptogram, 9a and 9b (in that order). Since the last page is half empty, this may have been the end of the codex.[49]

Thus, there have been identified in the first half of the 1970s at Cologne, the Bibliothèque Bodmer, and the Chester Beatty Library (that is, in three of the places where Bodmer Papyri were acquired) seven manuscripts: one of Pachomian letters in Coptic on parchment in Cologne; one of Pachomian letters in Greek on parchment in *rotuli* form at Dublin; one of Pachomian letters in Coptic on papyrus in Dublin; one of Pachomian letters in Coptic on parchment at Geneva; one of

46. Quecke, *Die Briefe*, 73–86; Veilleux, *Pachomian Koinonia*, 3:4.

47. Quecke, "Briefe Pachoms," 97–98 and n. 12.

48. Veilleux, *Pachomian Koinonia*, 3:4.

49. Quecke, *Die Briefe*, 42–43. See also, Quecke, "Ein neues Fragment," 66–82.

Theodore's Letter 2, "On Remission," in Coptic in *rotuli* form at Dublin, two of Horsiesios's Letters 3–4 in Coptic on papyrus in Dublin. This is not a completely fortuitous collection in Pachomian terms. If one may assume that materials of Pachomius would automatically be included in an archive, then the selection of those of Theodore and Horsiesios are explainable as documents calling for the assembly at the end of the year, around the first of Mesore on remission (in the case of the letter of Theodore) and for the assembly at Easter (in the case of the letters of Horsiesios). The only previously known letter of Theodore was a call to the Easter assembly, and Pachomius's Letter 7, previously known in Jerome's Latin collection as well as in Greek, present in the Chester Beatty collection, is a call to the assembly at the end of the year, upon which the beginning of Theodore's call to this assembly is modeled. As a pastiche of biblical allusions, such letters do not lose their relevance after a specific occasion has passed but have permanent validity as models of piety.

DATING THE BURIAL

The bulk of the Bodmer Papyri is dated from the third to the fifth century, with the exception of the Coptic Pachomian materials of the Chester Beatty Library (dated to the sixth century). Apart from these exceptions and the Coptic Pachominan letters at Cologne (dated by Hans Quecke to the fifth century), hardly any of this material is actually dated firmly as late as the fifth century.[50] For the fifth century is cited in the *editiones principes* usually in the spectrum of fourth or fifth century.[51] In one of these cases, P. Bodmer VI, the editor has subsequently expressed a preference for the fourth century,[52] and in the case of the second, P. Bodmer XIX, he has narrowed his dating to the end of the Fourth Century.[53] In the case of the third, P. Bodmer XXII = Mississippi Coptic Codex II,

50. Kropp and Hermann, *Demotische und koptische Texte*, 81–82, date the hands to the fifth or sixth century. But Quecke, *Die Briefe*, 41, attributes the two sheets to the same hand and concludes: "The script is an uncial probably of the Fifth Century."

51. *Papyrus Bodmer* VI, 5; *Papyrus Bodmer* XIX, 5; *Papyrus Bodmer* XXII, 13.

52. Kasser, "Les dialects coptes," 81: "The manuscript [P. Bodmer VI] that attests [the Paleo-Theban dialect] is of the Fourth (perhaps the Fourth-Fifth) Century."

53. *Papyrus Bodmer* XIX, 8, n. 3: "Assuming that the copy was effected at the latest at the end of the Fourth Century . . ."

William H. Willis has preferred the fourth century.[54] To be sure, Martin Krause has contested the dating by A. F. Shore of Bodmer XXI = Chester Beatty 1389 to the first half of the fourth century,[55] preferring a fifth century date.[56] Yet the bases for such a late dating are derived from codicological considerations shown by E. G. Turner to be no longer valid.[57] Concerning one unpublished codex there is wide divergence in dating, which indicates the degree of subjectivity still inherent in the dating process. Mississippi Coptic Codex I (the Crosby Codex) was dated by William H. Willis to the third century, and by E. G. Turner to the third or fourth century. However Stuart George Hall has postulated "probably Sixth Century."[58] But experts to whom I have shown my photocopy, including Professor Tito Orlandi, suggest the sixth, or at earliest the fifth, century.

Similarly, Hans Quecke has dated a Coptic codex of Pachomius's letters (Chester Beatty Glass Container 54) and a Coptic letter of a successor to Pachomius at the Chester Beatty Library (Ms Ac. No. 1486), perhaps of the same provenience, to the sixth century.[59] He has also accepted the dating of the fifth or sixth century given to P. Colon. Copt. 1–2 by Kropp and Hermann. Furthermore, he has also dated Palau Ribes 181–182 of Barcelona to the fifth century.[60]

To be sure, the second repair of Papyrus Bodmer XIX is placed in the sixth century, but no reasons are given for this dating other than the need for sufficient time to elapse for the deterioration to have taken place, a factor which varies widely depending on the circumstances.[61]

54. Willis, "New Collections of Papyri," 391. See also Willis's letter of February 25, 1980: "I know of nothing in the Bodmer-Mississippi-Beatty-Barcelona group that requires a date of deposit later than A.D. 400."

55. Shore, *Joshua I–VI*, 11. See also, *Papyrus Bodmer* XXI, 5: ". . . probably of the Fourth Century."

56. Krause, "Schätze aus dem zweiten grossen Fund," 442.

57. Turner, *Typology of the Early Codex*. See the discussion of this point in Robinson, et al., *Introduction*.

58. Willis, "New Collections of Papyri," 389; Turner, *Typology of the Early Codex*, 137; Hall (editor), Melito of Sardis, *On Pascha and Fragments*, xlv and xvii, n. 8.

59. Quecke, "Ein Brief von einem Nachfolger," 426–33 and plate 42.

60. Quecke, *Das Lukasevangelium saïdisch*, 13 (see also ibid., 88): "Admittedly I would put a question mark beside 'first half,' since the script of P stands in a certain proximity to that of the Vienna Dioskurides codex that was written around 512."

61. *Papyrus Bodmer* XIX 8, n. 3: "Assuming that the copy was effected at the latest

In the case of the fragments from a Sahidic codex of Genesis found in the cartonnage of Nag Hammadi Codex VII, Rodolphe Kasser considered fifty years sufficient to render this codex so worn as to be no longer reparable.[62] Only the Coptic Pachomian materials of the Chester Beatty Library would necessarily extend the time beyond the fifth century.

THE CHALCEDONIAN-MONOPHYSITE CONTEXT

Only a few years ago, a Coptic manuscript from the Pierpont Morgan Library was published that tells of the takeover by Justinian of the monastery of Phbow (also spelled *Pbau* and *Pbou*) and the resultant abandonment of the monastery by the Monophysite monks who had lived there. Since our own tradition is on the Chalcedonian side of this schism, it may be helpful to sketch the situation in this language of a memorial service in honor of a Pachomian monk who left Phbow rather than submit to the heresy of our Chalcedonian faith.[63] The parchment codex M 579 was written in 822–23. Three fragments of the same text, apparently from a second codex also of the ninth century, are scattered at Paris, Ann Arbor, and London. Stephen, later Bishop of Henen-nesut, (i.e., of Heracleopolis Magna, at the southern edge of the Fayyum), was a monk at the Monastery of Isaac, of which Isaac was also a monk. Judging by the amount of sixth-century detail in the text, it probably was written in that century, presumably in Coptic (Sahidic).

> Now when he who was at that time successor in the ministry of these men [Pachomius, Theodore, and Horsiesios] saw the holy Apa Apollo, he knew by the piety of his manner and the strictness of his habits that he was an honoured vessel, pleasing to the Lord and ready for every good work. He then received him with

---

at the end of the fourth century, and assigning prudently the last reparation to the sixth century, we are obliged to admit that in spite of all the efforts exerted to rejuvenate the codex, it took less than two hundred years to transform the new book into a relic, no doubt venerable, but mutilated and almost unusable."

62. Kasser, "Fragments du livre biblique," 69–70:

> As long as a codex was reparable, it was repaired. But obviously the time came when the leaves, tired by too long a use, finally became exhausted or split across the pages. From then on the book had become irreparable. And it is probably what happened to our codex of Genesis . . . Under these circumstances how many years did it take for it to become irreparable? Fifty? . . . This estimation, quite hypothetical, does not seem to me to be unacceptable a priori.

63. Kuhn, *Panegyric on Apollo*.

> honour and, as it is further written, held him by his right hand, took him into his holy monastery and girded him with the armour of righteousness; I am referring to the holy monastic habit. (395.3)
>
> For it was said concerning our father the prophet, Apa Apollo, that in the beginning, when he went to Pbow, he devoted himself to many vigils, so that he spent three years without ever lying down to sleep during the whole night and day. And if he wished to give way to refreshing sleep for a little, he would do this for a brief moment, squatting on his toes, that the natural sweetness of sleep should not beguile him. (395.7)
>
> For it was testified about him that often at baking time, when the ovens were left at the evening baking, he would go there while they were still hot and stand upon them and pray until morning, remembering the struggle of the three holy children, so that the ground under him became like mud because of the greatness of the heat and the amount of sweat that came down on it. But in the days of winter he would do the opposite. For the garment which he wore he would soak with water and put on and stand in frost and dew all through the night praying. Sometimes also he would go down to places filled with water and stand in them so that the pain of the freezing water should banish the sensation of sleep. (395.9–10)

Such an "athlete" for the faith could only be utterly appalled by what transpired:

> Now the wretched bishops who had come together at Chalcedon became food for perdition and death and error, but their sins continue to be active. And their wickedness was unending and their punishment also is unceasing. For the fire of apostasy which those wretched bishops kindled everywhere drew to itself the laments and tears of the holy prophets unto the end. (395.11)
>
> But those of the Council of Chalcedon renounced this apostolic doctrine and true teaching of all the teachers of truth ["he is not divided into two natures, God forbid, or two persons as it seemed good to the foul council, but he is one Lord, one Christ, one and the same without change and division"], and they divided according to the thought of the Jews' religion this single one, our Lord Jesus Christ, into two natures and two persons, and instead of the holy Trinity they advanced an unlawful quaternity. (395.12)

As this language would indicate, the Egyptian church refused to go along.

> For indeed it was not only the apostolic throne of Alexandria which displayed its light, the holy Dioscorus [444–51], set at that time by Christ upon the high-priestly lampstand, but (so did) almost the whole country of Egypt and in addition also the holy community of Pbow, which was reached by the aforementioned tempest not only in former times but also in the days of the Emperor Justinian. (395.12)

Of course Justinian took steps to get Egypt back into line.

> The emperor called also the patriarch of Alexandria, our father Theodosius [535–36, died 566], to him to Constantinople, outwardly as if honouring his priesthood, but actually he wanted to detain him with him in order that his ordination should be invalidated. (395.12–13)

It was inevitable that a comparable power play was directed at the order of St. Pachomius.

> They who came together at Chalcedon mixed the cup of the Jews' religion, and he who shall drink it, his reward is the office of archimandrite of Pbow. O wicked demand, O bitter conflict! The command came, the wolf advanced, the emperor's edict went forth. And as it is written, that emperor sent forth his darts. He troubled the brethren of the holy community. He multiplied his threats to scatter the sheep of the Lord, if they did not want to transgress the faith of the Lord. (395.13)

A mass exodus of monks resulted.

> For when the holy brethren saw that their faithful shepherd, the latter-day patriarch, Abraham, who was archimandrite at that time, was taken away from them, and that the transgressor whom the emperor had sent was appointed to stand in the place of this man, all who loved godliness acted with great zeal and chose to leave the dwelling-place of their fathers lest they should make themselves strangers to the God of their Fathers. (395.13)

It was as part of this grand exodus that Apa Apollo left Phbow and founded the Monastery of Isaac presumably near the Fayyum, where Stephan became a Bishop.

> For our holy father Apa Apollo is in truth a lily who uprooted himself from among the thorns of the heretics. And thus he departed from Pbow at that time, having kept as apostolic the Constitution of the Apostles which says: If the ungodly seize a monastery, flee far away . . . As one taught by God, thus did our father take upon himself the retreat (from the world), wandering in the deserts and ravines and holes of the earth, being a sojourner in an alien region, in want, distressed, and grieved . . . And after many wanderings he came to this very mountain. (395.13–14)

A Greek papyrus, also dated to the sixth century, refers to Justinian troops quartered "in the monastery of Bau," which was one of the several Greek spellings of *Phbow*, and hence may refer to this same situation of upheaval resulting from the imposition of a Chalcedonian abbot and the resultant abandonment of the monastery by the bulk of the monks.

> Paid by the church of Apollonopolis [Edfu] on account of supplies for the most noble Justinian Scythians quartered in the monastery of Bau, being the 2nd half-yearly quota of the fourteenth indiction, two gold solidi twenty-one carats according to the standard, total 2 sol. 21 car. standard. I, Colluthus, distributor, represented by me his brother Victor, agree to having received two solidi twenty-one carats standard, total 2 sol. 21 car. standard, as above. [Endorsed] From the church of Apollonopolis, 14th indiction, 2 solidi 21 carats.[64]

The inscription of the opening lines of Psalms on Cave 8 at the Jabal al-Ṭārif have been dated on the basis of photographs by Manfredo Manfredi at about the sixth century. The cave, on the floor of which coins dated from the late fifth to early seventh centuries have been located, could well have been a way station in the wanderings of such scattered Pachomian monks.

There is a cave at the Jabal al-Ṭārif some 500 meters south of the site of the discovery of the Nag Hammadi codices and some five kilometers south of the site of the discovery of the Bodmer Papyri—some five kilometers southwest of Phbow—that is in full view from the cliff. This cave, numbered 8 in the sequence of 158 niches and caves that I numbered with black paint from south to north in August 1974, is one of several that were expertly carved out presumably in the Sixth Dynasty, to judge by those such as numbers 73 and 66 that retain their carving and can be

64. Hunt and Edgar, *Public Documents*, 493.

dated as the tombs of Thauti and Udi of the Sixth Dynasty.[65] Half of the clasp of a necklace in bronze was found in the rubble on the floor of the cave. It had a hieroglyphic inscription "Idi, the hereditary prince and the governor of Southern Upper Egypt."[66] The four corners of the ceiling of cave 8 as well as part of the doorway still retain the expert carving of the intact tombs, but the rest of the surfaces have been chipped away to produce an irregular sunken surface, a vandalism no doubt intended as the pious act of removing pagan texts and images from a room to be used for Christian worship. For on the east wall, just south of the entrance, there has been inscribed in a very ragged way into this irregular sunken surface in dull red paint the opening lines of Psalms 51–90 (LXX) in Coptic (Sahidic). Even the number of each psalm is given at the beginning, so that the inscription in part consists in columns of numbers. These opening lines are often hardly edifying, since they are references to the choirmaster or the occasion for the psalm, rather than an uplifting spiritual message. This suggests that the inscription was intended, much like the beads in a Rosary, as an *aide memoire* for the recitation of memorized psalms, in that the worshipper needed to be reminded which psalm came next, but once the reminder had been provided in the form of the opening line, the rest of the psalm could be readily recited from memory.

This inscription was published in 1931.[67] The editor, Paul Bucher, hazarded the fifth or sixth century as a date, and Manfredo Manfredi has more recently suggested a sixth-century date, both on the basis of photographs. In some regards the *editio princeps* is in need of correction. For example, the four columns actually contain, from left to right, the openings of Psalms 87–90, 81–86, 51–80 (with Psalm 52 not below, but to the right of, Psalm 51). Also in various instances, a word or letters have been omitted or incorrectly transcribed in the *editio princeps*. But the most shocking difference between the publication and the present state of the wall is that huge segments of the inscription are missing, no doubt hacked out to sell on the antiquities market. In the rubble of chipped rocks that littered the floor, a number were found with small bits of the red paint on them, indicating this vandalism of modern times.

65. Montet, "Les tombeaux dits de Kasr-el-Sayad," 81–129.

66. Habachi, "Sixth-Dynasty Discoveries in the Jabal al-Tarif."

67. Bucher, "Les Commencements des Psaumes LI à XCIII," 157–60.

Thus, ten letters are missing from the middle of the line from Psalm 59, a loss that broadens to twenty-six missing letters from Psalm 79. Beneath Psalms 51–80, the openings of Psalms 91–93 were seen and transcribed by Bucher, with a note that about fourteen more lines followed that were too effaced to transcribe; none of this material that he saw below the main segment is now visible, though a cross beneath the text (as well as one on the north face of the doorway) does indicate it to be a Christian inscription.[68]

The Psalms cave had a floor littered with what were largely chips from the walls—rubble that rose one to two meters in height. It has now been cleared by Charles W. Hedrick in the excavation conducted by the Institute for Antiquity and Christianity in 1975 and 1977, except for the area just beneath the Psalms inscription, left to provide easier access to the inscription and as an indication of the situation prior to the clearing. In the clearing of this rubble, fifty-six Byzantine copper coins were found. They fall within two groups: twenty-five *folles* that date from the reign of Anastasius I (491–518) until 538, the year when Justinian I changed the coinage to use a full-face portrait of the emperor and a dated reverse—a new style not represented in the find. Then there are thirty-one *dodecanummia* from reigns that span the period 578–646 (only one prior to the Persian withdrawal from Egypt in 627 and the latest dated probably no later than the Arab conquest of Upper Egypt in 641–642). It is unclear whether the break in the dating indicates use at two distinct periods, or whether the more worn condition of, by and large, the older group suggests (as is also suggested by a similar distribution in the case of three hoards that have been found in Palestine) that *folles* from the older period were in use at the later period attested by the *dodecanummia*. Whether these copper coins fit with monastic usage or whether they reflect secular habitation is not clear. The coins were scattered widely over the room, and hence a specific burial of a hoard is not archeologically attested. But the lack of stratigraphy in the rubble leaves as an open question whether there was a disturbance of the rubble subsequent to such a burial.

68. Goehring, "Byzantine Hoard from Upper Egypt," 9–10; Goehring, "Two New Examples," 218–23; Goehring, "Byzantine Coins from the Jabal al-Ṭārif in Upper Egypt"; Robinson and Van Elderen, "First Season of the Nag Hammadi Excavation." See also van Elderen, "Nag Hammadi Excavation," esp. 226–28.

Appendix 1

The Pachomian Monastic Library at the Chester Beatty Library and the Bibliothèque Bodmer[1]

The first Christian monastic order was founded in Upper Egypt by Pachomius early in the fourth century. What was left of its library was buried in the seventh century, to judge by the date of the latest material produced (ac. 1494, item 6 in the Inventory of Pachomian letters, a small papyrus roll containing an archival copy of Horsiesios' Letter 3 in Sahidic). It was discovered late in 1952 in Upper Egypt near Dishnā, and hence is referred to locally as the Dishnā Papers, though it has been known to scholars up to the present primarily as the Bodmer Papyri. This nomenclature has obscured the fact that much of the material is scattered among some seven other repositories,[2] of which the Chester Beatty Library is the most important. I would like to lay this fascinating story before you by describing first the Pachomian Monastery Library, then the Discovery and Marketing of the Library, then the Acquisition by Sir Chester Beatty and Martin Bodmer, followed by an Inventory of the approximate contents of the Library. Finally, I end by describing how

1. An earlier version of this Appendix appeared in *Manuscripts of the Middle East* 5 (1990–91) 26–40.

2. One of these codices, originally acquired by the University of Mississippi and named Mississippi Coptic Codex I (The Crosby Codex) has been acquired by Martin Schøyen, distinguished Norwegian bibliophile, and has been published through the Institute for Antiquity and Christianity: Goehring, ed., *The Crosby-Schøyen Codex: Ms 193 in the* Schøyen *Collection*.

the basic facts about the discovery and marketing of the library were established.

THE PACHOMIAN MONASTERY LIBRARY

Right after the conversion of the Roman Empire Pachomius founded the first monastic order of Christianity. It would be anachronistic to make inferences about its library from medieval monastic libraries. But something can be inferred from the Pachomian Order's own legends and rules.

The First Greek Life of Pachomius 63 gives some information about how books were viewed in the Pachomian Order: "He [Pachomius] also used to teach the brothers not to give heed to the splendor and the beauty of this world in things like good food, clothing, a cell, or a book outwardly pleasing to the eye."[3]

The First Greek Life of Pachomius 59 gives some impression of a Pachomian Library:

> No one would do anything in the house without permission from those in charge, not even visit a brother in his cell. In each house, the housemaster or the second keeps all the surplus clothings locked in a cell until the brothers need them to wash and put on again those they are using. The books, which were in an alcove, were also under the care of these two. The brothers have no money, still less anything of gold; some of them died having never known such things. Only those entrusted with a ministry used money; and when they returned to the monastery they kept nothing with themselves for a single day and gave everything to the steward until they might go out again. And all that government is written in detail in the book of the stewards.[4]

What is here referred to as "the book of the stewards" is apparently the extant *Precepts*,[5] where a rather massive literacy program is envisaged and occasional references to books and to the Library occur (*Precepts* 139, 140, 82, 100, 101):[6]

3. Veilleux, trans., *Pachomian Koinonia* 1:341.
4. Ibid., 338–39.
5. Veilleux, trans., *Pachomian Koinonia* 2:414–15.
6. Ibid., 166, 260–62.

> Whoever enters the monastery uninstructed shall be taught first what he must observe; and when, so taught, he has consented to it all, they shall give him twenty psalms or two of the Apostle's epistles, or some other part of the Scripture. And if he is illiterate, he shall go at the first, third, and sixth hours to someone who can teach and has been appointed for him. He shall stand before him and learn very studiously with all gratitude. Then the fundamentals of a syllable, the verbs, and nouns shall be written for him, and even if he does not want to, he shall be compelled to read.
>
> There shall be no one whatever in the monastery who does not learn to read and does not memorize something of the Scriptures. [One should learn by heart from] at least the New Testament and the Psalter.
>
> No one shall have in his own possession little tweezers for removing thorns he may have stepped on. Only the housemaster and the second shall have them, and they shall hang in the alcove in which books are placed.
>
> No one shall leave his book unfastened when he goes to the *synaxis* or to the refectory.
>
> Every day at evening, the second shall bring the books from the alcove and shut them in their case.

Official letters of Pachomius in Coptic were translated into Greek and then in 404 CE translated by Jerome into Latin. Only the Latin translation has survived, copied down through the centuries for the edification of European monks. The Coptic and Greek letters have not been seen since—until, at the same time, from the same dealer, and (with but one exception) at the same repositories as the Dishnā Papers, they suddenly reappeared. The inference seems inescapable that they were part of the same discovery. As a matter of fact, the site of the discovery near the foot of the Jabal Abū Manāᶜ was in full view of the headquarters monastery of the Pachomian Order, at the foot of the cliff to which funeral processions moved from the monastery, itself not above the inundation level, to bury their dead on higher ground, according to their records, and apparently to secrete their Library or Archives as well. High up in the Wādī Shaykh ᶜAlī there is an overhang cut by a prehistoric torrent that is everywhere inscribed in scrawling red paint with the graffiti of pious monks.

The holdings of the Chester Beatty Library that come from the jar at the foot of the cliff, and even before that from the little alcove in the

Pachomian monastery where the tweezers were kept, give a direct impression of the primitiveness of some of the books that made up the Library.

The eight leaves of ac. 1390 (Inventory item 23) begin with a schoolboy's Greek exercises in solid geometry that rendered the rest of the quire of little financial value, the kind of material a Pachomian monastery might be able to afford. On the empty pages a few chapters of the Gospel of John in Coptic were written in a non-literary, cursive hand, beginning in the middle of a sentence. This may be explainable as the place where the mutilated text being copied had begun. Or perhaps ac. 1390 was one in a series of cheap writing materials, the only one to have survived, onto which the complete Gospel was copied. The preceding (lost) writing surface on which the Gospel was being copied would have ended in the middle of a verse, which would explain why the text that has survived begins there, just where the other happened to break off. Thus ac. 1390 may give some insight into the limitations of the monastic effort to build its collection.

A similar impression of primitiveness may be conveyed by the largely uninscribed ac. 1499 (Inventory item 25) containing a Greek grammar and a Graeco-Latin lexicon for deciphering Pauline epistles. One of the uninscribed quires of this codex has leaves not yet cut apart at the growing edge, like French paperback books used to be. This not only reflects the fact that this codex was never completed, but also documents how unusual its construction had been.[7] For the standard way to make a quire for a papyrus codex was to cut a roll into a stack of sheets and fold the stack down the middle, a procedure that produced no growing edges that needed to be cut apart. The very fact that this codex was not fully inscribed has left this aberration in the manufacturing procedure intact. The codex was apparently produced outside the main tradition of book manufacture, or in any case made use of a technique that did not gain general acceptance.

Another experiment at economy is ac. 2554 (Inventory item 28), a largely uninscribed and unbound folded stack of sheets constructed by pasting face to face two used rolls and cutting them into the sheets of a quire, on whose unbound leaves administrative records had begun to be inscribed, with the result that such a makeshift quire, left still largely

7. Robinson and Wouters, "Chester Beatty Accession Number 1499." See also Wouters, *Chester Beatty Codex Ac. 1499*.

uninscribed, would provide writing material that would not have been expensive at all.

It may be no coincidence that much of the material of the highest quality in the collection is older than the Pachomian Order itself, suggesting that it entered the Library as gifts from outside, perhaps contributed by prosperous persons entering the Order. This might be the most obvious way to explain non-Christian texts in a monastic library, such as the Homeric and Menander material. But some such explanation is also needed for such excellent early Greek New Testament texts as P. Bodmer II (P^{66}, the Gospel of John, Inventory item 3), and P. Bodmer XIV–XV (P^{75}, the Gospels of Luke and John, Inventory item 8), where one might even think of Athanasius living in hiding with the Order while in exile as the source of such gifts.

The bulk of Christian codices date from the first century of the Pachomian Order's existence, namely the early fourth to the early fifth century, and often present the competence of a trained scriptorium, though without adornment. But there is no specific indication that they came from a single scriptorium or that such a scriptorium belonged to the Order.

Some texts in the collection, such as some of the archival copies of letters from Pachomian Abbots, again suggest, in the primitiveness of the material employed, that the usual standards of a scriptorium were lacking. Ac. 1486, an archival copy of a Coptic letter from the Pachomian Abbot Theodore (item 4 in the Inventory of Pachomian letters), was written in the fifth or sixth century on a long thin irregular skin, obviously the leg of an animal that could not be used to produce leaves for a codex. Chester Beatty Ms. W. 145 (item 3 in the Inventory of Pachomian letters) makes a similar impression. It is a fourth-century copy of a letter of Pachomius.

The presence of relatively unskilled products alongside of relatively professional codices may indicate a plurality of places of origin, and perhaps a contrast between what was produced within the Order and what came from outside.

If discipline relaxed and the demand for reading material waned with the passage of time, as the center of Coptic learning shifted downstream to the White Monastery of Shenouda at Sohag, such a Pachomian collection could have become more a geniza than an active library. The identity of increasingly fragmentary items in the collection would be lost from sight, especially in the case of the old non-Coptic material, if one may assume that the Greek House did not retain its original vigor at Fāw Qiblī, once the Order had a monastery near Alexandria where Greek-speaking monks would be more at home. It would have been enough that the remains represented the venerated relics of the beginnings of the Order, worthy to be included along with copies of official letters of the early Abbots (about the only thing they continued to copy), in a jar no doubt intended to rescue for posterity the surviving symbols of continuity with the Order's legendary past.

This is illustrated in another way by the fate of the excellent early third-century copy of the Gospel of Luke and John (P^{75}, Inventory item 8) in the Bibliothèque Bodmer (P. Bodmer XIV–XV), from whose cover new fragments of John have been recovered: This very valuable old codex was rebound in late antiquity, by pasting fragmentary leaves of the quire together as cartonnage to thicken the leather cover, and by sewing the binding thongs through the inner margin of the quire so near the writing that the codex could not be opened wide enough to be actually read. One is inclined to think that the codex had become a relic, the Library a Museum, or, in view of the copies of official Pachomian letters, an Archive.

Except for the copies of official Pachomian letters, datings as late as the fifth century are not strongly represented. For it is usually mentioned by editors in the spectrum of fourth or fifth century. In the course of the fifth century the source of supply seems to have been drying up, or new production was being attracted to the White Monastery. But when one turns to the archival copies of letters of Pachomian Abbots, the situation is the converse. Whereas the earliest material is by the nature of the case no earlier than the fourth century, only one text (item 3 in the Inventory of Pachomian letters) has been dated simply to the fourth century,[8] and only one (number 1) to the fourth or fifth century.[9] One (number 5) is dated simply to the fifth century,[10] and two (numbers 8 and 9) to the

8. Quecke, "Die Briefe Pachoms," 98 n. 13, advocates the fourth century and reports that the same date was already proposed by T. C. Skeat in a letter of 17 December 1970. Quecke's *editio princeps* is *Die Briefe Pachoms*.

9. Orlandi, de Vogüé, Quecke, and Goehring, *Pachomiana Coptica*. The dating is from an early draft of the typescript by de Vogüé.

10. Krause, "Der Erlassbrief Theodors," esp. 221: "with every reservation, the fifth century."

fifth or sixth century.[11] Three (numbers 2, 4 and 7) are dated simply to the sixth century,[12] and one (number 6) to the seventh century.[13] Thus it is clear that the letters of the Pachomian Abbots continued being copied much later than did the literary texts themselves and represent the clearest indication of the narrowly limited interest of those responsible for the preservation of the Library or Archive in its latest period and hence presumably for its ultimate burial.[14]

Perhaps these relics were buried for safe keeping in the period of decline following the imposition of Chalcedonian orthodoxy on the traditionally Monophysite order, as the dating of the latest material in the seventh century might suggest.[15]

THE DISCOVERY AND MARKETING OF THE LIBRARY

The discovery of the Dishnā Papers was made by Ḥasan Muḥammad al-Sammān and Muḥammad Khalīl al-ʿAzzūzī, both of whom come from Abū Manāʿ "Bahri." This hamlet is on the right bank of the Nile in the

11. Number 8: Kurth, Thissen, and Weber, *Kölner Ägyptische Papyri*, 100–102. Quecke, "Die Briefe Pachoms," 97, cites with apparent approval the dating "fifth or sixth century" by Alfred Hermann in his very inadequate *editio princeps* (that Quecke in other regards corrected), "Homilie in sahidischem Dialekt," esp. 82.

Number 9: Kurth, Thissen, and Weber, *Kölner Ägyptische Papyri*, 103–8. Quecke, "Die Briefe Pachoms," 97, cites with apparent approval the dating "fifth or sixth century" as that of Angelicus Kropp, OP in his very inadequate *editio princeps* (that Quecke also corrected in other regards), "Ein Märchen als Schreibübung," esp. 81, where Kropp wrote "end of the fifth century."

12. Number 2: Quecke, "Ein neues Fragment," esp. 67: "probably from the sixth century."

Number 4: Quecke, "Ein Brief, esp. 427: "probably of the sixth century."

Number 7: Orlandi, "Nuovi Testi," esp. 242, where he referred to Guglielmo Cavallo for a dating "a bit older than that of the preceding roll" (see the following note). Quecke, "Eine Handvoll."

13. Orlandi, "Nuovi Testi," 241, cited Guglielmo Cavallo for a dating to the seventh century. Quecke, "Eine Handvoll," 222: "The hand is a very artificial uncial, which one would like to place considerably later" [than a sixth-century dating]; see preceding note.

14. Already Quecke has recognized the nonaccidental nature of the five Pachomian texts acquired by the Chester Beatty Library. "Eine Handvoll," 221: "It is to be suspected that the five ieces belong together, and thus, as it were, present a 'hoard' of Pachomian material. The five Pachomian pieces can indeed hardly have come together accidentally in the Chester Beatty Library." And Orlandi, "Nuovi Testi," 241, considers the material to come from "the library of a Pachomian monastery."

15. For a legend about such upheavals, see Kuhn, *Panegyric on Apollo*.

area of Upper Egypt where it flows from east to west, and hence literally on the north bank. Abū Manāʿ lies some 4 km from the river's edge, near the foot of the cliff Jabal Abū Manāʿ, which is 12 km east of the cliff Jabal al-Ṭārif where the Nag Hammadi Codices were discovered. It is 5 km northeast and in full view of Fāw Qiblī, ancient Pabau (Greek), Pbaw or Pbow (Sahidic), or Phbow (Bohairic), the site of the headquarters of the Pachomian Monastic Order. Put in more modern terms, the site is 5.5 km northwest of Dishnā, the larger town at the river with a railroad station, which thus played the role of regional center in this discovery corresponding to that of the town Nag Hammadi in the case of the Nag Hammadi Codices. Abū Manāʿ itself is 10 km east of Hamrah Diim, the hamlet that controls the site of the discovery of the Nag Hammadi Codices, much as does Abū Manāʿ in the case of the Dishnā Papers. This whole Dishnā Plain, important already in prehistoric times, seems to have been an important center of Egyptian Christianity.

Ḥasan and Muḥammad were digging for *sabakh* (fertilizer) some 300 meters out from the foot of the cliff Jabal Abū Manāʿ at al-Qurnah ("the corner"), when Ḥasan uncovered a large earthen jar containing the books. He broke the jar with his mattock, leaving the sherds where they fell. Some fragmentary parts of the find were burnt on the spot, and others were given away to passersby, who incidentally terrified Ḥasan with the mythic idea that they were books of monsters. Yet he carried the bulk of the discovery home in his *jallabīyah*, the typical peasant ground-length robe. Muḥammad took for his part a wooden plank variously interpreted as a book cover, a mirror, or a catalogue of the library's contents.

Ḥasan lived in his wife's family home, presided over by her father ʿUmar al-ʿAbbādī. Her brother, ʿAbd al-ʿĀl, trafficked in the books, unsuccessfully at first, since they could not even be bartered for sugar. Some leaves of a large papyrus book were crushed up and used as fuel to light their water pipe; parchment burnt like an oil lamp. (Rural electrification reached the hamlet only in 1980.)

ʿAbd al-ʿĀl worked in the Dishnā jewelry shop of the goldsmith Ṣubḥī Qusṭandī Dimyān, to whom he sold a book. Ṣubḥī showed it to the Dishnā priest 'al-Qummuṣ' Manqaryūs, who was related to the priestly family of al-Qaṣr through whose hands Nag Hammadi material had passed, to inquire if it were equally valuable. 'Al-Qummuṣ' Manqaryūs told him it was worthless, hoping thus to be able to acquire it himself. But Ṣubḥī's son Jirjis taught at the same Coptic parochial school at Dishnā as did a member of the priestly al-Qaṣr family, Rāghib Andarāwus "al-Qiss" ʿAbd al-Sayyid, who had sold Nag Hammadi Codex III to the Coptic Museum in Cairo for £250. Jirjis showed his father's book at the Coptic Museum, where it was confiscated and he threatened with jail, until a powerful friend persuaded the Museum to return his book and press no charges. Jirjis sold the book to Zakī Ghālī, an antiquities dealer in Luxor, for a price said to be £400.

ʿAbd al-Raḥīm Abū al-Ḥājj, ʿUmar's nephew, was a village barber going from house to house to ply his trade, as well as a sharecropper working fields belonging to a Dishnā goldsmith, Riyāḍ Jirjis Fām. Riyāḍ began dirt poor, the son of a peasant who eked out a living making baskets from reeds taken from the edge of the Nile, but scrounged his way up to the role of the ruthless strongman of Dishnā. When he heard of the discovery, he took another goldsmith with him, Mūsā Fikrī Ashʿīyah, and went to the house of ʿAbd al-Raḥīm in Abū Manāʿ. The latter was afraid of the accompanying stranger and refused to deal with them, but on a subsequent visit when Mūsā Fikrī was not present sold Riyāḍ three or four books.

'Al-Qummuṣ' Manqaryūs became involved with Riyāḍ's acquisitions, along with Mūsā Fikrī and another goldsmith, Shafīq Ghubrīyāl. They thus created some kind of partnership, the priest providing a semi-educated assessment, ecclesiastical connections, and a haven free of police searches, whereas the goldsmiths no doubt provided the capital and Riyāḍ also the entrepreneurship.

Accompanied by his son Nuṣḥī, Riyāḍ returned to Abū Manāʿ and went directly to the house of ʿUmar al-ʿAbbādī, where he bought out the rest of what the family held. He was able to leave the hamlet with the loot thanks only to the armed escort of ʿUmar's sons as far as the paved highway. He went straight to the home of 'al-Qummuṣ' Manqaryūs, where he counted out to him "thirty-three books." Though this figure recurs repeatedly in the telling of the story, it is not clear whether it is meant to include the books Riyāḍ had already acquired, and whether it included material usually distinguished from the "books," namely ten small rolls the size of one's finger, three or four large rolls some 25 cm or more high, and a few triangular-shaped leaves some 15 cm high. In spite of such ambiguities, the figure does tend to indicate roughly the extent of the discovery, perhaps some three times that of the thirteen Nag Hammadi Codices.

Muḥammad, irritated at having been excluded from the sales and profits, had reported the discovery to the police, who had found concrete evidence with Maṣrī ʿAbd al-Masīḥ Nūḥ, the person who acquired the wooden board from Muḥammad. He implicated the others. Charges were not brought against the priest, but Riyāḍ and Mūsā Fikrī were charged. And, by a case of mistaken identity, Shafīq Muḥārib was charged instead of Shafīq Ghubrīyāl. Also charged were Ḥasan and the brother of ʿAbd al-ʿĀl as well as Abū al-Wafā Aḥmad Ismāʿīl, who had acquired a triangular parchment leaf. By a combination of threats and bribes Riyāḍ prevented them from testifying against him in their effort to exonerate themselves. His defense lawyer, Ḥilmī Bandarī, argued unsuccessfully before Judge Rabāʿ Tawfīq that the possession of antiquities was not illegal, that they were ignorant of what they had acquired, and that there was no incriminating evidence. All eight were sentenced to a year in jail. Engaging as their attorney Aḥmad ʿAlī Allūbā 'Pasha,' a Conservative Party politician from Cairo, Riyāḍ appealed the case at the Court of Appeals in Qinā. Six were acquitted, but two were sentenced to six months in jail; Maṣrī's sentence was suspended and only Ḥasan served time.

During this trying time, 'al-Qummuṣ' Manqaryūs was concerned that his house might be searched. For the books were being kept in his home, no doubt on the assumption that a police search of a priest's home was less likely than of a goldsmith's home. The box in which they were kept was hidden at times under the floor, no doubt the dirt floor of the patio, at times behind rafters in the ceiling. But as the pressure mounted, he secreted them in a cupboard built under his divan, and asked his neighbor, Saʿīd Diryās Ḥabashī, if he could sun the divan in his patio, where there was more sun than in his own, to free it of fleas. When he recuperated the divan, he found the best book missing. Saʿīd Diryās denies having taken it, saying he was unaware of the divan's contents, otherwise he would have taken them all. Riyāḍ traced the book to Fāris, a tailor of Dishnā, who is reported to have paid £30 for it and then to have sold it for £700 to Phocion J. Tano, the distinguished Cypriote antiquities dealer of Cairo who had acquired most of the Nag Hammadi Codices, where Riyāḍ later saw it.

Riyāḍ retrieved the rest of the material from 'al-Qummuṣ' Manqaryūs, apparently except for a few fragments. For Distinguished Professor Emeritus ʿAzīz Suryāl ʿAṭīyah of the University of Utah has reported that the priest's son 'al-Qummuṣ' Ṭānyūs showed him a fragment at his home in the fashionable Cairo suburb Maadi. And Saʿīd Diryās has reported that a Spanish priest obtained some material about 1966 from the priest's son 'al-Qummuṣ' Ṭānyūs. The parish diary of the Franciscan Church adjoining the Sugar Factory near Nag Hammadi records that a José O'Callaghan Martinus of Barcelona (and the Pontifical Biblical Institute in Rome) with passport number 95912 came "to look for papers" on 14–20 November 1964 and for a second visit beginning 1 February 1965. The widow of "al-Qummuṣ" Manqaryūs thought there were fragments in the home when I interviewed her on 18 December 1976, but she could not find them.

Riyāḍ was under virtual house arrest. For he was not permitted to go as far as Cairo, but was limited in his movements to Upper Egypt, the region from Luxor to Sohag, for trips up to ten hours, and then only with police permission. So he turned to a lifelong friend, Fatḥallāh Dāʾūd, who had gone on pilgrimage to Jerusalem with him in 1945 (as their almost identical tattoos validate), to take books to Cairo to market. Though Fatḥallāh Dāʾūd was instructed to report to "al-Qummuṣ" Manqaryūs, Mūsā Fikrī, and Shafīq Ghubrīyāl a lower price than he actually received, so that their proportion of the profit would be correspondingly less, he actually told them the truth. Having his own profit thus appreciably reduced, Riyāḍ plotted revenge to recuperate his loss. He hired members of the Abū Bahbuh family to break into Fatḥallāh Dāʾūd's house and kidnap a son to be held for the equivalent ransom. In the dark of night they by mistake took a daughter, Sūsū. Rather than paying the ransom, Fatḥallāh Dāʾūd appealed by telegram to President Nasser. Within a week police sent from Cairo secured the release of Sūsū unharmed. Riyāḍ himself seeks to put a good (or less bad) light on the incident by maintaining that the Abū Bahbuh family was planning to kill Fatḥallāh Dāʾūd for their own reasons, but Riyāḍ had talked them out of that unprofitable venture in favor of a slightly less (?) inhumane and in any case more profitable procedure.

Riyāḍ then made friends with the two police guards posted at his home, plying them with alcohol on Saturday evenings until they were in a drunken stupor in time for him to catch the midnight train to Cairo. There he would take a few books at a time to Tano's home, receiving profits he has reported to be in the thousands of pounds, and return Sunday night in time to get into his home under the cover of darkness before dawn Monday. The death of Riyāḍ's son Waṣfī in a brawl some years later, which Fatḥallāh Dā'ūd interpreted as divine retribution, led Riyāḍ to move to Cairo, where he lives on the top, fifth floor of a large modern duplex apartment house in Heliopolis which he had purchased.

Photographs supplied by Émile Tawfīq Saʿd, the son of an Alexandrian antiquities dealer named by Ishāq Ayyūb Isḥāq, Inspector of the Department of Agriculture for Dishnā, as having acquired some "Dishnā Papers," were identified as Papyrus Bodmer XXIV (the Psalms in Greek, Inventory item 15) and Papyrus Bodmer XL, the unpublished Coptic Song of Songs (Inventory item 19). This then led to the identification of the "Dishnā Papers" with the famous discovery known in academic circles as the "Bodmer Papyri."

This identification of the Dishnā Papers with the Bodmer Papyri has then been variously confirmed. The contents as described by the peasants fit quite well the Bodmer Papyri, including such details as the balled-up condition of P. Bodmer XXII = Mississippi Coptic Codex II (Inventory item 13) stuck in the bottom of a piriform jar. The same dealer Tano, who according to Riyāḍ had funded a clandestine excavation of the site, has also been identified as their source by the main repositories of the materials in Geneva, Dublin and Cologne. The time frame of the discovery (1952) and that of the arrival of the material in Europe (P. Bodmer I, Inventory items 1–2, was published in 1954, and the bulk was acquired in 1955–56), given the trying circumstances, is what one might expect. And the site of the discovery, initially stated by the publications of the Bodmer Papyri either to be unknown or to be variously and vaguely located somewhere between Panopolis (Achmim near Sohag) and Thebes (Luxor), has finally been conceded to agree with our investigations in the most recent of these publications. This identification of the site has subsequently been located also in the Registry of Accessions of the Chester Beatty Library, on a typed slip of paper appended at ac. 1390, apparently written by Tano himself, to judge by the English: "Small village DESHNA just after NAGHI HAMADI about 2 hours before LUXOR by train. Probably from the Library of a Monastery. Found in a Jar in a cemetery."[16]

16. It was this identification of the remains of this codex as part of the Dishnā Papers that led to the decision to publish it through the Institute for Antiquity and Christianity: Brashear, Funk, Robinson, and Smith, eds., *Chester Beatty Codex Ac 1390.*

THE ACQUISITIONS BY SIR CHESTER BEATTY AND MARTIN BODMER

Sir Chester Beatty[17] and Martin Bodmer were the most distinguished bibliophiles in the period just before and after World War II. It is hence understandable that both felt a sense of competitiveness, as well as a sense of camaraderie in the rarified atmosphere of their shared hobby. This relationship was only intensified by the fact that both were long-standing customers of Tano.

Tano kept his collection in part in Cyprus, as he was able to get it out of Egypt. He spent summers in the family home at Nicosia, where he could correspond freely about his business affairs and ship antiquities and receive payment without difficulty. Tano was even from time to time on the continent. Sir Chester had known Tano personally during the winters he had spent in the "Blue House" at Giza near Cairo; and when Sir Chester came to prefer Nice for his winters the personal contacts continued there. This relationship outside of Egypt was not only convenient from the point of view of customs and payments, but was also diplomatically advantageous, as is reflected in a comment of Beatty in a letter of 21 March 1958 concerning ac. 2554 (Inventory item 28): 'We can honestly say it was bought in Europe; we need not say where or when."

Sir Chester had in fact been acquiring papyri and other antiquities from Tano for many years. The following may illustrate this relationship just prior to the acquisitions with which we are concerned: On 8 September 1947 he paid Tano £24 for four leaves from a codex, care of the Ottoman Bank, Famagusta, Cyprus. On 16 April 1948 Tano sent him four wooden tablets through the good offices of his brother-in-law, William Acker, an officer in the RAF. In 1950 Beatty ordered on approval Coptic materials offered by Tano for £235. That same year Tano wrote Sir Chester from New York not to involve his American-based nephew Frank J. Tano in any transactions, but to remit directly to the Ottoman or Bartley Banks of Famagusta, Cyprus. On 12 September 1951 Tano wrote Beatty's secretary, John Marsh, in London: "I asked to [sic] a friend in Paris to forward threw [sic] you for Mr. Chester Beatty a collection

17. Wilson, *Life and Times of Sir Alfred Chester Beatty*, presents an informed biography, including, however, all too few brief discussions of the bibliophile dimension of Beatty's activity. Kennedy, *Alfred Chester Beatty*, reports considerably more about the founding of the Chester Beatty Library; see esp. 49, 125–27 concerning the relations with Martin Bodmer.

of Coptic parchemains [sic]. Please wen [sic] you receive them, kindly forward the parcel to Mr. Chester Beatty's address."

On 25 March 1954, Beatty's secretary, John Wooderson, recorded in a memorandum: "Mr. A. Chester Beatty asked John Wooderson to see Mr. Tano and find out if he had any Coptic writing or vellum or pages of papyri in Greek; and if so, what they would cost, and if they could be examined in London . . . Mr. Tano said he had no stock in Cairo or Cyprus at present but that he would write later if he found anything interesting."

But by this time Martin Bodmer had established a business relationship with Tano that seemed even more efficient. Bodmer had visited Egypt as early as 1950, when he approached Tano to secure manuscripts for his library. Father Louis Doutreleau, SJ, one of the editors of the series Sources Chrétiennes in Lyon, was at the time stationed in Cairo, and has described Bodmer's acquisition procedure. For Doutreleau had an arrangement with Bodmer to provide him with an expert assessment of manuscripts Tano showed Doutreleau for this purpose. Sometimes Tano gave him direct contact with a peasant who owned manuscripts, whom Doutreleau knew only as "the Bey of papyrus," but who may well have been Riyāḍ. Tano referred to the Dishnā Papers as "Nag Hammadi Two," to designate the region of Egypt from which they came that would be more readily recognizable to foreigners and that would incidentally suggest a value comparable to that famous discovery. Tano exported to Cyprus material at times through the diplomatic pouch, at times through a friend who worked at the customs office in Alexandria. From Cyprus he went to Geneva in September 1955. It was at that time that P. Bodmer II (the Gospel of John, Inventory item 3) and III (the Gospel of John and Genesis 1:1—4:2, Inventory item 4) reached Geneva.

Bodmer himself was in Cairo at the end of January 1956, returning from a trip to Indonesia as a diplomat for the International Red Cross. On 8 October 1956 Gilles Quispel was told by Ludwig Keimer, an Austrian in Cairo who was close to Doutreleau and Tano, that at the beginning of February 1956 Bodmer had bought from Tano P. Bodmer XIV–XV (the Gospels of Luke and John, Inventory item 8) and much of XXV–IV–XXVI (Menander, Inventory item 5). These codices reached Geneva shortly thereafter. Bodmer's secretary, Odile Bongard, visited Tano in Cairo in March 1956. A rather steady stream of acquisitions during the subsequent months was interrupted by the Suez Crisis in

October 1956, though a shipment did arrive that month. Efforts by Mlle Bongard to complete the acquisitions were only successful to a limited extent. She was able to sift through Tano's residue of fragments and find a few belonging to P. Bodmer II (the Gospel of John, Inventory item 3). Tano also showed Doutreleau several leaves of Menander (Inventory item 5) in 1958. They were then deposited at the Tunisian Embassy in Cairo for export, but the shipment was delayed several years by a breaking of diplomatic relations between Egypt and Tunisia. When the shipment finally reached Geneva, part of it was missing.

On 2 April 1956 Sir Chester wrote his librarian, James Vere Stewart Wilkinson, from Nice that he had seen Tano and "got some very interesting things from him." In a letter of 5 April 1956 to Wilfred Merton, his papyrological consultant in Dublin, Sir Chester was more specific about the "very interesting things" he had acquired, distinguishing the following items clearly enough for us to identify them, in the light of later information: "The two books with the original bindings are very interesting. One seems to be complete [ac. 1389, Inventory item 12] and the other was never finished. About half of the papyrus pages are blank [ac. 1499, Inventory item 25]."

A third item was described as follows: "It was evidently a scroll which was cut in pieces to make it appear like a book. It must have been pretty long, because it is quite thick—it must be 2″ at least—and the page is just the size of the section of a scroll. They just bend over, and I looked at a good many of the pages and they separate naturally, so I do not anticipate much trouble in having the proper experts separate them." [Ac. 2554, Inventory item 31.]

Sir Chester added: "I will, of course, deliver them at once to the British Museum when I arrive." On 15 April 1956 Wilkinson replied urging him to invite the leading authority on book bindings, Berthe van Regemorter, to come from Belgium to examine the bindings before the books were disassembled and the leaves glassed, a proposal with which he readily agreed. Mlle van Regemorter had recently been at the Bibliothèque Bodmer to examine the book bindings there and had sent Beatty a report concerning her findings. The ensuing discussion illustrates the way in which Bodmer and Sir Chester became involved in friendly competition for Tano's wares. For in a letter to Merton of 21 May 1956, Sir Chester commented: "You have seen the memorandum that Miss van Regemorter did on Bodmer's library. Apparently he got some good things from Tano. It was quite an important purchase, and I imagine it was the Gospel of St. John that he bought. I do not think he is making a general collection of papyri, but I think he bought a few very important things from Tano."

In a letter the same day to Wilkinson, Sir Chester conceded the loss to Bodmer but immediately began thinking of future acquisitions he might make from Tano: "He indicated to me that he had an important deal on with Bodmer. I imagine it is in connection with that Gospels. Anyhow, I hope we will get some other things, and I wrote to him about early wooden bindings. I imagine Bodmer is not going in for those, and he [Tano] may be able to clean up the market and get something fine there."

In a letter of 24 April 1956 to Merton, Sir Chester described his business procedure with Tano:

> You see, with the deal I had with 'X' [Tano], I pay so much for the whole lot, and if I do not want to buy the whole lot I pay another sum. I pay £800 if I take them all, but if I do not take the whole lot I pay £200, but I can pay this in sterling. In other words, the price was 10,000 Swiss francs, which is a little over £800, and it is done on the normal exchange basis. Then I have the right to pay in sterling. Of course, it is a good deal like buying a pig in a poke, because he does not know too much about them and I know nothing. They look old and they smell old, and I imagine they are old. That is the opinion of a real expert.

All this tends to suggest that Sir Chester acquired the residue of what had been offered to Bodmer in Swiss Francs, items that presumably were not considered "world literature," as Bodmer defined the scope of his collection,[18] but rather were the kind of artifacts, such as book bindings, that interested Sir Chester. The paradoxical outcome of this selectivity procedure is that Bodmer tended to acquire items that entered the Pachomian Monastery Library from outside, such as Homer, Menander, and the Greek Gospels, whereas Sir Chester tended to acquire the material more directly related to the Pachomian Order, such as the more primitively produced items and the bulk of copies of the official letters of Pachomian Abbots, precisely what was needed to identify the discovery as the Archives of the Pachomian Monastic Order.

18. Bodmer, *Eine Bibliothek der Weltliteratur.*

Sir Chester lacked the expertise provided to Bodmer in Cairo by Father Doutreleau, but was dependent on expertise he received once he had taken an option to buy and had directed the material to the British Museum. In a letter of 21 May 1956 to Merton, Sir Chester wrote how he planned to reach a decision as to whether to exercise his option:

> My idea is, soon after I arrive, to take the big papyrus which is cut apart [ac. 2554, Inventory item 28] and in that parcel there are two lots of loose leaves—one is supposed to be agnostic [?]—and have them identified at the British Museum. I will not do anything beyond identification, because I do not want to be forced to take the lot, in case the other two are of no value.
>
> . . . If she [Mlle van Regemorter] can come over we will take the other two books [ac. 1389, Inventory item 12, and ac. 1499, Inventory item 25] to [I. E. S.] Edwards and [T. C.] Skeat at the British Museum [so] she can study the bindings. In the meantime, we will have the option [for: opinion?] about the first lot.

On 7 January 1957 Beatty wrote from Nice to Merton of a second potential acquisition:

> I received a letter from Bodmer's secretary [Mlle Bongard] who had just come from Cairo, as he had sent her to go through all the fragments that Tano had in the hope of finding a few little fragments which had been overlooked of the St. John's Gospel, and she managed to find a few fragments. She told me that she had certain things which Tano wanted me to have, and she told me the price was 4,000 Swiss francs, and I asked her if she would leave them with me, as I wanted to get a little information on them, and I would probably take them. There are 8 items, of which 6 are papyrus, and one, curiously enough, a perfect mass of small fragments. In fact, they fill a small plastic box of about 4" long by 3 1/2" wide by 2" deep. Then there is a roll on vellum of some sermon which is quite early [ac. 1486, item 4 in the Inventory of Pachomian letters] . . . So when Lady Powerscourt went back, I sent samples of the find, with the exception of one item, to Edwards.

On 16 December 1956 Sir Chester had written to Edwards a letter following up his shipment of samples: "I should be very pleased if you would get the proper advice and find out if they are of any value. I do not know what to make of these fragments. One lot they say is from the same roll as the Greek papyrus we have of the time of Diocletian [ac.

2554, Inventory item 28], and there are two big lots of fragments which are still here and I will get to you later."

On 21 January 1957 Edwards wrote Wilkinson that "the latest Coptic documents . . . seem to me to be too fragmentary to be very promising."

There was a third acquisition in 1958, again mediated through Mlle Bongard of the Bibliothèque Bodmer. On 18 December 1957 Tano wrote to Sir Chester in Nice: "I wrote to Miss Odile Bongard to forward you some papyrus which completes some you bought before. Also if she received a lot of parchments in Coptic. In case she did, please their price send it if possible in Cyprus pounds."

On 19 April 1958 Bodmer wrote Sir Chester: "The package from Tano is also ready to be delivered to you!" The package seems to be an item distinct from the papyrus completing previous acquisitions, and presumably contained the "lot of parchments in Coptic."

Miss McGillighan of the staff of Sir Chester's library had written him on 10 April 1958: "I will be very pleased to go to Geneva and collect the papyrus from Mademoiselle Bongard, as you suggest. I had planned to leave Paris for Dublin on May the 18th and so it would be on May the 19th that I would go to the Bodmer Library and collect the papyrus."

On 23 May 1958 Miss McGillighan wrote Beatty: "I collected the package which contains some fragmentary leather bindings and 17 vellum folios with some fragments, one with a miniature, several with spiral ornamentation and several with coloured initials. They are in fairly good condition and Dr. Hayes thinks that the writing may be Greek, but I would opt for Coptic."

The papyrus that complemented previous acquisitions may well belong to the Dishnā Papers, in that, for example, further fragments were added to ac. 1390 (Inventory item 23) even after it had been conserved between glass panes at the British Museum and sent on to Dublin, necessitating a return of the material from Dublin to London for a reconservation. But the vellum folios can be identified no doubt as ac. 1933, manuscript 820, an item apparently no longer belonging to the Dishnā Papers.

If thus the competition and assistance in acquiring the Dishnā Papers by Sir Chester and Bodmer seems to have reached its conclusion in 1958, the personal relations between the two friends continued until near Sir Chester's death. Indeed on 17 October 1963 Bodmer wrote him a bold letter proposing they unite the two collections under a single foundation, while leaving them at the two separate repositories. Sir Chester responded on 20 November 1963 politely declining the offer.[19] In a previous letter of 29 October 1963 to Dr. Hayes concerning Bodmer's proposal Sir Chester had commented: "I do think we might work in very close co-operation with him, and it might be well for you to go down and see the Bodmer Library sometime. We could possibly loan them items and they might loan us items, as we supplement each other extremely well . . ."

A striking instance of such a supplementing of each other's holdings is the Pachomian Monastery Library Archives, which were brought together in a small cupboard shared with tweezers for thorns at Fāw Qiblī at the headquarters monastery in Upper Egypt, then some three centuries later were buried at the foot of the Jabal Abū Manāʿ for safekeeping for over a millennium, then late in 1952 were discovered by Ḥasan Muḥammad al-Sammān of Abū Manāʿ "Bahri," were acquired by the strong man of Dishnā Riyāḍ Jirjis Fām and then sold by him bit by bit to Phocion J. Tano, who sold the bulk of the material in the years around 1956 to Martin Bodmer and Sir Chester Beatty. A joint exhibit of the Archives of the Pachomian, Monastic Library would be a fascinating instance of such close co-operation as Sir Chester had in mind.

INVENTORY

The contents of the discovery, including the quite fragmentary items and those listed only with hesitation, are as follows (they are Greek papyrus codices, unless otherwise indicated):[20]

1. Homer, *Iliad*, Book 5 = P. Bodmer I, a roll on the verso of a roll of documentary papyri, = P. Bodmer L.
2. Homer, *Iliad*, Book 6 = P. Bodmer I, a roll on the verso of the same roll of documentary papyri, = P. Bodmer L.
3. Gospel of John = P. Bodmer II + a fragment from the Chester Beatty Library, ac. 2555, + P. Köln 214, = P^{66}.

19. Excerpts of the exchange of letters are quoted by Kennedy, *Alfred Chester Beatty*, 126–27.

20. The inventory presented here was also appended to the following essays: Robinson, "Manuscript's History," esp. xxviii–xxxii; Robinson, "Introduction," esp. 6–9; and Robinson, "First Christian Monastic Library," esp. 375–78.

4. Gospel of John and Genesis 1:1—4:2 in Bohairic = P. Bodmer III.
5. Menander, *Samia, Dyskolos, Aspis* = P. Bodmer XXV, IV, XXVI + P. Barc. 45 + Cologne inv. 904 = P. Köln 3 + P. Rob. 38.
6. *Nativity of Mary = Apocalypse of James* (*Protevangelium of James*); Apocryphal Correspondence of Paul with the Corinthians; *Odes of Solomon* 11; the Epistle of Jude; Melito of Sardis *On the Passover*; a fragment of a liturgical hymn; the *Apology of Phileas*; Psalms 33–34; 1 and 2 Peter = P. Bodmer V; X; XI; VII; XIII; XII; XX (+ a fragment from the Chester Beatty Library, ac. 2555); IX; VIII.
7. Proverbs in Proto-Sahidic on parchment = P. Bodmer VI.
8. Gospels of Luke and John = P. Bodmer XIV–XV = P^{75}.
9. Exodus 1:1—15:21 in Sahidic on parchment = P. Bodmer XVI. (P. Bodmer XVII is generally agreed not to come from the same discovery.)
10. Deuteronomy 1:1—10:7 in Sahidic = P. Bodmer XVIII.
11. Matthew 14:28—28:20 + Romans 1:1—2:3, both in Sahidic on parchment, = P. Bodmer XIX.
12. Joshua in Sahidic = P. Bodmer XXI + Chester Beatty ac. 1389.
13. Jeremiah 40:3—52:34; Lamentations; Epistle of Jeremy; Baruch 1:1—5:5, all in Sahidic on parchment, = P. Bodmer XXII + Mississippi Coptic Codex II.
14. Isaiah 47:1—66:24 in Sahidic = P. Bodmer XXIII.
15. Psalms 17—118 = P. Bodmer XXIV.
16. Thucydides; Suzanna; Daniel; Moral Exhortations = P. Bodmer XXVII, XLV, XLVI, XLVII.
17. A satyr play on the confrontation of Heracles and Atlas, a papyrus roll, = P. Bodmer XXVIII.
18. Codex Visionum = P. Bodmer XXIX — XXXVIII. (For P. Bodmer XXXIX see the inventory of specifically Pachomian material below.)
19. Song of Songs in Sahidic on parchment = P. Bodmer XL.
20. *The Acts of Paul*, Ephesus Episode, in Subachmimic, = P. Bodmer XLI.
21. Fragments of the *Iliad* from a papyrus roll = P. Bodmer XLVIII.
22. Fragments of the *Odyssey* from a papyrus roll = P. Bodmer XLIX.

23. Mathematical exercises in Greek; John 10:7 — 13:38 in Subachmimic = Chester Beatty ac. 1390.
24. *The Apocalypse of Elijah* in Sahidic = Chester Beatty ac. 1493 = P. Chester Beatty 2018.
25. A Greek grammar; a Graeco-Latin lexicon on Romans, 2 Corinthians, Galatians, Ephesians = Chester Beatty ac. 1499.
26. Psalms 72:6—23, 25—76:1; 77:1—18, 20—81:7; 82:2—84:14; 85:2—88:20 = Chester Beatty ac. 1501 = P. Chester Beatty XIII = Rahlfs 2149.
27. Psalms 31:8–11; 26:1–6, 8–14; 2:1–8 = Chester Beatty ac. 1501 = P. Chester Beatty XIV = Rahlfs 2150.
28. Tax receipts of 339–47 A.D. from Panopolis (Achmim) in a largely uninscribed and unbound quire constructed from two papyrus rolls with correspondence of the Strategus of the Panopolitan nome of 298-300 A.D. = P. Beatty Panopolitanus = Chester Beatty ac. 2554.
29. Melito of Sardis *On the Passover*; 2 Maccabees 5:27—7:41; 1 Peter; Jonah; a homily or hymn, = The Crosby-Schøyen Codex = ms. 193 of The Schøyen Collection of Western Manuscripts.
30. Scholia to the *Odyssey* 1 from a papyrus roll = P. Rob. inv. 32 + P. Colon. inv. 906.
31. Achilleus Tatios from a papyrus roll = P. Rob. inv. 35 + P. Colon. inv. 901.
32. *Odyssey* 3–4 from a papyrus roll = P. Rob. inv. 43 + P. Colon. inv. 902.
33. A piece of ethnography or a philosophical treatise from a papyrus roll = P. Rob. inv. 37 + P. Colon. inv. 903.
34. Cicero, *in Catilinam*; Psalmus Responsorius; Greek liturgical text; Alcestis, all in Latin except the Greek liturgical text, = Codex Miscellani = P. Barcinonenses inv. 149–61 + P. Duke in L 1 [ex P. Rob. inv. 201].
35. Gospels of Luke; John; Mark, all in Sahidic = P. Palau Ribes 181–83.

The total quantity of material would involve what remains of some 37 books. They consist of 9 Greek classical papyrus rolls (numbers 1, 2, 17, 23, 24, 32–35) and 28 codices (numbers 3–16, 18–22, 25–31, 36, 37). The codices may be subdivided as follows: 21 are on papyrus (numbers 3–6, 8, 10, 12, 14-16, 18, 20, 22, 25–31, 36, 37), 5 on parchment (numbers 7, 9, 11, 13, 19), and of 1 the Bibliothèque Bodmer has not divulged the material (number 22). 10 are in Greek (numbers 3, 5, 6, 8, 15, 16, 18, 28–30), 2 in Greek and Latin (numbers 27, 36), and 1 in Greek and Subachmimic (number 25). 15 are in Coptic (numbers 4, 7, 9–14, 19–22, 26, 31, 37), of which 10 are in Sahidic (numbers 9–14, 19, 26, 31, 37), 1 in Bohairic (number 4), 1 in Proto-Sahidic (number 7), 1 in Subachmimic (number 20), and of 1 the Bibliothèque Bodmer has not divulged the dialect (number 22). 2 are non-Christian (numbers 5, 30), 21 Christian (numbers 3, 4, 6–15, 18–21, 26, 28, 29, 31, 37) and 4 partly each (numbers 16, 25, 27, 36). 11 contain something from the Old Testament (numbers 7, 9, 10, 12-16, 19, 28, 29) and 6 something from the New Testament (numbers 3, 8, 11, 21, 25, 37) and 3 something from each (numbers 4, 6, 31).

A distinctive part of this discovery consists of archival copies of official letters of Abbots of the Pachomian Monastic Order:

1. Pachomius' Letter 11b in Sahidic, a small parchment roll, = P. Bodmer XXXIX.
2. Pachomius' Letters 9a, 9b, 10, 11 b, from a papyrus codex, in Sahidic = Chester Beatty Glass Container No. 54 = ac. 2556.
3. Pachomius' Letters 1–3, 7, 10, 11a in Greek, a small parchment roll in rotuli format, = Chester Beatty Ms. W. 145 + Cologne inv. 3288 = P. Köln 174 = three fragments from Letter 7.
4. Theodore's Letter 2 in Sahidic, a small parchment roll in rotuli format, = Chester Beatty Library ac. 1486.
5. A second copy of Theodore's Letter 2, a small parchment roll in rotuli format in an unidentified private German collection, published by Martin Krause.
6. Horsiesios' Letter 3 in Sahidic, a small papyrus roll, = Chester Beatty Library ac. 1494.
7. Horsiesios' Letter 4 in Sahidic, a small papyrus roll, = Chester Beatty Library ac. 1495.
8. Pachomius' Letter 8 in Sahidic, a small parchment roll, = Cologne inv. 3286 = P. Colon. Copt. 2 = P. Köln ägypt. 8.
9. Pachomius' Letters 10-11a in Sahidic, a small parchment roll, = Cologne inv. 3287 = P. Colon. Copt. 1 = P. Köln ägypt. 9.

ESTABLISHING THE DISCOVERY AND MARKETING OF THE LIBRARY

It has taken more than a generation to establish the provenience of the Bodmer papyri, the approximate extent of their contents beyond the holdings of the Bibliothèque Bodmer, and the details of their discovery and marketing. The course of this development can be traced as follows.

Victor Martin listed Panopolis (Achmim) as the provenience on the basis of the land register on the recto of the rolls.[21] Yet Martin recognized that once the land register was no longer in use, the rolls could have been moved anywhere, in which connection he referred to Eric C. Turner,[22] where material from other nomes is reported to have been found at Oxyrhynchus. On 25 December 58 Martin wrote to William H. Willis: "That they were found in Achmim, though probable, is by no means certain." Willis, who quotes Martin, took the comment to apply to the Bodmer Papyri in general.[23]

But one may contrast Rodolphe Kasser in Papyrus Bodmer III: ". . . without the exact provenience having been revealed thus far. One said that all the pieces had been found together in Upper Egypt, and that it had to do with a private library. We do not know anything more."[24] Similarly Martin, in *Papyrus Bodmer IV*, listed the place of discovery as "unknown."[25] But Kasser, in *Papyrus Bodmer XVI*, reported that "we can admit, as a possibility if not probability, that these texts were copied between Achmim and Thebes, and, by preference, in the neighbourhood of the latter site."[26] The importance of Thebes is due to the Proto-Sahidic (previously called Proto-Theban) dialect Kasser identified in *Papyrus Bodmer VI*, an association made explicit by Michael Testuz, *Papyrus Bodmer VII–IX*, who hence supported Thebes as the place of origin of P. Bodmer VII–IX.[27]

21. Martin, *Papyrus Bodmer I*, 21.
22. Turner, "Roman Oxyrhynchus"; see also Turner, "Recto and Verso."
23. Willis, "New Collections of Papyri," 383 n. 1.
24. Kasser, *Papyrus Bodmer III*, 177.iii.
25. Martin, *Papyrus Bodmer IV*, 7.
26. Kasser, *Papyrus Bodmer XVI*, 7.
27. Testuz, *Papyrus Bodmer VII–IX*, 32.

Then Kasser, in *Papyrus Bodmer XXVIII*, stated: "Various indications, internal or external, would tend to orient our research a bit north of Thebes."[28] But the internal evidence, the dialects, is so variegated (Sahidic, Bohairic, Paleo-Sahidic, Subachmimic) as to make them a conflicting and hence unreliable indication of the site of the discovery.

Kasser's remark in *Papyrus Bodmer XXI*, p. 7, n. 1 might have seemed preferable: "Of course an admission of uncertainty is worth more than the affirmation of a 'certainty' based on false information."[29]

The source of the external information was not identified by Kasser, but by Olivier Reverdin in his Preface, 'Les Genevois et Menandre,' to Menandre, *La Samienne*, translated into French and adapted from the Greek by André Hurst, as presented on the French-language Swiss radio on 15 March 1975, published as a pamphlet in 1975, p. 1: "For a long time one had only quite vague indications about their provenience. Shortly before his death, however, the antiquities dealer who had sold them lifted the secret. He revealed that these papyri came from a village near Nag Hammadi . . . It is to Mr. Rodolphe Kasser, Professor of Coptic Language and Literature at the Faculty of Letters of Geneva, and editor of a large part of these papyri in the series *Papyrus Bodmer*, that he made his confession."

Then, with the resumption of publication of the monograph series, Kasser and Guglielmo Cavallo reported: 'Various converging indications (among them the dialects of the Coptic texts) make very plausible the localization of this discovery in Upper Egypt a bit to the east of Nag Hammadi."[30]

In the context of his 1984 statement Kasser referred explicitly to my having announced inappropriately in the *Bulletin of the Institute for Antiquity and Christianity*,[31] the discovery of the identity of the Bodmer Papyri with the Dishnā Papers. On receipt of that *Bulletin* he had requested further information, and on 23 June 1980 I obliged by mailing him a current draft of the relevant section of a book I had begun on the topic. Thus before announcing his final decision as to the provenience of the Bodmer Papyri (which agrees with the outcome of my investiga-

28. Kasser, *Papyrus Bodmer XXVIII*, 7 n. 1.

29. Kasser, *Papyrus Bodmer XXI*, 7 n. 1.

30. Kasser and Cavallo, *Papyrus Bodmer XXIX*, 100, n. 2.

31. Robinson, *Bulletin* 7/1 (March 1980) 6–7.

tions), he had access to my published and unpublished material reporting basically the same facts as found in the present essay, though no public acknowledgement is made to this effect.

Instead, in a recent article, Kasser has maintained that my investigations were based on no more than village "rumor" rendered irrelevant by the passing of 25 years.[32] Though this criticism is to be dismissed as simply not accurate, it does serve to indicate that it would be relevant to publish the sources of the information presented above in section 2 on the Discovery and Marketing of the Library.

My own investigation began as part of my efforts to track down the discoverers and middlemen of the Nag Hammadi codices. Jean Doresse had referred to a priest he thought had seen the Nag Hammadi codices, Abūnā Dāʾūd, whom I found after church on 20 November 1974 at the Deir al-Malāk where he had officiated, near al-Qaṣr not far from Nag Hammadi. Another priest there, to whom he introduced me, mentioned that the discovered codices had been for a time in the possession of a Dishnā priest named Manqaryus and his son Ṭānyūs. I added this secondarily to my essay "On The Codicology of the Nag Hammadi Codices,"[33] on the assumption that it had to do with the Nag Hammadi codices.

It was in the process of following up this lead that I interviewed the Inspector for Agriculture of the Dishnā Governorate, Isḥāg Ayyūb Isḥāq, who told me about what he referred to as the Dishnā Papers. He gave me on 12 September 1975 the name of an antiquities dealer in Alexandria, Tawfīq Saʿd, who, he said, had acquired some of them. On 30 December 1975, his son, a jeweller in Alexandria, Émile Tawfīq Saʿd, showed me pictures of antiquities his deceased father had sold. He even let me borrow the three pictures that had to do with manuscripts, which were soon identified as leaves of P. Bodmer XXIV (with the help of Albert Pietersma) and XL (with the help of Marvin W. Meyer and Hans Quecke).

I interviewed, repeatedly and year after year (in the Dishnā area alone: 18–21 November 1974; 11–13 January, 10–18 September, 25 November—20 December 1975; 30 November—6 December, 18–30 December 1976; 5–24 January 1978; 3–11 January, 15–20 December

32. Kasser, "Status quaestionis 1988," esp. 192 and n. 9.

33. Robinson, "On the Codicology," 16.

1980), the principals in the story (listed in the order in which they occur in the narrative):

- the widow of "al-Qummuṣ" Manqaryūs in Dishnā
- "al-Qummuṣ" Ṭānyūs (the son of "al-Qummuṣ" Manqaryūs) in Cairo
- Rāghib Andarāwus "al-Qiss" ʿAbd al-Sayyid in Dishnā, Nag Hammadi and Cairo
- Riyāḍ Jirjis Fām and his son Nuṣḥī, both in Heliopolis
- Mūsā Fikrī Ashʿiyah in Dishnā
- Abū al-Wafā Aḥmad Ismāʿīl in Fāw Qiblī
- Saʿīd Diryās Ḥabashī in Dishnā
- ʿAzīz Suryāl ʿAṭīyah in Claremont, California.

These investigations ultimately located the discoverer, Ḥasan Muḥammad al-Sammān, whom I interviewed at Abū Manāʿ 11 August 1981. During the interview someone from the back of the crowd called out that he too had been involved. I asked his name. He replied: ʿAbd al-ʿĀl ʿUmar, giving in the customary Arab way his and his father's name. I acknowledged the validity of his claim by adding his grandfather's name: al-ʿAbbādī, in this way incidentally accrediting myself as someone with the basic facts already in hand, which he then reported much as I had already heard more than once. Obviously in such repeated interviews there are minor fluctuations and contradictions, at times protestations of innocence and self-serving interpretations; but in the cross-examination procedure the basic facts were again and again confirmed.

Occasional details provided by Riyāḍ fit remarkably well the actual inventory as we know it. The small rolls the size of a finger that Tano told him were letters could well have been the archival copies of letters of Pachomian Abbots. Riyāḍ described one book as balled up, as if it had been forced into the bottom of a piriform jar. This corresponds to the balled-up condition in which P. Bodmer XXII = Mississippi Coptic Codex II was acquired. The approximate size of the discovery and its variegated contents, both rolls and codices, both papyrus and parchment, were reported by the middlemen, though of course they were not able to report on the language of the texts or their contents.

Written documentation, when available, has provided striking confirmation, such as the parish diary of the Franciscan Church near Nag

Hammadi confirming that Jose O'Callaghan had been there `to look for papers' in 1964-65, as Saᶜid Diryās Ḥabashī had maintained. Well after my investigations in Egypt had been completed, I located on 19 January 1984, stapled at ac. 1390 in the Accessions Book of the Chester Beatty Library, the typed note in Tano's wooden English and unusual spelling that summarized the conclusions regarding the provenience to which my investigations had already led me.

I am heavily indebted to Father Louis Doutreleau, SJ, who has written me over a period of years (1976–1980), with authorization to publish, details of the acquisition process in Cairo, together with memoranda he wrote in Cairo at the time and photographs taken in Cairo of materials he examined there for Bodmer that later became Bodmer Papyri. Kasser's repudiation of Father Doutreleau (whom he has never met) as too senile to be taken seriously is valid neither in terms of his age nor in terms of his detailed, intelligent letters and the earlier records he has supplied. I called to Kasser's attention a doctorate *honoris causa* Father Doutreleau had recently received from the University of Cologne. When I visited Father Doutreleau at the offices of Sources Chrêtiennes at Lyon on 26 May 1992, he took satisfaction in pointing out a second honorary doctorate framed and hung on his wall.

Confirmation has even belatedly come, as I searched secondary literature in this regard, from Kasser himself. In "Fragments du livre biblique de la Genese caches dans la reliure d'un codex gnostique," he reported: "I have serious reason to believe that they [the Bodmer Papyri] were found, like the Gnostic codices mentioned above, in a place near Nag Hammadi."[34] In "Les dialectes coptes," he sharpened the identification: "A bit to the east (north-east) of Nag Hammadi."[35] However it is quite inaccurate to describe[36] my identification of the site as an 'echo' of his vague allusions to a site to the east of Nag Hammadi (the earliest of which he cites being his essay "Le dialecte protosaïdique de Thèbes").[37] For I turned to secondary literature concerning the provenience of the Bodmer Papyri only after I had discovered that they were the same manuscript discovery that in Upper Egypt is known as the Dishnā Papers.

34. Kasser, "Fragments," 80.

35. Kasser, "Les dialects coptes," 81.

36. Kasser, "Status quastionis 1988," 192 and n.7.

37. Kasser, "Le dialecte protosaïdique de Thèbes," 77 n. 2.

Kasser reported that Tano gave "'Dabba' or 'Debba' (al-Dabba, 5 km to the east, slightly north-east, of Nag Hammadi)" as the location.[38] This village is too near the Nile to have preserved manuscripts intact over the years, in view of the annual inundations flooding this area prior to the construction of the High Dam. But it is the first railroad station upstream from Nag Hammadi, recommended in the 1914 English-language Baedeker as the station from which to visit the cliff area. It would be a more convenient point of departure for Abū Manāʿ than would be Dishnā (and for the Jabal al-Ṭārif than would be Nag Hammadi), if one planned to go by foot or donkey, but would have been replaced by Dishnā (or Nag Hammadi) once a taxi came in question (al-Dabba lacks a taxi stand). It was in fact the first name used to locate the Nag Hammadi codices (by the Abbot Étienne Drioton, General Director of the Department of Antiquities, in a letter of 13 February 1948 to Jean Doresse, reporting on an interview with the same Tano, and referring to "the discovery of Daba"). Tano liked to associate the Dishnā Papers with the Nag Hammadi codices for financial reasons. But since the main middlemen trafficking in the Dishnā Papers were located at Dishnā, that has become the local designation.

Kasser reported having waited in publishing his own view about the location of the discovery until Bodmer's secretary [Odile Bongard] revealed her view "a few months ago."[39] When it turned out to disagree with that of Kasser, the documentation I had entrusted to him may have strengthened his hand in resisting her conclusion. For I was, in response to his query, able to clarify for him that the Dishnā to which I had referred was, in spite of the divergent French spelling, located in the area conformable to his rather than Mlle Bongard's view of the provenience. She had "affirmed in all certainty" that the site of the discovery was near a village named Mina or Minia in the Asyūt region.[40] Kasser was not able to identify there a village with any such name,[41] and hence rejected her view. The only way that she has then been able to reconcile her information with Kasser's alternative is (according to Kasser) to the effect that the Asyūt region may have been the provenience only of P. Bodmer

38. Kasser, "Status quastionis 1988," 192.

39. Ibid., 192, and n. 6.

40. Ibid., 193.

41. Ibid., 193 n. 12.

XVII, which is generally recognized to derive from a different discovery than that of the bulk of the Bodmer Papyri. In fact the local Copts of the Dishnā region offer the popular etymology to the effect that Abū Manāʿ derives from the name of the Coptic saint, Mina, which may help to explain the garbled report by Mlle Bongard.

Kasser's own view is based on information given to him by Tano 19 years after the discovery.[42] Kasser had previously maintained that such information was irrelevant: "One knows the little credence one can give to the reports of antiquities dealers when they cannot be confirmed by any archeological investigation."[43] Kasser's revised position that his interview with Tano was an exception to the usual unreliability of dealers in antiquities, in view of a special "friendship" with Tano and the fact that Tano's death was imminent, needs to be taken with a grain of salt. I interviewed Tano about the Nag Hammadi codices the same day (20 December 1971, when Kasser and I were both together in Cairo at a work session of the Technical Sub-Committee of the International Committee for the Nag Hammadi Codices and staying in the same hotel, the Garden City House). Tano seemed quite aggressive in spirit and in good health for a person his age. He died 9 February 1972. Dealers in antiquities assure all of us of special bonds of friendship ("You are my brother!"), which one should not take too seriously. But as a matter of fact, over the years Tano was telling the truth regarding the provenience with a remarkable degree of consistency to persons he trusted. Since he funded a clandestine excavation of the site of the discovery directed by Riyāḍ Jirgis Fām, Tano apparently had the correct information.

In his article on the Bodmer Papyri in *The Coptic Encyclopaedia*, Kasser has summarized his criticism of my results:

> Thus, there are nineteen codices if one considers only the reliable information gathered by the Bodmer Foundation at the time the Bodmer papyri came to be included in the library. There are some scholars who, on the basis of much later research (some thirty years after the presumed date of discovery of the Bodmer papyri), think that they can also include in the Bodmer papyri various other famous manuscripts such as the P. Palau-Ribes from Barcelona (the Gospels of Mark, Luke, and John in Sahidic Coptic, edited by H. Quecke), and, above all, various letters of

42. Ibid., 191–92.

43. Kasser, *Papyrus Bodmer VI*, viii n. 1.

> Pachomius, one of which is preserved in the Bodmer Foundation but with nothing to indicate that it might be part of the Bodmer papyri. Their suggestion is that the actual library of the famous Monastery of Saint Pachomius at Faw al-Qibli has been rediscovered. This hypothesis is certainly very tempting, but the reliable information referred to above tends to weaken rather than strengthen it.[44]

Actually, information originally available to the Bibliothèque Bodmer seems to have been lost from sight. On 26 July 1956 Father Doutreleau had written to Victor Martin: "It is quite certain that this find of some thirty codices (in the region of Nag Hammadi, like the Gnostic papyri) cannot remain the act of a single individual." If Kasser can identify only 19 at the Bibliothèque Bodmer, where does he assume the others are to be found? Apparently he was simply unaware of some of the "reliable information gathered by the Bodmer Foundation at the time the Bodmer papyri came to be included in the library," such as the correspondence of which Doutreleau gave me a copy.

The total quantity of material would involve what remains of some 35 books (plus the 9 copies of letters of Pachomian Abbots). They consist of 10 Greek classical papyrus rolls (numbers 1, 2, 17, 21, 22, 30–33) and 26 codices (numbers 3–16, 18–20, 23–29, 34, 35). The codices may be subdivided as follows: 21 are on papyrus (numbers 3–6, 10, 12, 14–16, 18, 20, 23–29, 34, 35), and 5 on parchment (numbers 7, 9, 11, 13, 19). 10 are in Greek (numbers 3, 5, 6, 8, 15, 16, 18, 26–28), 2 in Greek and Latin (numbers 25, 34), and 1 in Greek and Subachmimic/Lycopolitan (number 23). 13 are in Coptic (numbers 4, 7, 9-14, 19, 20, 24, 29, 35), of which 10 are in Sahidic (numbers 9–14, 19, 24, 29, 35), 1 in Bohairic (number 4), 1 in Proto-Sahidic (number 7), and 1 in Subachmimic/Lycopolitan (number 20). 2 are non-Christian (numbers 5, 28), 20 Christian (numbers 3, 4, 6–15, 18–20, 24, 26, 27, 29, 35), and 4 partly each (numbers 16, 23, 25, 34). 11 contain something from the Old Testament (numbers 7, 9, 10, 12–16, 19, 26, 27), 5 something from the New Testament (numbers 3, 8, 11, 23, 35), and 3 something from each (numbers 4, 6, 29).

It is quite arbitrary to limit one's information about the provenience and the contents of the discovery to that of the Bibliothèque Bodmer. The amount of fragments in one repository that belong to codices in another link the materials in Barcelona, Cologne, Dublin, and Mississippi

44. Kasser, "Bodmer Papyri," 49.

just as firmly with the materials in the Bibliothèque Bodmer as does Kasser's comment that "not a single shred belonging to the Gnostic library [of Nag Hammadi] has been found among the Bodmer papyri and vice versa"[45] effectively serve to indicate that we have to do with two quite distinct discoveries. The reasoning is the same, and hence consistent conclusions should be drawn in both cases.

Actually, Kasser's list of 19 items does include two not represented in the Bibliothèque Bodmer (items 29 and 34), precisely because Bodmer acquired fragments of material in Barcelona and Mississippi and was kind enough to turn them over to the repository that held the bulk of the codex. Since Sir Chester acquired fragments from Tano belonging to codices acquired by Bodmer, it would be reasonable to assume other acquisitions by Sir Chester acquired at the same time from Tano should, at least as a working hypothesis, be considered part of the same discovery. This assumption has been confirmed by a note from Tano in the Book of Accessions in the Chester Beatty Library identifying one item (ac. 1390) as coming from Dishnā, with the conjecture that it was "from the Library of a Monastery." When Bodmer's assistant Mlle Bongard was later permitted to sort through Tano's fragments for vestiges of Bodmer's acquisitions, it was a matter of course that Bodmer made available to Sir Chester those that he did not identify as belonging to his acquisitions, just as he gave to Barcelona and Mississippi fragments of their acquisitions he had unknowingly acquired.

Father Doutreleau emphasized to me on my visit with him in Lyon on 26 May 1992 that Martin Bodmer and Mlle Bongard knew hardly anything about the discovery and middlemen, and that the little they knew they had learned from him. Kasser's "reliable information" is thus a secondhand version of the information I received firsthand from Doutreleau and the Copts who had been directly involved.

To discredit such research as 'some thirty years after the presumed date of the discovery' is neither accurate nor relevant. The discovery in 1952 preceded by 22 years my investigations that began in 1974, which compares not too unfavorably with the 19 years that elapsed before Tano confided in Kasser information about the provenience that Kasser took at face value. Since my research included interviews with the principals, made use of the notes Father Doutreleau made at the time of the

45. Ibid.

acquisitions, and has been confirmed by written records where available, it is hard to see how the presentation by Kasser, based on none of these sources, has a higher claim to be accurate. It is not as if he had retraced my steps and come to different conclusions; he has simply used the authority implicit in his status as an editor of the material at the Bibliothèque Bodmer to assert his view to be correct, as if he did not have to give the reasons for his claims.

In the case of P. Palau Ribes 181–183, it was put in last place in my Inventory, as being least certain. Hans Quecke had expressed skepticism to me in view of the considerably better condition of this codex compared to that of the Bodmer papyri. Kasser may hence be right that it is from a different provenience. But his negative conclusion is reached without considering the information I received from the parish diary of the Franciscan Church near Dishnā, to the effect that José O'Callaghan, who acquired the materials for the Palau Ribes collection, was actively searching in 1964–65 "for papers" in the Dishnā region, and from Saʿīd Diryās of Dishnā to the effect that O'Callaghan had obtained some material from the local Dishnā priest. When I wrote O'Callaghan to inquire if he had secured any Nag Hammadi material (which was my interest at the time), he replied that he had not, though he might have secured something from the same provenience as the Bodmer papyri. Of course O'Callaghan may have had something other than P. Palau Ribes 181–183 in mind. And of course these reports can be discredited, if one can establish reasons to do so. However they should not simply be dismissed out of hand, but rather should be investigated as to whether there may be some truth in them. Kasser was apparently unaware of them.

To postulate an independent discovery of the archival copies of letters from Abbots of the Pachomian Monastery Order, which then by pure coincidence passed through the same canals to reach the same European repositories as those which obtained Dishnā Papers at about the same time, is of course theoretically possible, but hardly probable. After all, the Coptic and Greek Pachomian letters had been completely unattested for 1500 years. Riyāḍ's report that Tano told him that the small rolls the size of a finger, among the manuscripts Riyāḍ had for sale, were letters, seems to confirm the converse probability that the Pachomian materials belong with the Dishnā Papers Riydd was trafficking.

Part of the difficulty in carrying on such a discussion is that Kasser's opinion is based on undocumented claims. He maintains that "the reliable information referred to above tends to weaken rather than strengthen" the view that one has to do with the archival remains of a Pachomian monastic library. But he does not provide that information for consideration. Michel Testuz, in *Papyrus Bodmer VII–IX*, speculated: "The content of this anthology shows that the book was produced by Christians of Egypt, probably on the order of a well-to-do member of their community, who intended it for his own library."[46] Such pure speculation is not "reliable information"; if there is such, it should be made public.

Three unpublished items included in these earlier publications were not mentioned by Rodolphe Kasser in his article on the Bodmer Papyri in *The Coptic Encyclopedia*, and for lack of confirming evidence, have also been omitted from the present Inventory:

- P. Bodmer XLII, "2 Corinthians in Coptic (dialect and material unknown)." Wolf-Peter Funk has determined that it is in Sahidic on parchment. There may be some unstated reason to assume it is not part of the Dishnā discovery. Hence one may await further information or its publication.
- P. Bodmer XLIII, "an Apocryphon in Coptic (identity, dialect and material unknown)." Kasser mentioned at a meeting on the Apocryphal Acts in Lausanne on 16 May 1992 that this is only a fragment of no significance. Though there was no further elucidation, it may be omitted pending further information or its publication.
- P. Bodmer XLIV, "Daniel in Bohairic." Wolf-Peter Funk has determined that it is in classical Bohairic on parchment, to be dated from the 10th to the 12th centuries. Hence it presumably does not come from the Dishnā discovery.

P. Bodmer I, from the *Iliad*, the verso of P. Bodmer L, as well as the Homeric fragments P. Bodmer XLVIII and XLIX, are also not mentioned by Kasser, no doubt because of the original ascription to a provenience at Panopolis (Achmim), in view of the fact that the land register on the recto comes from there. But that does not determine where the roll was later kept and reused. Furthermore, this did not originally deter Kasser from considering P. Bodmer I as belonging to the same discovery as the

46. Testuz, *Papyrus Bodmer VII–IX*, 9.

bulk of the Bodmer Papyri. For once he had edited in 1960 Bodmer Papyrus VI, in the Proto-Sahidic dialect that he at that time localized in Thebes and hence called Proto-Theban, he simply merged this Theban orientation with the Achmim orientation in 1965 into the compromise "between Achmim and Thebes, and, by preference, in the neighbourhood of the latter site" (see above). This location proved to be more or less correct, a location that he at that time conceded could have included material from Achmim. No further information has been subsequently reported as having emerged to associate the provenience of P. Bodmer I with a different discovery. Hence Kasser's original inclusion of it in the same discovery is here retained.

Appendix 2

List of Papyrus Bodmer Publications

BIBLIOTHÈQUE BODMER, COLOGNY NEAR GENEVA

Papyrus Bodmer I. Iliade, chants 5 et 6. Published by Victor Martin. Bibliotheca Bodmeriana 3. Cologny-Geneva: Bibliothèque Bodmer, 1954.

Papyrus Bodmer II. Évangile de Jean chap. 1–14. Published by Victor Martin. Bibliotheca Bodmeriana 5. Cologny-Geneva: Bibliothèque Bodmer, 1956.

Papyrus Bodmer II. Supplément. Évangile de Jean chap. 14–21. Published by Victor Martin. Cologny-Geneva: Bibliothèque Bodmer, 1958.

Papyrus Bodmer II. Supplément. Évangile de Jean chap. 14–21. Nouvelle édition augmentée et corrigée avec reproduction photographique complète du manuscrit (chap. 1–21). Published by Victor Martin and J. W. B. Barns. Cologny-Geneva: Bibliothèque Bodmer, 1962.

[P. Bodmer II] Seider, Richard. *Paläographie der griechischen Papyri.* Vol. 2. Stuttgart: Hiersemann, 1970.

[P. Bodmer II] Aland, Kurt. "Neue neutestamentliche Papyri III: 2. Neue Fragmente zu P^{66}." *New Testament Studies* 20 (1974) 376–81.

Papyrus Bodmer III. Évangile de Jean et Genèse I–IV,2 en bohairique. Edited by Rodolphe Kasser. Corpus Scriptorum Christianorum Orientalium 177. Scriptores Coptici 25. Louvain: Secrétariat du CorpusSCO, 1958.

Papyrus Bodmer III. Évangile de Jean et Genèse I–IV,2 en bohairique. Translated by Rodolphe Kasser. Corpus Scriptorum Christianorum Orientalium 178. Scriptores Coptici 26. Louvain: Secrétariat du CorpusSCO, 1958.

Papyrus Bodmer IV. Ménandre: Le Dyscolos. Published by Victor Martin. Cologny-Geneva: Bibliothèque Bodmer, 1958 [1959]. See also with P. Bodmer XXVI below.

[P. Bodmer IV] *Papyrus Bodmer XXVI. Ménandre: Le Bouclier. En appendice: compléments au Papyrus Bodmer IV. Ménandre: Le Dyscolos.* Published by Rodolphe Kasser with Colin Austin. Cologny-Geneva: Bibliothèque Bodmer, 1969.

[P. Bodmer IV] Turner, E. G. "Emendations to Menander's *Dyskolos*." *Bulletin of the Institute of Classical Studies of London University* 6 (1959) 61–72.

[P. Bodmer IV] Van Groningen, B. A. *Menander Dyskolos met inleiding en commentaar uitgegeven*. Griekse en Latijnse Schrijvers met Aantekeningen 66. Leiden: Brill, 1960.

[P. Bodmer IV] Van Groningen, B. A. *Le Dyscolos de Ménandre: Étude critique du texte*. Verhandelingen der Koninklijke Nederlandse Akademie van Wetenschappen, Afd. Letterkunde, nieuwe reeks 67.3. Amsterdam: N. V. Noord-Hollandsche Uitgevers Maatschappij, 1960.

[P. Bodmer IV] Marzullo, Benedetto. *Menandro, Il Misantropo*. Universale Einaudi 35. Turin: Einaudi, 1959.

[P. Bodmer IV] Gallavotti, Carlo. *Menandro, Dyscolos: Testo critico e interpretazione*. Ricerche Filologiche 2. Naples: Glaux, 1959.

[P. Bodmer IV] Sphyroeras, N.B. Athens: Papyros, 1959.

[P. Bodmer IV] Diano, Carlo. Menandro, *Dyskolos, ouvero sia Il Selvatico*. Proagones: Collezione di Studi e Testi. Testi 1. Padua: Antenore, 1960.

[P. Bodmer IV] Mette, Hans Joachim. *Menandros Dyskolos*. Göttingen: Vandenhoeck & Ruprecht, 1960; 2nd improved edition, 1961.

[P. Bodmer IV] Bingen, Jean. Menander, *Dyscolos: Critical Edition*. Textus Minores 26. Leiden: Brill, 1960; 2nd enlarged edition, 1964.

[P. Bodmer IV] Treu, Max. Menander, *Dyskolos: Griechisch und deutsch mit textkritischem Apparat und Erläuterungen herausgegeben*. Tusculum-Bücherei. Munich: Heimeran, 1960.

[P. Bodmer IV] Handley, E. W. *The Dyskolos of Menander*. London: Methuen, 1965.

[P. Bodmer IV] Arnott, W. C. *Menander*. Vol. 1. The Loeb Classical Library. Cambridge: Harvard University Press; and London: Heinemann, 1979.

[P. Bodmer IV] Kraus, Walther. *Der Menschenfeind (Dyskolos), herausgegeben und übersetzt*. Lebendige Antike. Zurich: Artemis, 1960.

[P. Bodmer IV] Kraus, Walther. *Menanders Dyskolos mit einem kritischen Kommentar*. Österreichische Akademie der Wissenschaften, Philosophisch-historische Klasse, Sitzungsberichte, 234. Band, 4. Abhandlung. Vienna: Hermann Böhlaus Nachf., 1960.

[P. Bodmer IV] Lloyd-Jones, H. *Menandri Dyscolus*. Scriptorum Classicorum Bibliotheca Oxoniensis. Oxford: Clarendon, 1960.

[P. Bodmer IV] Martin, Jean. *Ménandre: L'Atrabilaire: Édition, introduction et commentaire*. "Erasme": Collection de textes grecs commentés. Paris: Presses Universitaires de France, 1961.

[P. Bodmer IV] Foss, Otto. *Dyskolos*. Kopenhagen: Gyldendal, 1960.

[P. Bodmer IV] Jacques, Jean-Marie. *Ménandre, Le Dyscolos*. Paris: Societé d'Édition 'Les Belles Lettres,' 1963.

[P. Bodmer IV] Koch, Wilhelm. *Dyskolos*. Aschendorffs Sammlung lateinischer und griechischer Klassiker. Münster: Aschendorff, 1960.

[P. Bodmer IV] Stoessl, F. *Menander, Dyskolos: Kommentar*. Paderborn: Schöningh, text 1961; "Erlaüterungen," 1963.

[P. Bodmer IV] Blake, Warren E. *Menander's Dyscolus: Introduction, Text, Textual Commentary and Interpretive Translation*. Philological Monographs 24. New York: American Philological Association, 1966.

[P. Bodmer IV] Sandbach, F. H. *Menandri reliquiae selectae*. Oxford: Clarendon, 1972.

[P. Bodmer IV] Treu, Kurt, and Ursula Treu. *Menander*. Reclams Universal-Bibliothek 626. Leipzig: Reclam, 1975.

[P. Bodmer IV] Treu, Kurt, and Ursula Treu. *Menander—Herondas: Werke in einem Band.* Bibliothek der Antike, Griechische Reihe. Berlin: Aufbau-Verlag, 1980. Pp. 3–46.

[P. Bodmer IV] Gaulis, Louis, and Hurst, André. *Ménandre Théâtre (Les trois comédies du papyrus de Cologny): La Samienne; Cnemon le misanthrope (Dyscolos); Le Bouclier.* "Lettres Universelles." Lausanne: Éditions de l'Aire, 1981.

Papyrus Bodmer V. Nativité de Marie. Published by Michel Testuz. Cologny-Geneva: Bibliothèque Bodmer, 1958.

[P. Bodmer V] De Strycker, Émile. *La forme la plus ancienne du Protévangile de Jacques: Recherches sur le Papyrus Bodmer 5 avec une édition critique du texte grec et une traduction annotée.* Subsidia Hagiographica 33. Bruxelles: Société des Bollandistes, 1961.

Papyrus Bodmer VI. Livre des Proverbes. Edited by Rodolphe Kasser. Corpus Scriptorum Christianorum Orientalium 194. Scriptores Coptici 27. Louvain: Secrétariat du CorpusSCO, 1960.

Papyrus Bodmer VI. Livre des Proverbes. Translated by Rodolphe Kasser. Corpus Scriptorum Christianorum Orientalium 195. Scriptores Coptici 28. Louvain: Secrétariat général du CorpusSCO, 1960.

Papyrus Bodmer VII–IX. VII: L'Épître de Jude; VIII: Les deux Épîtres de Pierre; IX: Les Psaumes 33 et 34. Published by Michel Testuz. Cologny-Geneva: Bibliothèque Bodmer, 1959.

[P. Bodmer VIII] Martini, Carolus M. *Beati Petri Apostoli Epistulae: Ex Papyro Bodmeriana VIII Transcriptae.* Milan: Pizzi, 1968.

Papyrus Bodmer X–XII. X: Correspondance apocryphe des Corinthiens et de l'apôtre Paul; XI: Onzième Ode de Salomon; XII: Fragment d'un Hymne liturgique. Manuscrit du IIIe siècle. Published by Michel Testuz. Cologny-Geneva: Bibliothèque Bodmer, 1959.

[P. Bodmer XI] Lattke, Michael. *Die Oden Salomos in ihrer Bedeutung für Neues Testament und Gnosis.* Volume 1: *Ausführliche Handschriftenbeschreibung, ediert mit deutscher Parallel-Übersetzung, Interpretation der Oden Salomos in der Pistis Sophia.* Orbis Biblicus et Orientalis 25.1. Göttingen: Vandenhoeck & Ruprecht, 1979.

[P. Bodmer XI] Charlesworth, James H. *Papyri and Leather Manuscripts of the Odes of Solomon.* Dickerson Series of Facsimiles of Manuscripts Important for Christian Origins 1. Durham, NC: International Center for the Study of Ancient Near Eastern Civilizations and Christian Origins, Duke University, 1981.

[P. Bodmer XII] Perler, Othmar. *Ein Hymnus zur Ostervigil von Meliton? (Papyrus Bodmer XII).* Paradosis: Beiträge zur Geschichte der altchristlichen Literatur und Theologie 15. Freiburg, Switzerland: Universitätsverlag, 1960.

[P. Bodmer XII] Hall, Stuart George. Melito of Sardis, *On Pascha and Fragments.* Oxford Early Christian Texts. Oxford: Clarendon, 1979, p. 85.

[P. Bodmer XII] Perler, Othmar. Méliton de Sardes, *Sur la Pâque et fragments.* Sources chrétiennes 123. Paris: Cerf. 1966. Pp. 128ff.

Papyrus Bodmer XIII. Méliton de Sardes, Homélie sur la Pâque. Manuscrit du IIIe siècle. Published by Michel Testuz. Cologny-Geneva: Bibliothèque Bodmer, 1960.

[P. Bodmer XIII] Perler, Othmar. Méliton de Sardes, *Sur la Pâque et fragments.* Sources chrétiennes 123. Paris: Cerf. 1966.

[P. Bodmer XIII] Hall, Stuart George. Melito of Sardis, *On Pascha and Fragments.* Oxford Early Christian Texts. Oxford: Clarendon, 1979.

Papyrus Bodmer XIV. Évangile de Luc chap. 3–24. Published by Victor Martin and Rodolphe Kasser. Cologny-Geneva: Bibliothèque Bodmer, 1961.

Papyrus Bodmer XV. Évangile de Jean chap. 1–15. Published by Victor Martin and Rodolphe Kasser. Cologny-Geneva: Bibliothèque Bodmer, 1961.

[P. Bodmer XIV–XV] Aland, Kurt. "Neue neutestamentliche Papyri III: 3. Neue Fragmente zu P^{75}." *New Testament Studies* 22 (1976) 375–81.

Papyrus Bodmer XVI. Exode I–XV,21 en sahidique. Published by Rodolphe Kasser. Cologny-Geneva: Bibliothèque Bodmer, 1961.

[Papyrus Bodmer XVII. *Actes des Apôtres; Épîtres de Jacques, Pierre, Jean et Jude*. Published by Rodolphe Kasser. Cologny-Geneva: Bibliothèque Bodmer, 1961. Not from the shared provenience.]

Papyrus Bodmer XVIII. Deutéronome I–X,7 en sahidique. Published by Rodolphe Kasser. Cologny-Geneva: Bibliothèque Bodmer, 1962.

Papyrus Bodmer XIX. Évangile de Matthieu XIV,28–XXVIII,20; Épître aux Romains I,1–II,3 en sahidique. Published by Rodolphe Kasser. Cologny-Geneva: Bibliothèque Bodmer, 1962.

Papyrus Bodmer XX. Apologie de Philéas évêque de Thmouis. Published by Victor Martin. With an "Essai de reconstruction du texte original grec," bound separately. Cologny-Geneva: Bibliothèque Bodmer, 1964.

[P. Bodmer XX] Halkin, Fr. "L'Apologie du Martyr Philéas de Thmouis (Papyrus Bodmer XX) et les Actes latins de Philéas et Philoromus." *Analecta Bollandiana* 81 (1963) 5–27.

[P. Bodmer XX] Pietersma, Albert. *The Acts of Phileas Bishop of Thmuis (Including Fragments of the Greek Psalter): P. Chester Beatty XV (With a New Edition of P. Bodmer XX, and Halkin's Latin Acta)*. Geneva: Cramer, 1984. Pp. 85–99.

Papyrus Bodmer XXI. Josué VI,16–25, VII,6–XI,23, XXII,1–2,19–XXIII,7,15–XXIV,23 en sahidique. Published by Rodolphe Kasser. Cologny-Geneva: Bibliothèque Bodmer, 1963.

[Chester Beatty Library, Accession No. 1389 (Joshua 1–6) = P. Bodmer XXI] *Joshua I–VI and Other Passages in Coptic, edited from a Fourth-Century Sahidic Codex in the Chester Beatty Library, Dublin*. Edited by A. F. Shore. Chester Beatty Monographs 9. Dublin: Hodges Figgis, 1963.

[Chester Beatty Library, Accession No. 1389 (Joshua 1–6) = P. Bodmer XXI] Kasser, Rodolphe. *L'Évangile selon saint Jean et les versions coptes de la Bible*, pp. 93–167. Bibliothèque théologique. Neuchâtel: Delachaux et Niestlé. 1966.

Papyrus Bodmer XXII et Mississippi Coptic Codex II. Jérémie XL,3–LII,34; Lamentations; Épître de Jérémie; Baruch I,1–V,5 en sahidique. Published by Rodolphe Kasser. Cologny-Geneva: Bibliothèque Bodmer, 1964.

Papyrus Bodmer XXIII. Esaie XLVII,1–LXVI, 24 en sahidique. Published by Rodolphe Kasser. Cologny-Geneva: Bibliothèque Bodmer, 1965.

Papyrus Bodmer XXIV. Psaumes XVII–CXVIII. Published by Rodolphe Kasser and Michel Testuz. Cologny-Geneva: Bibliothèque Bodmer, 1967.

[P. Bodmer XXV] Roca-Puig, Ramon. "Fragment de 'La Samia' de Ménandre, Papir de Barcelona, inventari no 45." *Boletin de la Real Academia de Buenas Letras de Barcelona* 32 (1967–68) 5–13.

[P. Bodmer XXV] Roca-Puig, Ramon. "Un Fragmento de 'La Samia' de Ménandro: P. Barc. 45." *Estudios Clasicos* 12 (1968) 375–83.

Papyrus Bodmer XXV. Ménandre: La Samienne. Published by Rodolphe Kasser with Colin Austin. Cologny-Geneva: Bibliothèque Bodmer, 1969.

[P. Bodmer XXV and XXVI] Austin, Colin. *Menandri Aspis et Samia*. I. *Textus (cum apparatu critico) et indices*; II. *Subsidia interpretationis*. Kleine Texte für Vorlesungen und Übungen 188a, 188b. Berlin: de Gruyter, 1969, 1970.

[P. Bodmer XXV] Jacques, Jean-Marie. Ménandre, *La Samienne*. Collection des universités de France. Paris: Les Belles Lettres, 1971.

[P. Bodmer XXV] Hurst, André. Ménandre, *La Samienne*. Off-print of *Bastions de Genève* (Revue published by the Association des Universitaires de Genève.) 1974. (French translation only.)

[P. Bodmer XXV] Hofmann, Heinz. "A New Interpretation of Certain Aspects in Menander's Samia." In *Proceedings of the XIV International Congress of Papyrologists Oxford, 24–31 July 1974*, 167–75. London: Egypt Exploration Society for the British Academy, 1975. [Interpretation only.]

[P. Bodmer XXV] Sandbach, F. H. *Menandri reliquiae selectae*. Oxford: 1972.

[P. Bodmer XXV] Treu, Kurt, and Ursula Treu. *Menander*. Reclams Universal-Bibliothek 626. Leipzig: Reclam, 1975.

[P. Bodmer XXV] Treu, Kurt, and Ursula Treu. *Menander—Herondas: Werke in einem Band*. Bibliothek der Antike, Griechische Reihe. Berlin: Aufbau-Verlag, 1980. Pp. 47–86.

[P. Bodmer XXV] Gaulis, Louis, and Hurst, André. *Ménandre Théâtre (Les trois comédies du papyrus de Cologny): La Samienne; Cnemon le misanthrope (Dyscolos); Le Bouclier*. "Lettres Universelles." Lausanne: Éditions de l'Aire, 1981.

[P. Bodmer XXVI = Cologne Inv. 904] Merkelbach, Reinhold. "Wartetext 2: P. Colon. inv. 904: Komödienfragment." *Zeitschrift für Papyrologie und Epigraphik* 1 (1967) 103–4.

[P. Bodmer XXVI = Cologne Inventory Number 904 = P. Köln 3] Kramer, Bärbel. "Menander, Aspis 482–497; 520–535." *Kölner Papyri (P. Köln)* 1. Papyrologica Coloniensia 7.1. Opladen: Westdeutscher Verlag, 1976. Pp. 18–20.

Papyrus Bodmer XXVI. Ménandre: Le Bouclier. En appendice: compléments au Papyrus Bodmer IV. Ménandre: Le Dyscolos. Published by Rodolphe Kasser with Colin Austin. Cologny-Geneva: Bibliothèque Bodmer, 1969.

[P. Bodmer XXVI] Sandbach, F. H. *Menandri reliquiae selectae*. Scriptorum classicorum bibliotheca Oxoniensis. Oxford: Clarendon, 1972.

[P. Bodmer XXVI] Treu, Kurt, and Ursula Treu. *Menander*. Reclams Universal-Bibliothek 626. Leipzig: Reclam, 1975.

[P. Bodmer XXVI] Treu, Kurt, and Ursula Treu. *Menander—Herondas: Werke in einem Band*. Bibliothek der Antike, Griechische Reihe. Berlin: Aufbau-Verlag, 1980. Pp. 139–60.

[P. Bodmer XXVI] Gaulis, Louis, and André Hurst. *Ménandre Théâtre (Les trois comédies du papyrus de Cologny): La Samienne; Cnemon le misanthrope (Dyscolos); Le Bouclier*. "Lettres Universelles." Lausanne: Éditions de l'Aire, 1981.

[P. Bodmer XXVII] Carlini, Antonio. "Il papiro di Tucidide della Bibliotheca Bodmeriana (P. Bodmer XXVII)." *Museum Helveticum* 32 (1975) 33–40 + plates 1–3.

[P. Bodmer XXVII] Carlini, Antonio et al. *Papiri Letterari Greci*. Biblioteca degli Studi Classici e Orientali 13. Pisa: Giardini Editori e Stampatori, 1978. Pp. 65–77.

[P. Bodmer XXVIII] Turner, Eric G. "Papyrus Bodmer XXVIII: A Satyr-Play on the Confrontation of Heracles and Atlas." *Museum Helveticum* 33 (1976) 1–23.

[Codex Visionum 1,1—9,19 = "Vision of Dorotheos"] *Papyrus Bodmer XXIX. Vision de Dorotheos.* Published by André Hurst, Olivier Reverdin, and Jean Rudhardt. Cologny-Geneva: Fondation Martin Bodmer, 1984.

Codex Visionum 9,20—10,17 = Poem "on Abraham" = P. Bodmer XXX.

Codex Visionum 10,18—14,11 = Poem "on the Just" = P. Bodmer XXXI.

Codex Visionum 14,12—15,16 = "[. . .] of the Lord Jesus" = P. Bodmer XXXII.

Codex Visionum 15,17–39 = Murder of Abel by Cain 1 = "What Would Say Cain Having Murdered [Abel]" = P. Bodmer XXXIII.

Codex Visionum 15,40—16,31 = "The Lord to the [. . .]" = P. Bodmer XXXIV.

Codex Visionum 16,32—19,2 = The Murder of Abel by Cain 2 = "[. . .] Abel Destroyed by Cain" = P. Bodmer XXXV, unpublished.]

Codex Visionum 19,3—20,37 = Poem with a Mutilated Title = P. Bodmer XXXVI.

Codex Visionum 21–22 = Hymn? = P. Bodmer XXXVII.

Codex Visionum 23–44 = Shepherd of Hermas, Visiones 1,12—21,4 = P. Bodmer XXXVIII, entrusted to Antonio Carlini?

[P. Bodmer XXXIX; see under Pachomiana]

P. Bodmer XL. Song of Songs in Coptic; assigned to Rodolphe Kasser.

P. Bodmer XLI. The Acts of Paul, Ephesus Episode, in Coptic; assigned to Rodolphe Kasser.

[P. Bodmer XLI The Acts of Paul, Ephesus Episode, in Coptic] Kasser, Rodolphe. "Acta Pauli 1959." *Revue d'histoire et de philosophie religieuses* 40 (1960) 45–57. [Though not an *editio princeps* (see p. 45 n. 4), the text is summarized on pp. 50–52 and paraphrased, indeed in part translated, on pp. 54–56.]

[P. Bodmer XLI. The Acts of Paul, Ephesus Episode, in Coptic] Kasser, Rodolphe. "Anfang des Aufenthaltes zu Ephesus (Nach einem bisher noch nicht edierten koptischen Papyrus)." In Edgar Hennecke. *Neutestamentliche Apokryphen in deutscher Übersetzung.* Third edition by Wilhelm Schneemelcher. 2. *Apostolisches: Apokalypsen und Verwandtes.* Tübingen: Mohr/Siebeck, 1964. Pp. 268–70. English translation: "The Beginning of the Stay in Ephesus." *New Testament Apocrypha.* 2. *Writings Relating to the Apostles; Apocalypses and Related Subjects.* Edited by R. McL. Wilson. Philadelphia: Westminster, 1964. Pp. 387–90.

P. Bodmer XLII. Second Corinthians in Coptic; assigned to Rodolphe Kasser.

P. Bodmer XLIII. An unidentified apocryphon in Coptic; assigned to Rodolphe Kasser.

P. Bodmer XLIV. Daniel in Bohairic, fragmentary, assigned to Rodolphe Kasser.

[P. Bodmer XLV and XLVI] Carlini, Antonio and Citi, Annamaria. "Susanna e la prima visione di Daniele in due papiri inediti della Bibliotheca Bodmeriana: P. Bodm. XLV e P. Bodm. XLVI." *Museum Helveticum* 38 (1981) 81–120.

P. Bodmer XLVII. Moral Exortations; assigned to Antonio Carlini.

P. Bodmer XLVIII. Iliad fragments not from P. Bodmer I; assigned to André Hurst.

P. Bodmer XLIX. Odyssey fragments; assigned to André Hurst.

[P. Bodmer XLIX = Cologne Inventory Number 902 = P. Köln 40] Kramer, Bärbel. "Odyssee gamma 87–94; 460–472; 489–496; delta 18; 20; 21; 106–111; 135, 138–140; 164–177; 199–206; 230; 257–264; 339–342, 344, 346–354." *Kölner Papyri (P. Köln)* 1. Papyrologica Coloniensia 7.1. Opladen: Westdeutscher Verlag, 1976. Pp. 89–97.

P. Bodmer L. Documentary texts from the recto of P. Bodmer I and miscellaneous facsimiles not previously published.

CHESTER BEATTY LIBRARY, DUBLIN

[Orlandi, Tito. "Les Manuscrits coptes de Dublin, du British Museum et de Vienne." Le Muséon 89 (1976) 323–27. Announcement only of Ac. No. 1389, 1390, 1486, 1493 [inaccurately listed as 1443], 1495, 1496, etc.]

[Chester Beatty Ac. No. 1389. Joshua 1–6 see with P. Bodmer XXI above.]

Chester Beatty Ac. No. 1390. Schoolboy's Exercise and Gospel of John. Brashear, William, Wolf-Peter Funk, James M. Robinson, and Richard Smith, eds. *The Chester Beatty Codex Ac. 1390: Mathematical School Exercises in Greek and John 10:7—13:38 in Subachmimic*. Chester Beatty Monographs 13. Leuven and Paris: Peeters, 1990 [1991].

[Chester Beatty Ac. No. 1493. Apocalypse of Elijah] Pietersma, Albert and Comstock, Susan Turner, with Attridge, Harold W. *The Apocalypse of Elijah based on P. Chester Beatty 2018*. Texts and Translations 19. Pseudepigrapha Series 9. Chico: Scholars Press, 1981.

[Chester Beatty Ac. No. 1499: van Regemorter, Berthe. "Le Papétier-Libraire en Égypte." *Chronique d'Égypte* 35 (1960) 278–80. Only a pre-publication announcement.]

[Chester Beatty Ac. No. 1499: Lowe, E. A., ed. *Codices Latini Antiquiores: A Palaeographical Guide to Latin Manuscripts Prior to the Ninth Century, Supplement*. Oxford: Clarendon, 1971. P. 5, and facsimile on facing page, item 1683: "Glossarium Graeco-Latinum; Paradigmata Verborum Graecorum." Only a pre-publication announcement.]

[Chester Beatty Ac. No. 1499: "An Unedited Grammatical and Lexicographical Papyrus Codex in Dublin." *Ancient Society* 3 (1972) 259–62. Only a pre-publication announcement.]

[Chester Beatty Ac. No. 1499: Wouters, Alfons. "A Greek Grammar and a Graeco-Latin Lexicon on St. Paul (Rom., 2 Cor., Gal., Eph.): A Note on E. A. Lowe, C.L.A., Supplement No. 1683." *Scriptorium* 31 (1977) 240–42. Only a pre-publication announcement.]

[Chester Beatty Ac. No. 1499: Wouters, Alfons. "An Unedited Papyrus Codex in the Chester Beatty Library Dublin containing a Greek Grammar and a Graeco-Latin Lexicon on Four Pauline Epistles." In *Actes du XVe Congres International de Papyrologues 3 (Problèmes Généraux—Papyrologie Littéraire)*. Papyrologica Bruxellensia 18. Brussels: Fondation Égyptologique Reine Elizabeth, 1979. Pp. 97–107. Only a pre-publication announcement.]

[Chester Beatty Ac. No. 1499] Wouters, Alfons. *The Chester Beatty Codex Ac. 1499. A Greek Grammar and a Graeco-Latin Lexicon on St. Paul*. Chester Beatty Monographs 12. Leuven: Peeters, 1988.

[Chester Beatty Ac. No. 1501] Pietersma, Albert. *Two Manuscripts of the Greek Psalter*. Analecta Biblical 77. Rome: Pontifical Biblical Institute Press, 1978.

[P. Beatty Panop.] Skeat, T. C. *Papyri from Panopolis in the Chester Beatty Library Dublin*. Chester Beatty Monographs 10. Dublin: Hodges Figgis, 1964.

[P. Beatty Panop.] Youtie, L. C., Dieter Hagedorn, and H. C. Youtie. "Urkunden aus Panopolis II. 19. Tax Receipts." *Zeitschrift für Papyrologie und Epigraphik* 8 (1971) 214–34.

FORMERLY UNIVERSITY OF MISSISSIPPI, NOW LONDON AND OSLO

[Mississippi Coptic Codex I (the Crosby Codex)] Metzger, Bruce M. "Recent Developments in the Study of the Text of the Bible." *Journal of Biblical Literature* 79 (1959) 13–20, esp. 15–16. [Only a pre-publication announcement.]

[Mississippi Coptic Codex I (the Crosby Codex)] Cabaniss, Allen. "The University of Mississippi Coptic Papyrus Manuscript: A Paschal Lectionary?" *New Testament Studies* 8 (1961) 70–72. [Only a pre-publication announcement.]

[Mississippi Coptic Codex I (the Crosby Codex); Mississippi Coptic Codex II] Willis, William H. "The New Collections of Papyri at The University of Mississippi." *Proceedings of the IX International Congress of Papyrology*. Oslo: Norwegian Universities Press, 1961. Pp. 381–92 and Plate 5, reproducing p. [104] = p. 30, and Plate 6, reproducing p. 96. [Only a pre-publication announcement.]

[Mississippi Coptic Codex I (the Crosby Codex); Mississippi Coptic Codex II] Kilpatrick, George D. "The Bodmer and Mississippi Collection of Biblical and Christian Texts." *Greek Roman and Byzantine Studies* 4 (1963) 33–47. [Only a pre-publication announcement.]

[Mississippi Coptic Codex 1 (the Crosby Codex)] Willis, William H. "An Unrecognized Fragment of I Peter in Coptic." In *Classical, Medieval and Renaisssance Studies in Honor of Berthold Louis Ullmann*. Edited by C. Henderson. Rome: Edizioni di Storia e Litteratura, 1964. [Only a pre-publication announcement.]

[Mississippi Coptic Codex I (the Crosby Codex)] Hall, Stuart George. Melito of Sardis. *On Pascha and Fragments*. Oxford Early Christian Texts. Oxford: Clarendon, 1979. [Melito, *On Pascha*, only variant readings are published, in Latin translation.]

[P. Duke inv. L 1 (ex P. Robinson inv. 201) = P. Barcin. Inv. No . 149–57; see under Fundacio "Sant Lluc Evangelista," Barcelona.]

PRIVATE COLLECTION, ENGLAND

[Mississippi Coptic Codex II = P. Bodmer XXII see above]

[Mississippi Coptic Codex II = P. Bodmer XXII] Kraus, H. P. *Cimelia*. Catalogue 165. New York: H. P. Kraus, 1983. P. 126, item 26, with plate reproducing pp. 92, 93, 108, 109.

DUKE UNIVERSITY, DURHAM, NORTH CAROLINA

[P. Duke inv. L 1 (ex P. Robinson inv. 201) = P. Barcin. Inv. No. 149–57; see under Fundacio "Sant Lluc Evangelista," Barcelona.]

[P. Robinson 38 = P. Bodmer XXVI, 55/56, Menander's *Aspis* lines 487–98, 524–32; see under Bibliothèque Bodmer.]

INSTITUT FÜR ALTERTUMSKUNDE OF THE UNIVERSITY OF COLOGNE

[Cologne Inventory Number 902 = P. Köln 40; see P. Bodmer XLIX] Kramer, Bärbel. "Odyssee gamma 87–94; 460–72; 489–96; delta 18; 20; 21; 106–11; 135, 138–40;

164–77; 199–206; 230; 257–64; 339–42, 344, 346–54." *Kölner Papyri (P. Köln)* 1. Abhandlungen der Rheinisch-Westfälischen Akademie der Wissenschaften. Sonderreihe Papyrologica Coloniensia 7.1. Opladen: Westdeutscher Verlag, 1976. Pp. 89–97.

[Cologne Inventory Number 904 = P. Köln 3; see P. Bodmer XXVI.]

[Cologne Inventory Number 3286 = P. Colon. Copt. 2 = P. Köln ägypt. 8: Pachomius, Letter 8; see under Pachomiana.]

[Cologne Inventory Number 3287 = P. Colon. Copt. 1 = P. Köln ägypt. 9: Pachomius, Letters 10–11a; see under Pachomiana.]

[Cologne Inventory Number 3288 = P. Köln 174 = Chester Beatty Manuscript W. 145: Pachomius, Letter 7; see under Pachomiana.]

FUNDACIO "SANT LLUC EVANGELISTA," BARCELONA

[P. Barcin. Inventory Number 45] see P. Bodmer XXV.

[P. Barcin. Inventory Numbers 149–57 + P. Robinson inv. 201] Roca-Puig, Ramon. *Himne a la Verge Maria: "Psalmus Responsorius," papir llati del segle IV*. Barcelona: Asociacion de Bibliofilos de Barcelona, 1965.

[P. Barcin. Inventory Numbers 149–57 + P. Robinson inv. 201] Lowe, E. A, ed. *Codices Latini Antiquiores: A Palaeographical Guide to Latin Manuscripts Prior to the Ninth Century, Supplement*. Oxford: Clarendon, 1971. P. 32, and facsimile on facing page, item 1782: "'Psalmus Responsorius.'" [Only an announcement.]

[P. Barcin. Inventory Numbers 149–57 + P. Robinson inv. 201] Emmett, Alanna. "A Fourth Century Hymn to the Virgin Mary? Psalmus Responsorius: P. Barc. 149b-153." In *Proceedings of the XIV International Congress of Papyrology Oxford, 24–31 July 1974*. London: Egypt Exploration Society for the British Academy, 1975. Pp. 97–102.

[P. Barcin. Inventory Numbers 149–57 + P. Robinson inv. 201] Willis, William H. "A Papyrus Fragment of Cicero." *Transactions and Proceedings of the American Philological Association*, edited by Donald W. Prakken. 94 (1963) 321–27.

[P. Barcin. Inventory Numbers 149–57 + P. Robinson inv. 201] Roca-Puig, Ramon. Cicero, *Catalinaries (I et II in Catilinam)*. Papyri Barcilonenses. Barcelona, 1977.

[Alcestis] Roca-Puig, Ramon. "New Literary Latin texts in the Papyri Barcelonensis Collection: Hexameters on Alcestis." In *Proceedings of the XIV International Congress of Papyrologists Oxford, 24–31 July 1974*. Egypt Exploration Society: Graeco-Roman Memoirs 61. London: Egypt Exploration Society for the British Academy, 1975. Pp. 111–12.

[Alcestis] Roca-Puig, Ramon. *Alcestis. Hexametres Llatins: Papyri Barcilonenses, Inv. no. 158–161*. Barcelona: Grafos, 1982.

[Alcestis] Lebek, Wolfgang Dieter. "Das neue Alcestis-Gedicht der Papyri Barcilonenses." *Zeitschrift für Papyrologie und Epigraphik* 52 (1983) 1–29.

[Alcestis] Parsons, P. J., R. G. M. Nisbet, and G. O. Hutchinson. "Alcestis in Barcelona." *Zeitschrift für Papyrologie und Epigraphik* 52 (1983) 31–36.

[Alcestis] Schwartz, Jacques. "Le papyrus latin d'Alceste et l'oeuvre de Claudien." *Zeitschrift für Papyrologie und Epigraphik* 52 (1983) 37–39.

PALAU RIBES COLLECTION, SEMINARIO DE PAPIROLOGIA, FACULTAD TEOLOGICA DE SAN CUGAT DES VALLES, BARCELONA

[P. Palau Ribes 182] Quecke, Hans. *Das Markusevangelium saïdisch. Text der Handschrift PPalau Rib. Inv.-Nr. 182 mit den Varianten der Handschrift M 569*. Papyrologica Castroctaviana: Studia et textus 4, directed by José O'Callaghan, SJ. Barcelona: Papyrologica Castroctaviana. 1972.

[P. Palau Ribes 181] Quecke, Hans. "Eine koptische Bibelhandschrift des 5. Jahrhunderts II (PPalau Rib. Inv.-Nr. 181)." *Studia Papyrologica* 16 (1977) 7–11. [An announcement only.]

[P. Palau Ribes 181] Quecke, Hans. *Das Lukasevangelium saïdisch. Text der Handschrift PPalau Rib. Inv.-Nr.* 181 *mit den Varianten der Handschrift M* 569. Papyrologica Castroctaviana: Studia et textus 6, directed by José O'Callaghan, SJ. Barcelona: Papyrologica Castroctaviana. 1977.

[P. Palau Ribes 183] Quecke, Hans. "Eine koptische Bibelhandschrift des 5. Jahrhunderts III (PPalau Rib. Inv.-Nr. 183)." *Studia Papyrologica* 20 (1981) 7–13. [An announcement only.]

[P. Palau Ribes 183] Quecke, Hans. *Das Johannesevangelium saïdisch. Text der Handschrift PPalau Rib. Inv.-Nr. 183 mit den Varianten der Handschrift M 569*. Papyrologica Castroctaviana: Studia et textus 7, directed by José O'Callaghan, SJ. Rome: Papyrologica Castroctaviana. 1984.

PACHOMIANA

[Cologne Inventory Number 3286 = P. Colon. Copt. 2 = P. Köln ägypt. 8: Pachomius, Letter 8] Hermann, Alfred. "Homilie in Sahidischem Dialekt." In *Demotische und Koptische Texte*. Papyrologica Coloniensia 2. Wissenschaftliche Abhandlungen der Arbeitsgemeinschaft für Forschung des Landes Nordrhein-Westfalens. Cologne: Westdeutscher Verlag, 1968. Pp. 82–85 + plate 3.

[Cologne Inventory Number 3287 = P. Colon. Copt. 1 = P. Köln ägypt. 9: Pachomius, Letters 10–11a] Kropp, Angelius, OP. "Ein Märchen als Schreibübung." In *Demotische und Koptische Texte*. Papyrologica Coloniensia 2. Wissenschaftliche Abhandlungen der Arbeitsgemeinschaft für Forschung des Landes Nordrhein-Westsfalens. Cologne: Westdeutscher Verlag, 1968. Pp. 69–81 + plates 1–2.

[Cologne Inventory Numbers 3286–87 = P. Colon. Copt. 2–1 = P. Köln ägypt. 8 and 9: Pachomius, Letters 8; 10–11a] Quecke, Hans. "Briefe Pachoms in koptischer Sprache: Neue deutsche Übersetzung." In *Zetesis: Album Amicorum door vrienden en collega's aangeboden aan Prof. Dr. E. de Strijcker*. Antwerp: De Nederlandsche Boekhandel, 1973. Pp. 655–63. (German translation only.)

[Cologne Inventory Numbers 3286–87 = P. Colon. Copt. 2–1 = P. Köln ägypt. 8 and 9: Pachomius, Letters 8; 10–11a] Quecke, Hans. *Die Briefe Pachoms: Griechischer Text der Handschrift W. 145 der Chester Beatty Library, eingeleitet und herausgegeben*. Textus Patristici et Liturgici 11. Regensburg: Pustet. 1975. Pp. 112 (Letter 8), 113–14 (Letter 10), 114–16 (Letter 11a).

[Cologne Inventory Numbers 3286–87 = P. Colon. Copt. 2–1 = P. Köln ägypt. 8 and 9: Pachomius, Letters 8; 10–11a] Kurth, Dieter, Heinz-Josef Thissen, and

Manfred Weber. *Kölner ägyptische Papyri (P. Köln ägypt.)* 1. Abhandlungen der Rheinisch-Westfälischen Akademie der Wissenschaften, Sonderreihe Papyrologica Coloniensia 9. Cologne: Westdeutscher Verlag, 1980. Pp. 100–102, 103–8.

[Cologne Inventory Numbers 3286–87 = P. Colon. Copt. 2–1 = P. Köln ägypt. 8 and 9: Pachomius, Letters 8; 10–11a] Veilleux, Armand. *Pachomian Koinonia.* Vol. 3. *Instructions, Letters, and Other Writings of Saint Pachomius and His Disciples.* Cistercian Studies Series 47. Kalamazoo, MI: Cistercian Publications, 1982. Pp. 71–72 (Letter 8), 74–75 (Letter 10), 75–76 (Letter 11a). (English translation only.)

[Chester Beatty Glass Container No. 54: Pachomius, Letters 9a, 9b, 10, Cryptogram, 11b] Quecke, Hans. "Ein neues Fragment der Pachombriefe in koptischer Sprache." *Orientalia* 43 (1974) 66–82.

[Chester Beatty Glass Container No. 54: Pachomius, Letters 9a, 9b, 10, Cryptogram, 11b] Quecke, Hans. *Die Briefe Pachoms: Griechischer Text der Handschrift W. 145 der Chester Beatty Library, eingeleitet und herausgegeben.* Textus Patristici et Liturgici 11. Regensburg: Pustet. 1975. Pp. 116–17 (Letter 9a), 118 (Letter 9b), 113–14 (Letter 10), 116 (Cryptogram), 112–13 (Letter 11b).

[Chester Beatty Glass Container No. 54: Pachomius, Letters 9a, 9b, 10, cryptogram, 11b] Veilleux, Armand. *Pachomian Koinonia.* Vol. 3. *Instructions, Letters, and Other Writings of Saint Pachomius and His Disciples.* Cistercian Studies Series 47. Kalamazoo, MI: Cistercian Publications, 1982. Pp. 72–73 (Letter 9a), 73–74 (Letter 9b), 74–75 (Letter 10), 76 (Cryptogram), 77–78 (Letter 11b). (English translation only.)

[Chester Beatty Manuscript W. 145: Pachomius, Letters 1–3, 7, 10, 11a] Quecke, Hans. *Die Briefe Pachoms: Griechischer Text der Handschrift W. 145 der Chester Beatty Library, eingeleitet und herausgegeben.* Textus Patristici et Liturgici 11. Regensburg: Pustet. 1975.

[Chester Beatty Manuscript W. 145: Pachomius, Letters 1–3, 7, 10, 11a: Quecke, Hans. "Die griechische Übersetzung der Pachombriefe (Dublin, Chester Beatty Library, Ms. W. 145)." *Studia Papyrologica* 15 (1976) 153–59.

[Chester Beatty Manuscript W. 145: Pachomius, Letters 1–3, 7, 10, 11a: Funk, Wolf-Peter. "Quecke, Hans: Die Briefe Pachoms." *Theologische Literaturzeitung* 105 (1980) 117–19. Book review.]

[Chester Beatty Manuscript W. 145: Pachomius, Letters 1–3, 7, 10, 11a] Veilleux, Armand. *Pachomian Koinonia.* Vol. 3. *Instructions, Letters, and Other Writings of Saint Pachomius and His Disciples.* Cistercian Studies Series 47. Kalamazoo, MI: Cistercian Publications , 1982. Pp. 51–52 (Letter 1), 52–53 (Letter 2), 53–59 (Letter 3), 69–71 (Letter 7). (English translation only.)

[Cologne Inventory Number 3288 = P. Köln 174 = Chester Beatty Manuscript W. 145: Pachomius, Letter 7] Römer, Cornelia. "Aus dem siebten Brief des Pachom: Fragmente zur Pergamentrolle der Chester Beatty Library." *Kölner Papyri (P. Köln)* 4. Papyrologica Coloniensia 7.4. Opladen: Westdeutscher Verlag, 1982. Pp. 90–98.

[P. Bodmer XXXIX: Pachomius' Letter 11b] Orlandi, Tito, A. de Vogüé, Hans Quecke, and James Goehring. *Pachomiana Coptica.*

[P. Bodmer XXXIX: Pachomius' Letter 11b] Veilleux, Armand. *Pachomian Koinonia.* Vol. 3, *Instructions, Letters, and Other Writings of Saint Pachomius and His Disciples.* Cistercian Studies Series 47. Kalamazoo, MI: Cistercian Publications, 1982. Pp. 77–78. (English translation only.)

[Chester Beatty Library Ms. Ac. 1486 = Theodore's Letter 2] Quecke, Hans. "Ein Brief von einem Nachfolger Pachoms (Chester Beatty Library Ms. Ac. 1486)." *Orientalia* 44 (1975) 426–33 and plate 42.

[Chester Beatty Library Ms. Ac. 1486 = Theodore's Letter 2] Quecke, Hans. "Eine Handvoll pachomianischer Texte." *Zeitschrift der Deutschen Morgenländlischen Gesellschaft*, Supplementum III,1 (1977 = 19. Deutscher Orientalistentag 1975). Pp. 221–29. (German translation only.)

[Chester Beatty Library Ms. Ac. 1486 = Theodore's Letter 2] De Vogüé, Adalbert. "Épîtres inédites d'Horsiese et de Théodore." In *Commandements du Seigneur et Liberation évangelique*. Studia Anselmiana 70. Rome: Editrice Anselmiana, 1977. Pp. 244–57, esp. 255–57. (French translation only.)

[Chester Beatty Library Ms. Ac. 1486 = Theodore's Letter 2] Veilleux, Armand. *Pachomian Koinonia*. Vol. 3. *Instructions, Letters, and Other Writings of Saint Pachomius and His Disciples*. Cistercian Studies Series 47. Kalamazoo, MI: Cistercian Publications, 1982. Pp. 127–29. (English translation only.)

[Private German collection = Theodore's Letter 2, another copy] Krause, Martin. "Der Erlassbrief Theodors." In *Studies Presented to Hans Jakob Polotsky*. Edited by Dwight W. Young. East Gloucester, MA: Pirtle & Polson, 1981. Pp. 220–38 + plate 6.

[Chester Beatty Library Ac. 1494 = Horsiesios' Letter 3] De Vogüé, Adalbert. "Épîtres inédites d'Horsiese et de Théodore." *Commandements du Seigneur et Liberation évangelique*. Studia Anselmiana 70. Rome: Editrice Anselmiana, 1977. Pp. 244–57, esp. 245–49. (French translation only.)

[Chester Beatty Library Ac. 1494 = Horsiesios' Letter 3] *Veilleux, Armand. Pachomian Koinonia*. Vol. 3. *Instructions, Letters, and Other Writings of Saint Pachomius and His Disciples*. Cistercian Studies Series 47. Kalamazoo, MI: Cisterian Publications, 1982. Pp. 157–60 (English translation only).

[Chester Beatty Library Ac.1495 = Horsiesios' Letter 4] De Vogüé, Adalbert. "Épîtres inédites d'Horsiese et de Théodore." In *Commandements du Seigneur et Liberation évangelique*. Studia Anselmiana 70. Rome: Editrice Anselmiana, 1977. Pp. 244–57, esp. 250–54. (French translation only.)

[Chester Beatty Library Ac. 1495 = Horsiesios' Letter 4] Veilleux, Armand. *Pachomian Koinonia*. Vol. 3. *Instructions, Letters, and Other Writings of Saint Pachomius and His Disciples*. Cistercian Studies Series 47. Kalamazoo, MI: Cisterian Publications, 1982. Pp. 161–65. (English translation only.)

A SIMILAR *ROTULI* ROLL

[P. Yale Inv. 1779 = Ps. 76–77] *A Collection of Papyri: Egyptian—Greek—Coptic—Arabic: Showing the Development of Handwriting Mainly from the Second century B.C. to the Eighth Century A.D.* Introduction by Theodore C. Petersen. New York: H. P. Kraus, n. d. (ca. 1962). The frontispiece (reduced) and the fold-out at p. 28 present the facsimile; Petersen's description is on p. 29.

[P. Yale Inv. 1779 = Ps. 76–77] Vergote, Joseph, and Parássoglou, George M. "Les Psaumes 76 et 77 en Copte-Sahidique d'après le P. Yale Inv. 1779." *Le Muséon* 87 (1974) 531–41.

Collectors, Dealers, Scholars, and Institutes

Kurt Aland (1915–1994). German New Testament text critic. He was Professor at the University of Münster, West Germany, and founding Director of the Institut für neutestamentliche Textforschung / Institute for New Testament Textual Research.

ʿAziz Suryāl ʿAṭīya (1898–1988). Egyptian professor of Coptology and medieval history. He founded the Institute of Coptic Studies in Cairo, Egypt, and the Middle East Center at the University of Utah.

Stanley Baker. Senior Museum Assistant in the Egyptian Department of the British Museum.

Sir A. Chester Beatty (1875–1968). Major collector of manuscripts and papyri. He founded the Chester Beatty Library. Born in the U.S., he became a naturalized citizen of Great Britain, and was an honorary citizen of Ireland. He made his fortune mining copper in the U.S. and around the world.

Bey of Papyrus. The nickname of the middleman who supplied Tano with papyri. "Bey" is a Turkish term for chieftain.

Bibliothèque Bodmeriana. The Bodmer Library, located in Cologny, Switzerland (near Geneva). It was founded in the 1920s by Martin Bodmer. Just prior to Bodmer's death in 1971, a permanent foundation was established, and the library became part of the Fondation Martin Bodmer. Web site: *www.fondationbodmer.org*.

Martin Bodmer (1899–1971). Swiss philanthropist, bibliophile, and manuscript collector. He founded the Bibliothèque Bodmeriana.

Odile Bongard. The secretary of Martin Bodmer. In 1956 she traveled to Egypt to reactivate Tano, and re-enlisted Fr. Doutreleau to aid in evaluating the manuscripts Tano had for sale.

Hans Braun. Director of the Bibliothèque Bodmeriana.

British Museum. Founded in 1753 as the first national public museum in the world. It is located in the Bloomsbury district of London. Web site: *www.britishmuseum.org.*

E. A. Wallis Budge (1857–1934). British Egyptologist and Keeper of the Egyptian and Assyrian Antiquities at the British Museum.

Guglielmo Cavallo (b. 1938). Italian papyrologist and Professor of History and Paleography at La Sapienza University in Rome.

Chester Beatty Library. Located in Dublin, Ireland. It was originally housed in Shrewsbury Road, but relocated in 2000 to a new facility on the grounds of Dublin Castle. Web site: *www.cbl.ie.*

Nisim Cohen. Jewish rug dealer who also sold manuscripts to Bodmer.

Coptic Museum. The largest collection of Egyptian Christian artifacts and art works, located in Cairo, Egypt. It was founded in 1910 by Marcus Simaika Pasha on property provided by the Coptic Orthodox Church of Alexandria. In 1931 it became a state museum. It houses the Nag Hammadi manuscript collection. Web site: *www.copticmuseum.gov.eg/english/default.htm.*

Jean Doresse (b. 1917). French Egyptologist and papyrologist. He was in the research department at the Centre National de Recherche Scientifique.

Louis Doutreleau, SJ (1909–2005). French patristics scholar and Jesuit priest. One of the editors of the series *Sources chrétiennes*. He worked in Cairo in the 1950s, during which time he served as a link between Tano, the antiquities dealer, and the Bibliothèque Bodmeriana.

René Draguet (1896–1980). Belgian patristics scholar and editor of CSCO in Leuven.

Abbot Étienne Drioton (1889–1961). French Egyptologist and archaeologist. He was the Director General of Antiquities of Egypt at the Egyptian Museum in Cairo, Egypt (1936–57). He became Head Curator at the Louvre in 1957.

Stephen Emmel. Professor of Coptology at the Institute of Egyptology and Coptology at the University of Münster. He was one of the original members of the team that edited the Nag Hammadi Library and produced *The Nag Hammadi Library in English*; and he is past president of the International Association for Coptic Studies.

Michel van Esbroeck, SJ (1934–2003). Belgian Jesuit priest and scholar of Eastern Christianity. He was Professor at Rome, then Paris, then Munich. He edited a Georgian text in one of the Bodmer Papyri.

Fatḥallāh Daʾūd. A friend of Riyāḍ from Dishnā.

Fundacio Sant Lluc Evangelista. Located in Barcelona, Spain, this institute holds biblical and classical manuscripts and codices in Greek and Coptic. It was founded in 1952 by Ramon Roca-Puig.

Graeco-Roman Museum. An antiquities museum located in Alexandria, Egypt. Riyāḍ purportedly attempted in vain to sell the museum books.

Jean Guitton (1901–1999). French Catholic philosopher and theologian.

John Sykes Hartin (1916–1989). Director of Libraries at the University of Mississippi.

Ḥasan Muḥammad al-Sammān. One of the two Egyptian discoverers of the Dishnā Papers. He was from Abū Manaʿ "Baḥrī."

Institut für Altertumskunde. A classics-oriented research institute at the University of Cologne, Germany. They have a substantial collection of papyri.

Institute for Antiquity and Christianity. Founded in 1967, it is located in Claremont, California, and associated with the Claremont Graduate University. James M. Robinson was the founding Director in addition to being the Director of the Coptic Gnostic Library Project. That project resulted in the publication of the *Facsimile Edition of the Nag Hammadi Codices* and *The Nag Hammadi Library in English*. Web site: *iac.cgu.edu*

Institut für neutestamentliche Textforschung / Institute for New Testament Textual Research. Located at the University of Münster, Germany, it was founded by Kurt Aland in 1959. Web site: *www.uni-muenster.de/INTF.*

Paul Kahle (1875–1964). German Semitist. He was Professor at the universities of Giessen, Bonn, and Oxford. After World War II he returned to Germany as emeritus professor.

Rodolphe Kasser (b. 1927). Swiss Coptologist and archaeologist. He was Professor at the University of Geneva.

Ludwig Keimer (1893–1957). Austrian Egyptologist and ethnologist. He settled in Egypt in 1927 and became Professor at the University of Cairo in 1936. He was a confidant of Tano.

H. P. Kraus (1907–1988). A rare book dealer in New York. He bought and then sold Mississippi Coptic Codex I (the Crosby Codex) and bought Mississippi Coptic Codex II and Mississippi Coptic Codex III.

Martin Krause (b. 1930). German Coptologist and Professor at the University of Münster. He was the first President of the International Association for Coptic Studies.

E. A. Lowe (1879–1969). American paleographer.

Maguid Sameda. The Cairo antiquities dealer who sold the Mississippi Coptic Codices in 1955.

"al-Qummuṣ" Manqaryūs (died c. 1966). A priest in Dishna. He was involved with Riyāḍ in the assessment and marketing of the Dishnā Papers.

Victor Martin (1886–1964). Papyrologist and paleographer.

Reinhold Merkelbach (1918–2006). German classicist at the University of Cologne. He founded the Arbeitstelle für Papyrologie, Epigraphik und Numismatik der Nordrhein-Westfälischen Akademie der Wissenschaften und der Künste, which is a research center at the Institut für Altertumskunde.

Wilfred Merton (1888–1957). A close friend of Sir Chester Beatty. Merton was also a collector of ancient papyri and advised Beatty on papyrological and codicological matters.

Muḥammad Farag al-Shir. Antiquities dealer in Cairo.

Muḥammad Khalīl al-ʿAzzūzi. One of the two Egyptian discoverers of the Dishnā Papers. He was from Abū Manaʿ "Baḥrī."

Mūsā Fikrī Ashʿiyah. A goldsmith from Dishnā. He was an associate of Riyāḍ involved in the acquisition and selling of the Dishnā Papers.

José O'Callaghan, SJ (1922–2001). A Spanish papyrologist and biblical scholar, as well as a Jesuit priest. He was Professor at S. Cugat del Vallés, Pontifical Biblical Institute (Rome), and then the University of Barcelona. He founded the journal *Studia Papirologica*.

Tito Orlandi. Italian Coptologist and Professor at La Sapienza University, Rome. He was President of the International Association for Coptic Studies (2000–2004). He is Director of Corpus dei Manoscritti Copti Letterari.

Carroll Osburn. Professor of New Testament at Harding Graduate School of Religion in Memphis, Tennessee (later at Pepperdine University and then Abilene Christian University). He was engaged by H. P. Kraus to examine the two codices offered for sale by the University of Mississippi and specifically to provide a detailed report of Mississippi Coptic Codex I (the Crosby Codex).

Pax ex Innovatione Foundation. Located in Vaduz, Liechtenstein. It was the location of the Mississippi Coptic Codex I (the Crosby Codex) = the Savery Codex.

Gilles Quispel (1916–2006). Dutch Coptologist and scholar of Gnosticism. He was Professor at Utrecht University.

Berthe van Regemorter. Belgian bookbinder.

Riyāḍ Jirjis Fām. An Egyptian goldsmith from Heliopolis. He was the primary middleman for the purchase of the Bodmer Papyri.

Colin H. Roberts. British New Testament text critic, papyrologist and Fellow at St. John's College, Oxford.

David M. Robinson (1880–1958). Professor of Classics at the University of Mississippi. He purchased the Mississippi Coptic Codices in 1955 from Maguid Sameda in Cairo. The David M. Robinson Memorial Collection of Greek and Roman Antiquities is located at the University of Mississippi Museum.

James M. Robinson (b. 1924). Professor of New Testament and Coptologist at Claremont Graduate University (emeritus). He was the founding Director of the Institute for Antiquity and Christianity, Director of the Coptic Gnostic Library Project, and the editor of the Nag Hammadi Library.

Ramon Roca-Puig (1906–2001). Spanish (Catalan) papyrologist and Roman Catholic priest. He was the founder of the Fundacio Sant Lluc Evangelista. He taught classical languages in the Balmes Institute of Barcelona and the University of Barcelona.

Winsor T. Savery. Businessman from Houston, Texas. Owner of the Pax ex Innovatione Foundation and of the Mississippi Coptic Codex I (the Crosby Codex) = the Savery Codex.

Shafiq Ghubrīyāl. A goldsmith and partner of Mūsā Fikrī in Dishnā. He partnered with Riyāḍ in the selling of the Dishnā Papers.

A. F. Shore (1924–1994). Classicist and Egyptologist at the British Museum (1957–1974). Later he was Brunner Professor of Egyptology at Liverpool Universtiy (1974–1991).

T. C. Skeat (1907–2003). Papyrologist and Keeper of Manuscripts at the British Library.

Sultan Sameda. The son of Maguid Sameda. He took over his father's antiquities business.

Phokion J. "Phoqué" Tano (d. 1972). A Cypriote antiquities dealer in Cairo. He told Kasser in interviews in 1969 and 1971 about the Nag Hammadi provenience of some of the papyri.

"al-Qummuṣ" Tānyūs (1914–1970). Son of "al-Qummuṣ" Manqaryūs. He sold some of the Dishnā Papers to Prof. José O'Callaghan.

Michel Testuz. A scholar of Arabic. He has worked in various positions for the International Committee of the Red Cross around the world, including Cairo, Egypt.

Eric G. Turner (1911–1983). British papyrologist.

J. V. S. Wilkinson (d. 1957). Librarian of the Chester Beatty Library.

William H. Willis. Professor of Classics at the University of Mississippi, and later Duke University.

John Wooderson. The secretary of Sir Chester Beatty.

Zakī Basṭā. Antiquites dealer in Qinā. He sold Nag Hammadi Codices II and VII to Tano.

Zakī Ghālī. An antiquities dealer in Luxor. He was the first dealer to take possession of any of the Dishnā papers, sold to him by Jirjis Ṣubḥi Qustandi.

Glossary of Technical Terms

Akhmimic. A dialect of the Coptic language, named after the modern region of Akhmim (ancient Panopolis) in Upper Egypt.

bifolio. A single sheet of papyrus folded to make two leaves.

Bohairic. A dialect of the Coptic language, also known as Memphitic. It is the liturgical language of the Coptic Orthodox Church.

cartonnage. Layers of papyrus used as filler in the binding of ancient codices.

codex (pl. codices). A book made of leaves, which are then made into quires, and then into book form, often on some form of leather or papyrus.

codicology. The study of books: their materials, construction, use, and development.

Coptic. The Egyptian language in alphabetic script. It is categorized as a northern Afro-Asiatic language. It was spoken from the first century until the seventh century. As a literary language, it flourished through the thirteenth century.

Egyptian pound (written £E). The currency of Egypt since 1834. During the 1960s the exchange rate was £E1=$2.80.

editio princeps (pl. *editiones principes*). The principal edition of a text, often the original publication of a work that previously had only been in manuscript form.

folio. The leaf of a book.

lacuna (pl. lacunae). A gap in a manuscript. This might be a hole, a damaged section, a torn-off section, or a missing leaf.

Oxyrhynchite. A dialect of Coptic, also known as Mesokemic. It takes its name from the town of Oxyrhynchus (ancient Per-Medjed) in Middle Egypt.

papyrology. The study of writings on papyrus, but more broadly used as the study of ancient manuscripts on other surfaces as well.

papyrus (pl. papyri). The writing material made from the pith of papyrus reeds developed in ancient Egypt.

parchment. A medium for bookmaking. It is made of skins from cows, goats, or sheep, and limed but not tanned.

quire. A gathering of sheets in a codex.

rotulus (pl. *rotuli*). A papyrus or parchment strip wound around a stick and written on one side.

Sahidic. A dialect of the Coptic language, also known as Thebaic.

scholia. Comments on an ancient text made by ancient scribes and scholars.

scriptorium. A room in which scribes copied manuscripts.

Sub-Akhmimic. The Lycopolitan dialect of the Coptic language, also known as Assiutic.

textual criticism. The study of the manuscript witnesses to texts including: text types, scribal practices, variants between manuscripts, etc.

Thebaic. *See* Sahidic.

Bibliography

Aland, Kurt. "Papyrus Bodmer II: Ein erster Bericht." *Theologische Literaturzeitung* 82 (1957) 161–84.

———. *Repertorium der griechischen christlichen Papyri*. Patristische Texte und Studien 18. Berlin: de Gruyter, 1976.

ʿAtīyah, ʿAziz Suryāl. *A History of Eastern Christianity*. London: Methuen, 1968.

Baedeker, Karl. *Egypt and the Sudan: Handbook for Travellers*. 7th remodelled ed. Leipzig: Baedeker, 1914.

Baud, Marcelle, and Magdelaine Parisot. *Égypte: Le Nil égyptien et soudanais du Delta à Khartoum*. Les guides bleus. Paris: Hachette, 1956.

Bodmer, Martin. *Eine Bibliothek der Weltliteratur*. Zurich: Atlantis, 1947.

———. *Variationen zum Thema Weltliteratur*. Frankfurt: Suhrkamp, 1956.

Bober, Harry. "On the Illumination of the Glazier Codex: A Contribution to Early Coptic Art and Its Relation to Hiberno-Saxon Interlace." In *Homage to a Bookman: Essays on Manuscripts, Books and Printing Written for Hans P. Kraus on His 60th Birthday Oct. 12, 1967*, edited by Hellmut Lehmann-Haupt, 31–49. Berlin: Mann, 1967.

Böhlig, Alexander. "Die Arbeit an den koptischen Manichaica." In *Mysterion und Wahrheit: Gesammelte Beiträge zur spätantiken Religionsgeschichte*, 177–87. Arbeit zur Geschichte des Spätjudentums und Urchristentums 6. Leiden: Brill, 1968.

Bonner, Campbell, editor. *The Homily on the Passion, by Melito, Bishop of Sardis; with Some Fragments of the Apocryphal Ezekiel*. Studies and Documents 12. London: Christophers, 1940.

Bonner, Campbell, editor, with Herbert C. Youtie. *The Last Chapters of Enoch in Greek*. Studies and Documents 8. London: Christophers, 1937.

Boon, Armand, editor. *Pachomiana Latina: Règle et Épîtres de S. Pachome, Épître de S. Théodore et "Liber" de S. Orsiesius: Texte latin de St. Jérôme*. Bibliothèque de la Revue d'histoire ecclésiastique 7. Louvain: Bureaux de la Revue, 1932.

Bouriant, Urbaine. "Notes de voyage. l. Catalogue de la Bibliothèque du Couvent d'Amba Helias." In *Recueil de Travaux relatifs à la Philologie et l'Archéologie Égyptiennes et Assyriennes pour servir de Bulletin à la Mission française du Caire*, edited by Gaston Maspero, 131–38. Onzième Année. Paris: Beuillon, 1889.

Brashear, William, Wolf-Peter Funk, James M. Robinson, and Richard Smith, editors. *The Chester Beatty Codex Ac 1390: Mathematical School Exercises in Greek and John 10:7—13:38 in Subachmimic*. Chester Beatty Monographs 13. Leuven: Peeters, 1990.

Browne, Gerald M. "A Panegyrist from Panopolis." In *Proceedings of the XIV International Congress of Papyrologists Oxford, 24–31 July 1974*. London: Egypt Exploration Society for the British Academy, 1975.

Bucher, Paul. "Les Commencements des Psaumes LI à XCIII: Inscription d'une tombe de Kasr es Saijad." *Kemi* 4 (1933) 157–60.

Budge, E. A. Wallis. *Coptic Biblical Texts in the Dialect of Upper Egypt*. London: British Museum, 1912.

Cabaniss, Allen. "The University of Mississippi Coptic Papyrus Manuscript: A Paschal Lectionary?" *New Testament Studies* 8 (1961) 70–72.

Dummer, Jürgen. "Zum Problem der sprachlichen Verständigung in den Pachomius-Klöstern." *Bulletin de la Société d'Archéologie Copte* 20 (1971) 43–52.

Elston, Roy. *The Traveller's Handbook to Egypt and the Sudan*. Cook's Traveller's Handbooks: Egypt and Sudan. London: Simpkin & Marshall, 1929.

Goehring, James E. "Byzantine Coins from the Jabal al-Ṭārif in Upper Egypt." *Bulletin de la Société d'Archéologie Copte* 26 (1984) 31–41.

———. "A Byzantine Hoard from Upper Egypt." *Numismatic Fine Arts Quarterly Journal* 26 (1983) 9–10.

———, editor. *The Crosby-Schøyen Codex Ms 193 in the Schøyen Collection*. CSCO 521, Subsidia 85. Leuven: Peeters, 1990.

———. "Two New Examples of the Byzantine 'Eagle' Countermark." *Numismatic Chronicle* 143 (1983) 218–23.

Guitton, Jean. "Preface." In *Beati Petri Apostoli Epistulae ex Papyro Bodmeriano VIII Transcriptae*, by Carolus M. Martini. Würzburg: Biblia Rara, 1984.

Habachi, Labib. "Sixth-Dynasty Discoveries in the Jabal al-Ṭārif." *Biblical Archaeologist* 42 (1979) 237–38.

Haelst, Joseph van. *Catalogue des papyrus littéraires juifs et chrétiens*. Série Papyrologie 1. Paris: Publications de la Sorbonne, 1976.

Hagedorn, Dieter. "Papyri aus Panopolis in der Kölner Sammlung." In *Proceedings of the Twelfth International Congress of Papyrology*, edited by Deborah H. Samuel, 207–11. American Studies in Papyrology 7. Toronto: Hakhert, 1970.

Hayes, R. J. *The Chester Beatty Library, Dublin*. Dublin: Walker, 1958.

———, editor. *Plates of Chester Beatty Biblical Papyri IV, V, VII, VIII, and XI*. Dublin: Hodges Figgis, 1958.

Henrichs, Albert. "Scholia Minora zu Homer III: Nr. 8: Glossar zu *Od.*1.67–69, 79–116." *Zeitschrift für Papyrologie und Epigraphik* 8 (1971) 1–3 and plates 1–2.

Hermann, Alfred. "Homilie in sahidischem Dialekt." In *Demotische und Koptische Texte*, 82–85 + plate 3. Wissenschaftliche Abhandlungen der Arbeitsgemeinschaft für Forschung des Landes Nordrhein-Westfalens, Sonderreihe Papyrologica Coloniensia 2. Opladen: Westdeutscher Verlag, 1968.

Hogarth, James. *Egypt*. Prepared under the direction of Jean Sainte Fare Garnot, et al. Nagel's Encyclopedia-Guide. Geneva: Nagel, 1978.

Horn, Jürgen. "'Da berief er alle Vorsteher der Klöster ein' (Vita Prima Pachomii §106): Zur Gliederung des pachomianischen Klösterverbandes im Jahr der Amtsenthebung Theodors." In *Coptic Studies: Acts of the Third International Congress of Coptic Studies, Warsaw, 20–25 August, 1984*, edited by W. Goldlewski. Warsaw: PWN-Éditions scientifiques de Pologne, 1990.

Hunt, A. S., and C. C. Edgar, translators. *Public Documents*. Select Papyri 2. Loeb Classical Library. Cambridge: Harvard University Press, 1977–1992.

Ibscher, Rolf. "Die Wiederherstellung des Berliner Proverbiencodex: Der Weg einer neuen Konservierungsmethode für Papyri." *Zentralblatt für Bibliothekswesen* 73 (1959) 362–71.

Irgoin, Jean. "Les manuscrits grec 1931–60." *Lustrum* 7 (1962[63]) 1–93, 332–35.

Kahle, Paul Eric, editor. *Bala'izah: Coptic Texts from Deir el Bala'izah in Upper Egypt*. 2 vols. London: Oxford University Press, 1954.

Kasser, Rudolphe. "Bodmer Papyri." In *The Coptic Encyclopedia*, edited by Aziz S. Atiya, 8:48–53. New York: Macmillan, 1991.

———. *Compléments au Dictionnaire Copte de Crum*. Publications de l'Institut français d'archéologie orientale, bibliothèque d'études coptes 7. Cairo: Institut français d'archéologie orientale, 1964.

———. "Compléments morphologiques au Dictionnaire de Crum." *Bulletin de l'Institut français d'archéologie orientale* 64 (1966) 19–66.

———. "Fragments du livre biblique de la Genèse caches dans la reliure d'un codex gnostique." *La Muséon* 85 (1972) 65–89.

———. "Le dialecte protosaïdique de Thèbes." *Archiv für Papyrusforschung* 28 (1982) 67–82.

———. "Les dialects coptes." *Bulletin de l'Institut Français d'archéologie orientale* 73 (1973) 71–101.

———. "Les dialectes coptes *V*, fayoumique sans lambdacisme, illustré par quelques extraits de son témoin principal, le P. Mich. inv. no. 3520 (encore inédit)." *Enchoria* 19/20 (1992–93) 87–124.

———. *Papyrus Bodmer III: Évangile de Jean et Genèse I–IV,2 en bohairique*. CSCO 177–78. Scriptores Coptici 25–26. Louven: Secrétariat du CorpusSCO, 1958.

———. *Papyrus Bodmer VI: Livre des Proverbes*. CSCO 194–95. Scriptores Coptici 27–28. Leuven: Secrétariat du CorpusSCO, 1960.

———. *Papyrus Bodmer XXI: Josué VI,16–25, VII,6—XI,23, XXII,1–2, 19—XXIII,7,15—XXIV,23 en sahidique*. Cologny-Geneva: Bibliothèque Bodmer, 1963.

———. *Papyrus Bodmer XXVIII: Esaie XLVII,1—LXVI,24 en sahidique*. Cologny-Geneva: Bibliothèque Bodmer, 1965.

———. "Prolegomenes à un essai de classification systematique des dialectes et subdialectes coptes selon les critères de la phonétique." *Le Muséon* 93 (1980) 53–112; 237–97; 94 (1981) 91–152.

———. "Status Quaestionis 1988 sulla presunta origine dei cosiddetti Papiri Bodmer." *Aegyptus* 68/1–2 (1988) 191–94.

Kasser, Rodolphe, and Guglielmo Cavallo. "Appendice: Description et datation du Codex des Visions." In *Papyrus Bodmer XXIX = Vision of Dorothéos*, edited by André Hurst, Olivier Reverdin, et al., 99–120. Cologny-Geneva: Fondation Martin Bodmer, 1984.

Kasser, Rudolphe, and Guglielmo Cavallo. *Papyrus Bodmer XXIX: Vision de Dorotheos*. Cologny-Geneva: Foundation Martin Bodmer, 1984.

Kebabian, John S. "The Binding of the Glazier Manuscript of the Acts of the Apostles (IVth or IV/Vth century)." In *Homage to a Bookman: Essays on Manuscripts, Books and Printing Written for Hans P. Kraus on his 60th Birthday Oct. 12, 1967*, edited by Hellmut Lehmann-Haupt, 25–30. Berlin: Mann, 1967.

Kennedy, Brian P. *Alfred Chester Beatty and Ireland 1950–1968: A Study in Cultural Politics*. Dun Laoghaire: Glendale, 1988.

———. "Sir Chester Beatty—Friend and Patron of Ireland." *The Irish Times*, February 7, 1985, 10.

Kenyon, Frederic G. *The Chester Beatty Biblical Papyri: Descriptions and Texts of Twelve Manuscripts on Papyrus of the Greek Bible*. 8 vols. London: Emery Walker, 1933–1958.

Kraus, Hans Peter. *A Rare Book Saga: The Autobiography of H. P. Kraus*. New York: Putnam, 1978.

Krause, Martin. "Der Erlassbrief Theodors." In *Studies Presented to Hans Jacob Polotsky*, edited by Dwight W. Young, 220–38. East Gloucester, MA: Pirtle & Polson, 1981.

———. "Schätze aus dem zweiten grossen Fund koptischer Handschriften." *Orientalische Literaturzeitung* 62 (1967) 438–46.

———. "Zur Bedeutung des gnostisch-hermetischen Handschriftenfundes von Nag Hammadi." In *Essays on the Nag Hammadi Texts: In Honour of Pahor Labib*, edited by Martin Krause, 65–89. Nag Hammadi Studies 6. Leiden: Brill, 1975.

Kropp, Angelicus, OP. "Ein Märchen als Schreibübung." In *Demotische und Koptische Texte*, 68–81 + plates 1–2. Wissenschaftliche Abhandlungen der Arbeitsgemeinschaft für Forschung des Landes Nordrhein-Westfalens, Sonderreihe Papyrologica Coloniensia 2. Opladen: Westdeutscher Verlag, 1968.

Kropp, Angelicus, and A. Hermann. *Demotische und koptische Texte*. Vol. 2. Cologne: Westdeutscher Verlag, 1968.

Kuhn, K. H., translator. *A Panegyric on Apollo, Archimandrite of the Monastery of Isaac, by Steven, Bishop of Heracleopolis Magna*. CSCO 395. Scriptores Coptici 40. Louvain: Secrétariat du CorpusSCO, 1978.

Kurth, Dieter, Heinz-Josef Thissen, and Manfred Weber. *Kölner Ägyptische Papyri (P Köln ägypt.)*. Abhandlungen der Rehinishc-Westfälischen Akademie der Wissenschaften, Sonderreihe Papyrologica Coloniensia 9. Opladen: Westdeutscher Verlag, 1980.

Lehmann-Haupt, Hellmut, editor. *Homage to a Bookman: Essays on Manuscripts, Books and Printing Written for Hans P. Kraus on His 60th Birthday Oct. 12, 1967*. Berlin: Mann, 1967.

Lowe, E. A. *Codices Latinis Antiquiores: A Palaeographical Guide to Latin Manuscripts Prior to the Ninth Century, Supplement*. Oxford: Clarendon, 1971.

Martin, Victor. *Papyrus Bodmer I: Iliade, chants 5 et 6*. Bibliotheque Bodermeriana 3. Cologny-Geneva: Bibliothèque Boder, 1954.

———. *Papyrus Bodmer IV: Ménandre, Le Dyscolos*. Cologny-Geneva: Bibliothèque Boder, 1958 [1959].

———. *Papyrus Bodmer XVI: Exode I–XV,21 en sahidique*. Cologny-Geneva: Bibliothèque Bodmer, 1961.

Melito of Sardis. *On Pascha and Fragments*. Translated and edited by Stuart George Hall. Oxford Early Christian Texts. Oxford: Clarendon, 1979.

Montet, Pièrre. "Les tombeaux dits de Kasr-el-Sayad." *Kemi* 6 (1936) 81–129.

Nagel, Peter. "Der frühkoptische Dialekt von Theben." In *Koptologische Studien in der DDR*, 38–40. Wissenschaftliche Zeitschrift der Martin-Luther Universität Halle-Wittenberg: Sonderheft, 1965.

Orlandi, Tito. "Les Manuscrits coptes de Dublin, du British Museum et de Vienne." *Le Muséon* 89 (1976) 323–38.

———. "Nuovi Testi Copti Pachomiani." In *Commandements du Seigneur et Libération évangélique: Études monastiques proposées et discutées a Saint-Anselm, 15–17 février 1976*, edited by Jean Gribomont, 241–43. Studia Anselmiana 70. Rome: Editrice Anselmiana, 1977.

Orlandi, Tito, and Hans Quecke, editors. *Papyri della R. Universitá degli Studi Milano*. Vol. 5, *Lettre di San Paolo in Coto-Ossirinchita*. Milan: Istituto editoriale Cisalpino, 1974.

Orlandi, Tito, A. de Vogüe, Hans Quecke, and James E. Goehring. *Pachomia Coptica*. Unpublished manuscript.

Pellegrin, Elisabeth. *Manuscrits Latins de la Bodmeriana*. Cologny-Geneva: Fondation Martin Bodmer, 1982.

Petersen, Theodore C. "An Early Coptic Manuscript of Acts: An Unrevised Version of the Ancient So-called Western Text." *Catholic Biblical Quarterly* 26 (1964) 225–41.

Plummer, John, compiler. *The Glazier Collection of Illuminated Manuscripts*. New York: The Pierpont Morgan Library, 1968.

Quecke, Hans. "Ein Brief von einem Nachfolger Pachoms (Chester Beatty Library, Ms. Ac. 1486)." *Orientalia* 44 (1975) 426–33 + plate 42.

———. "Die Briefe Pachoms." In *Deutscher Orientalistentag XVIII*, edited by Wolfgang Voigt, 96–108. ZDMG Supplement 2. Wiesbaden: Steiner, 1974.

———. *Die Briefe Pachoms: Griechischer Text der Handschrift W. 145 der Chester Beatty Library*. Textus patristici et liturgici 11. Regensburg: Pustet, 1975.

———. "Briefe Pachoms in koptischer Sprache: Neue deutsche Übersetzung." In *Zetesis: Album amicorum door vrienden en collega's aangeboden aan Prof. Dr. E. de Strycker ter gelegenheid van zijn 65e verjaardag*, 655–64. Antwerp: Nederlansche Boekhandel, 1973.

———. "Ein Handvoll Pachomianischer Texte." In *XIX. Deutscher Orientalistentag: Vom 28. September bis 4. Oktober 1975 in Freiburg im Breisgau. Vorträge*, edited by Wolfgang Voigt, 1:221–29. Zeitschrift der Deutschen Morganländischen Gesellschaft, Supplement. Wiesbaden: Steiner, 1977.

———. "Ein neues Fragment der Pachombriefe in koptischer Sprache." *Orientalia* 43 (1974) 66–82.

———. *Das Johannesevangelium saïdisch: Text der Handschrift PPalau Rib. Inv.-Nr. 183 mit den Varianten der Handschriften 813 und 814 der Chester Beatty Library und der Handschrift M 569*. Papyrologica Castroctaviana 11. Rome: Papyrologica Castroctaviana, 1984.

———. *Das Lukasevangelium saïdisch: Text der Handschrift PPalau Rib. Inv.-Nr. 181 mit den Varianten der Handschrift M 569*. Papyrologica Castroctaviana: Studia et Texte 6. Barcelona: Papyrologica Castroctaviana, 1977.

———. *Das Markusevangelium saïdisch: Text der Handschrift PPalau Rib. Inv.-Nr. 182 mit den Varianten der Handschrift M 569*. Papyrologica Castroctaviana: Studia et Texte 4. Barcelona: Papyrologica Castroctaviana, 1972.

Regemorter, Berthe van. *Some Early Bindings from Egypt in the Chester Beatty Library*. Chester Beatty Monographs 7. Dublin: Hodges Figgis, 1958.

Reverdin, Oliver. "Les Genevois et Ménandre." In *Les trois comédies du papyrus de Cologny*, translated and adapted by Louis Gaulis and André Hurst. Lausanne: Éditions de l'Aire, 1981.

Roberts, Colin H. *Manuscript, Society and Belief in Early Christian Egypt*. Schweich Lectures 1977. London: Oxford University Press, 1979.

———. "Two Oxford Papyri." *Zeitschrift für die neutestamentliche Wissenschaft* 37 (1938) 184.88.

Roberts, Colin H., and T. C. Skeat. *The Birth of the Codex*. Rev. ed. London: Oxford University Press, 1983.

Robinson, James M. "Bodmer Papyri." *Bulletin of the Institute for Antiquity and Christianity* 7/1 (1980) 6–7.

———. "The Construction of the Nag Hammadi Codices." In *Essays on the Nag Hammadi Texts: In Honour of Pahor Labib*, edited by Martin Krause, 170–90. Nag Hammadi Studies 6. Leiden: Brill, 1975.

———. "The First Christian Monastic Library." In *Coptic Studies: Acts of the Third International Congress of Coptic Studies, Warsaw, 20–25 August 1984*, edited by W. Godlewski, 371–89. Warsaw: PWN-Panstwowe Wydawnictwo Naukowe, 1990.

———. "Introduction." In *The Chester Beatty Codex Ac 1390: Mathematical School Exercises in Greek and John 10:7—13:38 in Subachmimic*, edited by William Brashear et al., 3–32. Chester Beatty Monographs 13. Leuven: Peeters, 1990.

———. "The Manuscript's History and Codicology." In *The Crosby-Schøyen Codex Ms 193 in the Schøyen Collection*, edited by James E. Goehring, xvii–xlvii. CSCO 521, Subsidia 85. Leuven: Peeters, 1990.

———. "On the Codicology of the Nag Hammadi Codices." In *Les textes de Nag Hammadi: Colloque du Centre d'Histoire des Religions (Strasbourg, 23-25 octobre 1974)*, edited by Jacques É. Ménard, 15–31. Nag Hammadi Studies 7. Leiden: Brill, 1975.

Robinson, James M., and Bastiaan Van Elderen. "The First Season of the Nag Hammadi Excavation." *Newsletter of the American Research Center in Egypt* (Spring 1976) 18–24. Also in *Göttingen Miszellen* 22 (1976) 71–79.

Robinson, James M., and Alfons Wouters. "Chester Beatty Accession Number 1499: A Preliminary Codicological Analysis." In *Miscellania Papiròlogical Ramon Roca-Puig en el seu vuitantè aniversari*, edited by Sebastià Janeras, 297–306. Barcelona: Fondacio Salvador Vives Casajuana, 1987.

Robinson, James M. et al., editors. *The Facsimile Edition of the Nag Hammadi Codices, Published under the Auspices of the Department of Antiquities of the Arab Republic of Egypt, in Conjunction with the United Nations Educational, Scientific, and Cultural Organization*. Volume 1, *Introduction*. Leiden: Brill, 1984.

Rosenstiehl, Jean-Marc. *L'Apocalypse d'Élie: Introduction, traduction et notes*. Textes et études pour servir à l'histoire du Judaisme intertestamentaire 1. Paris: Geuthner, 1972.

Schenke, Hans-Martin. *Das Matthäus-Evangelium im mittelägyptischen Dialekt des Koptischen (Codex Scheide)*. Texte und Untersuchungen zur Geschichte der altchristlichen Literatur 127. Berlin: Akademie-Verlag, 1981.

Schmidt, Carl. "Die Evangelienhandschrift der Chester Beatty-Sammlung." *Zeitschrift für die neutestamentliche Wissenschaft* 32 (1933) 225–32.

———. "Die neuesten Bibelfunde aus Ägypten." *Zeitschrift für die neutestamentliche Wissenschaft* 30 (1931) 285–93.

Shore, A. F. *Joshua I–VI and Other Passages in Coptic*. Chester Beatty Monographs 9. Dublin: Hodges Figgis, 1963.

Skeat, T. C. "Papyri from Panopolis in the Collection of Sir Chester Beatty." In *Proceedings of the IX International Congress of Papyrology, Oslo, 19th–22nd August, 1958*, edited by Leiv Amundsen and Vergard Skånland, 194–99. Oslo: Norwegian Universities Press, 1961.

———, compiler. *Papyri from Panopolis in the Chester Beatty Library, Dublin*. Chester Beatty Monographs 10. Dublin: Hodges Figgis, 1964.

Testuz, Michael. *Papyrus Bodmer VII–IX, VII: L'Épître de Jude; VIII: Les deux Épîtres de Pierre; IX: Les Psaumes 33 et 34*. Cologny-Geneva: Bibliothèque Bodmer, 1959.

Till, Walter C. "Coptic Biblical Texts Published after Vaschalde's List." *Bulletin of the John Rylands Library* 42 (1959) 220–40.

Treu, Kurt. "Christliche Papyri 1940–1967." *Archiv für Papyrusforschung* 19 (1969) 169–214.

Turner, E. G. "The Dimensions of Papyrus and Parchment Codices." In *The Typology of the Early Codex*, 13–34. Haney Foundation Series 18. Philadelphia: University of Pennsylvania Press, 1977.

———. *Greek Manuscripts of the Ancient World*. Oxford: Clarendon, 1971.

———. *Greek Papyri: An Introduction*. Oxford: Clarendon, 1968.

———. *Greek Papyri: An Introduction*. 2nd ed. Oxford: Clarendon, 1980.

———. "Recto and Verso." *Journal of Egyptian Archaeology* 40 (1954) 102–6.

———. "Roman Oxyrhynchus." *Journal of Egyptian Archaeology* 38 (1952) 78–93.

———. *The Typology of the Early Codex*. Haney Foundation Series 18. Philadelphia: University of Pennsylvania Press, 1977.

Van Elderen, Bastiaan. "The Nag Hammadi Excavation." *Biblical Archaeologist* 42 (1979) 225–31.

Veilleux, Armand, translator. *Pachomian Koinonia*. Vol. 2, *Pachomian Chronicles and Rules*. Cistercian Studies Series 46. Kalamazoo, MI: Cistercian, 1981.

———. *Pachomian Koinonia*. Vol. 3, *Instructions, Letters, and Other Writings of Saint Pachomius and His Disciples*. Cistercian Studies Series 47. Kalamazoo, MI: Cistercian, 1982.

Vergote, Jozef, and Georges M. Parássoglou. "Les Psaumes 76 et 77 en Copte Sahidique: d'après le P. Yale Inv. 1779." *Le Muséon* 87 (1974) 531–41.

Willis, William H. "The New Collection of Papyri at the University of Mississippi." In *Proceedings of the IX International Congress of Papyrology*, 383–89. Oslo: Norwegian Universities Press, 1961.

———. "Papyrus Fragment of Cicero." *Transactions of the American Philological Association* 94 (1963) 321–27.

Wilson, A. J. *The Life and Times of Sir Alfred Chester Beatty*. London: Cadogan, 1985.

Winlock, Herbert Eustis, and W. E. Crum. *The Monastery of Epiphanius at Thebes*. Vol. 1, *The Archaeological Material*. Publications of the Metropolitan Museum of Art Egyptian Exhibition 3. New York: n.p., 1926.

Worrell, William H. *Coptic Sounds*. University of Michigan Studies. Humanistic series 26. Ann Arbor: University of Michigan Press, 1934.

Wouters, Alfons. *The Chester Beatty Ac. 1499. A Greek Grammar and a Graeco-Latin Lexicon on St. Paul*. Chester Beatty Monographs 12. Leuven: Peeters, 1988.

Youtie, L. C., Dieter Hagedorn, and H. C. Youtie. "Urkunden aus Panopolis I." *Zeitschrift für Papyrologie und Epigraphik* 7 (1971) 1–40.

———. "Urkunden aus Panopolis III." *Zeitschrift für Papyrologie und Epigraphik* 10 (1973) 101–70.

Index of Names

EGYPTIANS

WESTERNERS